EQEnglish.com
雅思口语高分的保障

MW01699184

徐小平 隆重推荐！

31种雅思口语高分必背公式

31 High-Scoring Formulas to Answer Every IELTS Question

主编：Jonathan Palley（美）
Adrian Li（英）
Oliver Davies（英）
编者：EQ英语雅思研发中心
Elliott Gibbons（英）
陈 娟

外语教学与研究出版社
FOREIGN LANGUAGE TEACHING AND RESEARCH PRESS
北京 BEIJING

图书在版编目(CIP)数据

31 种雅思口语高分必背公式 = 31 High-Scoring Formulas to Answer Every IELTS Question / (美) 帕利(Palley, J.)等主编；EQ 英语雅思研发中心等编 .— 北京：外语教学与研究出版社，2009.12 (2010.12 重印)
ISBN 978 - 7 - 5600 - 9178 - 5

Ⅰ. ①3… Ⅱ. ①帕… ②E… Ⅲ. ①英语—口语—高等教育—自学参考资料 Ⅳ. ①H319.9

中国版本图书馆 CIP 数据核字 (2009) 第 232303 号

出 版 人：于春迟
责任编辑：丁 宁 韩晓岚
封面设计：刘 冬
版式设计：黄 蕊
出版发行：外语教学与研究出版社
社　　址：北京市西三环北路 19 号 (100089)
网　　址：http://www.fltrp.com
印　　刷：北京双青印刷厂
开　　本：787×1092 1/16
印　　张：23
版　　次：2010 年 1 月第 1 版 2010 年 12 月第 2 次印刷
书　　号：ISBN 978 - 7 - 5600 - 9178 - 5
定　　价：45.00 元
* * *
购书咨询：(010)88819929 电子邮箱：club@fltrp.com
如有印刷、装订质量问题，请与出版社联系
联系电话：(010)61207896 电子邮箱：zhijian@fltrp.com

物料号：191780001

奇妙的缘分和共同的梦想
——分享EQ英语创始故事

信念让缘分出现

Adrian Li, 英籍华人，从小学习多种外语，但终因没有语言环境，无果。大学毕业后，来到北京学习汉语，有了良好的语言环境，他半年后就讲出了一口流利的普通话。他回顾以往语言学习经历，得出的经验是：良好的语言环境是学习语言的关键因素。由此，Adrian 萌生了这样的信念：创建一个语言学习平台，让第二语言学习者与母语人士在线一对一练习，抛弃“哑巴”口语的尴尬！

Adrian 通过在线搜索，无意中找到了 Virtual FlashCards 学习软件，此软件采用以教育技术为依托的交互学习方式，这正是 Adrian 所要找的技术。

梦想的碰撞

一封邮件后，Adrian 找到了 Virtual FlashCards 学习软件的创始人 Jonathan Palley。Jonathan 在斯坦福大学主修物理学与戏剧表演，收到邮件后，他异常兴奋，两人随即约见，发现彼此竟然还同住在一条街道。通过见面交谈，他们彼此分享对教育和科技的热情。两人都看到了互联网技术在全球教育体系中有巨大的潜能，于是达成共识，结成“草率联盟”。

EQ 英语初始与发展

经过不懈地努力，2006 年伊始，EQ 英语终于成立了。从语言市场的研究与开拓到全球雅思外教的招聘与培训，从语言学习内容的研究设计再到整个 EQ 英语学习平台技术的开发与整合，EQ 英语经历了一个又一个考验，通过不断的改进，完善，终于整合出一套强大而智能的教学体系。

信念成果的绽放

现如今，EQ 英语拥有全球最领先的雅思口语教学体系——31 种雅思口语高分必背公式，以及强大的一对一雅思外教团队。据粗略统计，通过在 EQ 英语的学习，在上万名雅思考生中有 98% 的考生经过 1 个月的学习，雅思口语分数至少提高了 0.5 分，圆了他们的出国深造梦想！

EQ 英语还为全国五十多所高校提供免费在线图书馆口语学习课程，希望帮助越来越多的中国学生说一口流利的英语。先进的互联网学习平台还得到了英国大使馆文化教育处的认可，通过共同的努力，把创新实时的教育技术学习介绍给全球的英语学习者，为彼此进一步合作奠定了基础。

作者简介

Jonathan Palley

Jonathan Palley，美国人，在斯坦福大学主修物理学和戏剧表演。在程序开发方面有很深的造诣，研发了 Virtual FlashCards 学习软件，这种软件已在世界范围内应用，被下载超过 50 万次。他始终致力于教育与技术的双重领域，对人机交互式学习有着十分透彻的理解，是在线语言教育的开拓者。

他于 2006 年来到中国，和 Adrian Li 合伙创办了 EQ 英语，从事在线语言培训，同时联合多位语言学专家共同研究总结了 EQ 英语学习法，为 31 种雅思口语高分必背公式进一步奠定了深厚的理论根基和坚实的科学基础。

他经常与世界各地的在线语言教育专家探讨研究，并多次应邀参加了英国大使馆、GloCALL（Globalization and Localization in Computer-Assisted Language Learning，全球化和本地化的计算机辅助语言学习）等举办的重大英语研讨会议，主讲 EQ 英语学习法，获得了与会人员的一致认可和好评。

Jonathan 还擅长即兴表演，曾出演过三十多个剧目，几乎每个月都能在北京的舞台上看到他的精彩表演。

Adrian Li

Adrian Li，英籍华人，曾获剑桥大学经济学学士和斯坦福大学 MBA 硕士学位。他曾学习多种语言：汉语、法语、拉丁语、德语、日语等，致力于第二语言学习方式的研究，认为掌握第二语言的最佳方式是学会该种语言的思维逻辑。

他曾在上海百事可乐公司（Pepsi）负责项目管理，成绩斐然；2001 于近千名竞争者中脱颖而出，成为伦敦摩根大通（JPMorgan）的投资顾问，为世界知名企业提供卓越分析和合理建议；2004 年，加盟社会企业孵化机构 Globalegacy，并策划了社会风险投资项目，为企业带来巨额利润。工作之余，孜孜不倦于第二语言学习领域的探索和研究。

他于 2006 年来到中国开办 EQ 英语，集九年研究成果，联合多位语言学专家，独创 EQ 英语逻辑学习法，从雅思口试中的英语答题逻辑提炼归纳成 31 种高分公式。只要掌握了这 31 种雅思口语高分必背公式，考生就可以在短短一个月内轻松获得雅思口语高分。

Adrian 曾应邀在全国“211 工程”大学做过一百多次演讲，介绍 EQ 英语逻辑学习法，并广受雅思口语考生的欢迎。

Adrian 心系中国教育事业，创立了国际性质的慈善机构——CNY Trust（Chinese New Year Trust，华新基金会），始终帮助着中国贫困地区的儿童。同时他还是一位耐力运动的热衷者，曾多次参加铁人比赛和马拉松赛跑并取得了不错的成绩。

Oliver Davies

Oliver Davies，英旅华学者，曾获威尔士大学宗教与哲学学士学位，之后在英国伦敦圣三一学院进修，获英语教学师资证书和英国伦敦工商会颁发的商务英语证书。

他曾在英国、摩洛哥、西班牙、埃及和中国等国家生活和工作，凭借其对语言与文化的热爱，最终走上了学术道路。从国际学校到跨国公司，对语言教学的兴趣使得他可以同时胜任翻译和教学两种工作。精通西班牙语的他还在探索更新颖、更高效的语言学习方法的同时，为英语母语者编写了两套西班牙语教材。

多元文化下的工作经历以及对语言教学理念的创新，引领他来到了 EQ 英语，在这里他成功地把语言教学搬上了互联网，让中国学生在家里就能学到地道的英语。在 2008 年 GloCALL 举办的英语研讨会上，Oliver 向与会专家介绍了 EQ 英语的语言学习平台，广受好评。

前言

EQ英语，雅思口语高分的保障

感谢你在本书前驻足并用心阅览。本书历时三年，由 Jonathan Palley, Adrian Li 和 EQ 英语雅思研发中心的语言学专家精心编撰而成。EQ 英语始终致力于雅思口语培训，不但拥有先进的语言教学平台，还拥有专业的雅思教师团队。通过对数万名雅思考生口语培训的总结和一对一测评的分析，经过与雅思口语专家及考官充分的交流和探讨，我们得出这样一个结论：取得雅思口语高分最有效的途径就是运用西方人的逻辑思维，即书中所讲的**英语答题逻辑**，回答雅思口试中的问题，从而使表达更加流利和精确。

EQ 英语现已将与雅思口试中相关的英语答题逻辑提炼、汇总成 31 种雅思口语高分公式，并结合高分语言点和实例编成此书，旨在帮助雅思考生备考口语，是考生取得雅思口语高分的保障。本书将教你如何正确使用 31 种雅思口语高分公式，掌握英语答题逻辑，从而能够让你准确地回答所有雅思口语考试的问题，获得雅思口语高分。同时，对于希望全面提高英语口语能力的人士，本书也能提供巨大的帮助。

一、雅思口语高分的“瓶颈”到底是什么？

首先请你回顾一下自己的口语经历或与外籍人士的最后一次交谈。你是否有以下问题：紧张得头脑里一点儿思路也没有？回答问题时，想到很多方面，却不知道从哪个方面去回答？知道怎么回答，却不能流利地用英语表达出来？出现以上现象的原因主要有以下两个：

1）缺乏英语答题逻辑；
2）缺乏与外教的沟通练习。

现在 EQ 英语把抽象的英语答题逻辑提炼成颇为具体的 31 种雅思口语高分必背公式，只要掌握了这 31 种高分公式，就可以从容回答雅思口语的所有问题，获得雅思口语高分。

二、理解英语答题逻辑，掌握雅思口语高分公式，获得雅思口语高分

1）EQ英语的英语答题逻辑是什么？

英语答题逻辑由 EQ 英语首次提出，并得到了众多语言学专家的认可。

英语答题逻辑是指英语母语者在回答问题和进行表达时的一种逻辑思维。中西方文化差异的表现之一就是回答和表达时的逻辑顺序和表现形式的不同，而当中国人用汉语逻辑思维进行英语表达时，很容易令西方人认为我们答非所问。在雅思口语考试中，考官常常感到，考生在

回答问题时，尽管可以明白考生每个句子要表达的意思，可是依然会觉得其表达颠三倒四、模糊混乱。事实上，导致这个问题的根本原因就是考生没有理解和掌握西方人的答题逻辑思维，即“英语答题逻辑”。

2）31种雅思口语高分必背公式的秘诀是什么？

考生在回答任何雅思口语考题时，31 种雅思口语高分必背公式将先教会你“说什么”，然后再教会你“如何说”。它们是根据 EQ 英语的英语答题逻辑并依据雅思口语考试真题提炼、汇总而成的 31 种高分公式，包括答题思路和高分语言点两个部分，答题思路教你“说什么”；高分语言点教你“如何说”。这 31 种高分公式几乎涵盖了雅思口语考试中所有的话题，考生将其熟练掌握，就可以**自然地、自信地回答雅思口语考试中的所有问题，获得口语高分。**

以一道常见的雅思口语考题为例，如考官问考生：“How often do you play sports?”，中国考生经常会这样回答：“Yes, I play sports every day.”。考生似乎正确地回答了问题，但却没有击中雅思口语考试中的得分点。实际上，对于这类题型，考官希望考生能够运用下面的答题思路和高分语言点来回答：

第一步，清楚地了解答题思路（教你说什么）

答题思路：

- Say how frequently you do the activity the examiner asks you about.
- Explain why you do it that frequently.

第二步，将高分语言点运用到答题思路之中（教你如何说）

高分语言点：

- Use a range of different adverbs of frequency correctly. (“I *never* go to the cinema.” / “I *regularly* watch DVDs.”)
- Use a variety of adverbs of infrequency to describe something you don’t do often. (“I *don’t always* eat at home.” / “*Every once in a while* I play sports.”)

如果考生能按照上述的答题思路并结合高分语言点答题，那么考生的答案就会显得完整而清晰。根据这个雅思口语高分公式，考生很容易就能给出相应的雅思口语高分答案：

“I play sports a few times a week. Usually I play basketball with my friends, but sometimes I play football instead. I think team sports are a great way to socialise and keep fit.”

我们可以很清楚地看出，上面这段完整的回答，与“Yes, I play sports every day.”相比，在内容上更加丰富、具体，在用词上更加准确、地道，在表达上更加完整、清晰。

只要采用这个雅思口语高分公式，一切关于“How often...”的问题就都能迎刃而解，例如：How often do you eat in restaurants? How often do you go for long walks? How often do you take public transport? 等。因此，掌握了本书中的 31 种雅思口语高分必背公式，考生就可以从容回答雅思口语考试的所有问题，获得口语高分。

3）31种雅思口语高分必背公式是如何帮你取得口语高分的?

31 种雅思口语高分公式可帮助雅思考生解决在口语考试中“不知道说什么”以及“不知道如何说”的问题——通过答题思路教会你说什么，再通过高分语言点教会你如何说，从而帮助考生取得雅思口语高分。

三、本书结构及使用指南

本书共分为三个部分：

第一部分——共 20 章，教授 20 种高分公式。此部分针对雅思口语考试 Part One 部分设计内容。

第二部分——共 4 章，每章分为 4 节，教授 4 种高分公式。此部分针对雅思口语考试 Part Two 部分设计内容。

第三部分——共 7 章，教授 7 种高分公式。此部分针对雅思口语考试 Part Three 部分设计内容。

每一部分的内容都是针对雅思口语考试而精心设计的，它涵盖了雅思口试所需的所有英语答题逻辑。

本书可供考生自学，亦可作为培训班的辅导资料。在这里，我们建议你按照以下方法进行学习：

1. 充分理解英语答题逻辑，类比口语考题，学习雅思口语高分公式；
2. 通过学习答题思路，学会“说什么”；
3. 通过学习高分语言点，掌握“如何说”；
4. 通过更多同类型问题的练习，熟练掌握高分公式；
5. 与专业的雅思外教进行一对一的密集练习；
6. 在练习的过程中，不断纠正自己的错误，使表达精确、流畅。

如果你找不到专业雅思外教进行一对一的练习，欢迎拨打 EQ 英语 24 小时雅思咨询热线：400-887-1020，我们将为你提供一次免费的口语测评。同时，EQ 雅思外教还将为你提供评估报告，一对一地指出你的不足，教你学会如何运用英语答题逻辑。

四、EQ学员的成功见证

目前，EQ 英语已经帮助成千上万的学子们取得了理想的雅思口语分数，实现了他们出国的梦想。我们真诚地希望这本书能够提高你的口语表达能力，协助你获得雅思口语高分，实现自己的梦想。下面让我们一起来见证一下 EQ 学员的成功：

雅思考生来信

考生姓名：王力达 **口语历史得分：5**	**职业：上班族** **口语实考分数：7**	**城市：北京**
我考雅思是为了移民。之前考过一次，口语只得了5分，而移民需要单项达到6分。在某日上完培训班后，很偶然地收到一张EQ英语发送的免费口语测评单页，于是决定试一试，跟随EQ英语的外教练习口语，背诵高分公式。一个多月下来，每天坚持上课、预习、复习。我变得越来越自信，考试那天一点都不紧张，只是后来7分的成绩还真是让我感到惊喜。感谢EQ英语，希望更多雅思考生可以认识你们，选择你们。		
考生姓名：时力倬 **口语历史得分：6.5**	**职业：学生** **口语实考分数：7**	**城市：广州**
我在广州上大学，两年前考过雅思，口语得了6.5分，但是分数已经过期。为了留学，我不得不再次参加考试。通过无忧雅思网认识了EQ英语。我每天至少花一个小时的时间学习雅思口语高分公式，并与外教练习，提高口语能力。考试的时候，所有的问题我都能套用高分公式进行回答。我真是又开心，又吃惊。最后分数出来了，我得了7分。我真幸运！		
考生姓名：贾佳 **口语历史得分：5**	**职业：上班族** **口语实考分数：6.5**	**城市：北京**
我是工作一族，因为每天需要上班，只有晚上才有时间学习。跟随EQ英语复习雅思，我发现这种学习方式非常适合我：只要有电脑有网络，我就随时都可以学习。每天白天我抽时间预习，晚上在家跟雅思外教练习，每节课下来我都得到很有针对性的反馈。我很感谢EQ英语帮助我取得6.5分的好成绩。尤其感谢所有的外教、口语分析师给我的帮助与支持。		

EQ 英语真挚地希望能够为英语学习者提供一种全新的口语学习方法，更重要的是，让他们懂得英语逻辑思维的重要性，也就是“要学的是思维，而不仅仅是语言”。在雅思口语的这片领域里，我们一直在努力，而且也会坚持下去，希望广大雅思考生和读者给我们提出宝贵的意见和建议——你们的支持，正是我们前进的动力。

EQ英语

目录

雅思口语考试概览
Overview of the IELTS Speaking Test

雅思口语考试介绍

雅思口试分为以下三个部分：

- 第一部分

雅思口语考试第一部分考试时间为 4 到 5 分钟。考官会问一些你比较熟悉的问题，比如你的家乡、家庭、兴趣爱好以及你所熟悉的人等。你需要简短、准确地回答问题并举例说明。

第一部分考查考生讨论熟悉话题及使用基础英语语法的能力。

高分口语小贴士

要想取得雅思口语高分，每一个回答都要完整，而且既不能太长也不能太短。高分公式将教会你如何组织一个完整的回答，包括：

—陈述一个关于你个人的观点或者感受

—说出原因：为什么会有这样的感受或这样的理解

—举出具体的例子、趣事等

有时，一个完整的回答仅仅包含几个句子，有时则需要更多的句子才能表达清楚。其实，你说的多少并不重要，回答是否完整才是至关重要的。

提示：永远不要只说“yes”或者“no”，也永远不要堆砌语句或者给出太过冗长的回答。

- 第二部分

雅思口语考试第二部分考试时间为 3 到 4 分钟。考官要求考生就某个话题做一段个人陈述，时间为 1 到 2 分钟。考官会给考生准备一张话题提示卡，上面写明考生需要表达的内容，考生有 1 分钟的时间进行准备。在准备过程中，考官会向考生提供笔和纸，考生可以做一些笔记。

第二部分考查考生条理清晰地用英语讲述完整故事的能力。

高分口语小贴士

“个人的轶闻趣事”是一些可以给你的回答增添趣味和色彩的小故事或者细节，高分公式将教会你怎样在第一和第二部分的回答中加入轶闻趣事，让你的回答显得更加生动有趣。

例题："Describe a park that you know."

低分表达：

"I really like the park in my building complex because there are lots of trees."

高分表达：

"I really like the park near my building complex because there are lots of trees. My little brother and I normally go there to play games when the weather is pleasant. There was one time that we played hide-and-seek when I searched everywhere but still couldn't find him. Later, I got so worried that I almost cried. In the end, Mom called and told me that he had gone home already. Only then did I realise that he was trying to trick me. In general, I always have a good relaxing time in the park."

注意：当回答第二部分的问题时，除了叙述轶闻趣事以外，你还应该在回答中增添一些相关的内容。例如，在回答一个关于地点的问题时，你应该说你多久去一次、和谁去以及你的感受等。EQ 英语将通过本书中的高分公式让你知道如何自然地、自信地回答问题。

- 第三部分

雅思口语考试第三部分考试时间为 4 到 5 分钟。考官将就一些比较广泛的社会问题与考生进行双向讨论。你需要清晰地表达并支持自己的观点，同时向考官展示自己能够运用英语母语者讨论问题的技巧，就一些不太熟悉的话题进行广泛而深入的讨论。

第三部分考查考生对有争论性的问题表达个人见解，并通过辩证分析讨论问题的能力。

高分口语小贴士

当你陈述一个观点时，高分公式会教你如何阐述其他不同的观点，运用辩证思维方式回答问题。

低分表达：

"I think Global warming is the largest problem facing the world."

高分表达：

"Some people believe that global warming is the biggest problem facing the world today, *while* others are quite skeptical about it. I think that people should make more efforts to take care of the natural environment, *not just* to reduce global warming, *but* to make our air cleaner, our water fresher and our daily lives more comfortable. It is important to boost the economy and give more people the opportunity to buy luxury goods and live a good life; *however*, people should also be aware that the natural environment is also important and consider the long-term effects of some of our action."

注意：从以上的表达可以再次看到，恰当地使用连接词可以让你的表达听起来更加清楚，回答也更加有条理。

如何学习31种雅思口语高分必背公式
How to Study the 31 High-Scoring Formulas

EQ 英语通过对雅思口语考试的充分研究，根据英语答题逻辑并依据雅思口语考试真题，研发了 31 种雅思口语高分必背公式。这 31 种高分公式为你备战雅思口语考试提供了一个框架，只要你掌握了这 31 种高分公式，就可以从容回答雅思口语的所有问题，获得口语高分。

本书分为三个部分，书中的 31 种雅思口语高分必背公式以雅思口语考试中的各种问题为基础，并与考试的三个部分相对应（详情请仔细阅读本书的“前言”）：

第一部分：针对 Part One 部分的 20 种高分公式
第二部分：针对 Part Two 部分的 4 种高分公式
第三部分：针对 Part Three 部分的 7 种高分公式

其中，每一个高分公式都包括答题思路和高分语言点，是最为核心的内容。答题思路教你“说什么”，高分语言点教你“如何说”；前者是口试时所应运用的答题逻辑，后者是在运用答题逻辑时需要用到的具体的词汇和语法（详情请仔细阅读本书的“前言”）。

以第一部分的高分公式“Formula 1: Do you prefer X or Y?”为例：

Answer Order

- State which one you prefer.
- Compare the two things the examiner mentions.
- Give reasons and examples to explain why.

Language Steps

1. Master prefer + verb-ing (“I *prefer walking*.”) and prefer + to verb (“I *prefer to walk*.”).
2. Use comparatives of convenience or greater benefit like a native speaker. (“Travelling by bus is *faster than* going by car.”)

使用本书时，建议读者依照课程顺序，由易到难、循序渐进地进行学习，打下坚实的口语基础，为获得口试高分做好铺垫。

本书建议读者采用如下步骤学习每一个高分公式：

1）了解学习目标，清楚该章的学习内容，并在学完每章后，通过对照学习目标，检验自己的学习效果。

2）熟悉答题思路和高分语言点。通过答题思路，学会用西方人的逻辑思维去组织答案；通过高分语言点，学会在回答问题时需要使用到的具体的词汇和语法。

3）识记并掌握英语词汇，完成相应的词汇练习，并把这些词汇运用到实际口语表达中，让你的英语听起来更加地道。

4）阅读答题范例，领会如何根据高分公式组织自己的答案。

5）学习高分语言点的范例解析和相关例句，并完成相应的强化练习，从而使你的表达更加精准，答案更加丰富。

建议：最好能有至少一个月的时间来准备雅思口语考试，同时，你需要深入理解口语高分公式，通过不断地练习，熟练地掌握它们，从而达到理想的学习效果。如果你是和朋友一起学习的，本书将提供更大的帮助，你们可以通过轮流提问和回答的形式来练习书中的雅思口语高分必背公式。

此外，EQ 英语还为你准备了更多的网上资源来辅助学习。登录 http://www.EQEnglish.com/book 并注册即可获得更多高分资源。

注册后，你可以：

1）**获得免费真人一对一雅思外教口语测评**——与真人外教进行一对一口语测评，并获得专业评估反馈。专家为你指出不足，提出提高建议。

2）**收听各分数段标准录音**——与自己的口语回答作对比，考前做到心中有数。

3）**得到量身订制的学习计划**——根据你的目标分数、考试时间、现有水平等因素，为你制订快速提高的学习计划。

4）**获得更多口语练习**——查漏补缺，步步为“赢”，让你打好坚实的口语基础并快速提高口语能力，得到口语高分。

如果你在雅思备考过程中有任何疑问，欢迎拨打 EQ 英语 24 小时雅思咨询热线 400-887-1020 进行咨询。

注：本书练习题的所有答案和关于高分公式的更多练习题可登录 http://www.EQEnglish.com/book 进行下载。

最后，EQ 英语欢迎你对本书提出宝贵建议与意见。

电话：400-887-1020

邮箱：book@EQEnglish.com

Part One 第一部分

第一部分高分公式介绍
INTRODUCTION TO PART ONE FORMULAS

雅思口语考试第一部分介绍

雅思口语考试第一部分考试时间为4到5分钟。

考官会问一些你比较熟悉的问题，比如你的家乡、家庭、兴趣爱好以及你所熟悉的人等。

你要简短、准确地回答问题并举例说明。

EQ英语课程第一部分概述

通过对雅思口试第一部分考题的研究和分析，EQ英语归纳并总结了雅思考官在口试第一部分提出的各种问题，从中发现了20种最常见的问题类型，并在此基础上提炼出相应的雅思口语高分公式。

如果掌握了这20种雅思口语高分公式，你就可以轻松应对雅思口试第一部分的所有问题。

每一种雅思口语高分公式都由答题思路以及高分语言点组成，这20种雅思口语高分公式是你在回答各种口试问题时所必须掌握的。

Formula 1: Do you prefer X or Y?

AIMS 学习目标

In this lesson you'll master the Formula for
"Do you prefer X or Y?" type questions.
本课的高分公式将教会你如何回答下列同类型的问题，比如：

- Do you prefer writing letters or sending emails?
- Do you prefer talking on the phone or chatting online?
- Do you prefer to travel by bike or on foot?

THE FORMULA 高分公式

When the examiner asks you "Do you prefer X or Y?" type questions, you must:

Answer Order

- State which one you prefer.
- Compare the two things the examiner mentions.
- Give reasons and examples to explain why.

Language Steps

1. Master prefer + verb-ing ("I *prefer walking*.") and prefer + to verb. ("I *prefer to walk*.")
2. Use comparatives of convenience or greater benefit like a native speaker. ("Travelling by bus is *faster than* going by car.")

NATIVE SPEAKER WORDS 英语母语词汇

让我们来学习一些英语母语词汇，这些词汇对于回答该类型的问题非常有用，并且能够帮助你理解下面的答案范例。

Native Speaker Word	Part of Speech	Definition	Example Sentence
convenient 方便的	adjective	fitting in well with a person's need or plans	I prefer to meet you on Friday afternoon. It's more convenient than Saturday.

续表

Native Speaker Word	Part of Speech	Definition	Example Sentence
actually 事实上，实际上	adverb	in fact, really, usually used for emphasising something that is true or a little surprising to the listener	Many people think that languages are difficult to learn, but actually, if you have a good teacher and plenty of confidence, they can be quite easy.
get stuck 陷入僵局，受困，堵塞		to get into a situation when you cannot move easily (It can be used in an abstract or specific. It is often used for when you can't move in a traffic jam.)	We always get stuck in traffic on the 3rd Ring Road at rush hour. There are too many cars!
traffic jam 交通堵塞		a lot of vehicles very close together so that they cannot move	Traffic jams are more and more common today because so many people are going to work in private cars.
means of transport 交通工具，运输方式		referring to all the different types of transport: cars, buses, trains, the subway, planes etc	Cars are becoming an increasingly popular means of transport.
smiley 表情符，笑脸符	noun	a small image used in chat rooms online by users to indicate different emotions (It also can be sent by mobile phone or email. Example: ☺)	Whenever I make a joke while chatting on line, I like to put a smiley after it.
online 在线的	adjective	on the Internet	I won't let my children surf the Web; there are too many dangerous and dirty things online.
sociable 好交际的，善社交的	adjective	to describe somebody who likes meeting new people or spending time with people	Mark is very sociable. He always goes out with friends in his spare time and loves to talk.

MODEL ANSWERS 答案范例

在完成下面的练习之前，阅读雅思考生Alice和David的参考答案。

Interviewer Do you prefer to travel by bike or by bus?

Alice I prefer cycling to travelling by bus. Cycling is so much more convenient than taking the bus if you're not travelling too far. Actually, it's often faster to go by bike because you don't get stuck in traffic jams! Cycling is also better for my health than all other means of transport because it's a form of physical exercise.

Interviewer Do you prefer chatting online or talking on the phone?

David Generally I prefer chatting online. I nearly always find that chatting online can be more sociable as you can speak to more than one person at the same time. Also, chatting online is often much more fun because you can send smileys, photos and even videos!

LANGUAGE STEP 1 Prefer 高分语言点 1 Prefer 的用法

我们来看一下雅思考生Alice和David是如何使用prefer的。

Alice I *prefer cycling to travelling* by bus...

David Generally *I prefer chatting online*...

Obviously, the first thing you need to tell the examiner for this type of question is whether you prefer X or Y. "Prefer" can be followed by either verb-ing or to verb.

Notice in the examples below that prefer + verb-ing can be followed by either "to" or "rather than", but prefer + to verb can only be followed by "rather than".

- prefer + verb-ing + to / rather than + verb-ing
  "I *prefer cycling to taking* the bus."
  "I *prefer eating to cooking*."
  "I *prefer baking* cakes at home *rather than buying* them in shops."
  "I *prefer reading* a newspaper *rather than watching* TV."

- prefer + to verb + rather than + verb
  "I *prefer to cycle rather than take* the bus."
  "I *prefer to eat rather than cook*."
  "I *prefer to bake* cakes at home *rather than buy* them in shops."
  "I *prefer to read* a newspaper rather than *watch* TV."

Both these forms are correct, and mean exactly the same. The "rather than" form, however, is a little more formal.

Exercise 1.1: Error Correction

Some of the sentences below are incorrect, some are correct. Identify the incorrect sentences and write the correct sentences in the spaces provided.

1. I prefer to go to the cinema to watch DVDs at home.

   ____

2. My sister prefers writing letters to write emails.

   ____

3. I prefer to talk with friends on the phone rather than using QQ.

   ____

4. I much prefer to live in a town rather than a big city.

____

5. My mother prefers shopping at the market more than in supermarkets.

____

6. My friends generally prefer to send text messages to talking on the phone.

____

LANGUAGE STEP 2 Comparatives 高分语言点 2 比较级

让我们再回顾一下雅思考生Alice 和David是如何使用比较级的。

Alice …Cycling is so much *more convenient than* taking the bus if you're not travelling too far. Actually, it's often *faster* to go by bike because you don't get stuck in traffic jams! Cycling is also *better* for my health than all other means of transport, because it's a form of physical exercise.

David …I nearly always find that chatting online can be *more sociable* as you can speak to more than one person at the same time. Also, chatting online is often much *more fun* because you can send smileys, photos and even videos!

After you have told the examiner whether you prefer X or Y, you should compare them, so it's very important to use comparatives correctly.

To form the comparative of an adjective you should:

- add "-er" if the adjective is one syllable long
- add "-ier" if the adjective is more than one syllable and ends in -y
- add "more" before the adjective if it is two or more syllables long

Look at the table below to see how these rules work.

Short Adjectives		-y Adjectives		Long Adjectives	
Adjective	Comparative Form	Adjective	Comparative Form	Adjective	Comparative Form
cheap	cheaper	easy	easier	expensive	more expensive
large	larger	heavy	heavier	comfortable	more comfortable
fast	faster	pretty	prettier	fashionable	more fashionable
slow	slower	ugly	uglier	useful	more useful

> 小贴士
>
> 以下几个形容词的比较级形式是不规则的。
> 形容词原级—比较级
> good — better bad — worse fun — more fun
> 如果要强调比较级，只需要在比较级前加much，比如：...*much* prettier，...*much* more convenient。

When you compare X and Y, you should use one of the following comparative structures:

- X + to be + comparative + than + Y
  "Watching TV is more interesting than listening to the radio."
  "Cars are prettier than buses."
- X + to be + not as + adjective + as + Y
  "Listening to the radio is not as interesting as watching TV."
  "Buses are not as fast as cars."

Exercise 1.2: Gap Fill

Write the words below in the correct spaces.

not as comfortable	peaceful	more independent	convenient
cheaper	more fun	faster	better

1. My mother prefers to eat at home than in restaurants because she says it's ____________ for one's health.
2. I think that I prefer student life to working life because we are allowed to be ____________ and express ourselves more.
3. Most people prefer taking the airport express light railway to taking a taxi to the airport because it is ____________.
4. I prefer going to parties with friends than going with family – partying with friends is so much ____________ because I can drink wine and let my hair down!
5. To be honest, I prefer to travel to work by bus rather than by foot because it's ____________ and I am lazy and don't like walking.
6. I dislike public transport. It's definitely ____________ as getting around in a private car.
7. I prefer sending text messages than making phone calls, especially when arranging a time to meet a friend. It's much more ____________, especially when you are in a noisy, crowded place.
8. Generally speaking, I prefer to travel alone, rather than travel with friends. I enjoy my own company and don't like to talk a lot, so I find it much more ____________ and relaxing.

EXTRA LANGUAGE POINT Discourse Markers
补充语言点语篇标记词

让我们来看看雅思考生Alice和David的回答中使用了哪些语篇标记词。

Alice …Cycling is so much more convenient than taking the bus if you're not travelling too far. *Actually*, it's often faster to go by bike because…

David …I nearly always find that chatting online can be more sociable as you can speak to more than one person at the same time. *Also*, chatting online is often much more fun because…

One reason why Alice's and David's answers are so good is that both candidates put extra little words (called discourse markers) into their answers in a very native way.

Try to use the following words more often when you speak English, as they will help make you sound more like a native speaker:

- actually / in fact

  "Actually" and "in fact" are very often used by native speakers to emphasise that something you say is really true, or introduce something that may come as a slight surprise to the listener.

  "It is *actually* a lot cheaper to go to that supermarket than the market!"

  "*In fact* public buses are a lot more environmentally friendly than many people think."

- needless to say

  "Needless to say" is another way of saying "obviously" or "everybody knows that…" without sounding rude or arrogant.

  "I like eating lots of cakes, but *needless to say*, that will make me fat."

  "He's done very badly in his exams, so *needless to say* he won't get into university this year."

- also

  We're sure you've already mastered "also"! Remember that "also" is used to add extra or further information.

  "I prefer cycling rather than driving a car because it helps me keep fit; it's better for the environment and it's *also* cheaper!"

- besides

  "Besides" at the beginning of a sentence means "as well as", whereas in the middle of a sentence it means "anyway".

  "*Besides* watching the TV and talking to my friends, I can relax while travelling on the subway." (as well as)

  "I like riding a bike as it's a very convenient way to travel. *Besides*, it's cheap and I can't afford a car." (anyway)

Exercise 1.3: Gap Fill

Write the words below in the correct spaces.

fact also needless to say besides actually

1. __________, after spending 3 days trekking in the mountains, I am exhausted and prefer to sit and relax than go out to the party this Friday.
2. Though most people prefer to eat out, I __________ prefer to eat at home than eat in restaurants.
3. Writing letters with a pen and ink is a more personal way to communicate. __________, I like writing by hand because I think it's more beautiful.
4. I prefer watching films at home to going to the cinema. It's a lot cheaper and it's __________ more comfortable.
5. Many people think it's dangerous to travel by aeroplane, but in __________ it's probably the safest means of transport available.

For more practice, please go to: www.EQEnglish.com

Formula 2: What do you usually / normally do?

AIMS 学习目标

In this lesson you'll master the Formula for
"What do you usually / normally do?" type questions.
本课的高分公式将教会你如何回答下列同类型的问题，比如：

- What do you do on an average day?
- What is your normal daily routine?
- Can you describe your typical day?
- What do you usually do on weekends?

THE FORMULA 高分公式

When the examiner asks you "What do you usually / normally do?" type questions, you must:

Answer Order

- Say what you do at the time the examiner asks you about.
- Say how often you do these things.

Language Steps

1. Use adverbs of frequency like a native speaker to show how frequently, or infrequently, you do things. ("I *often* meet up with my classmates." / "I *sometimes* go shopping.")
2. Use the present tense & times of day correctly for general habits. ("I *ride* my bike *every day* at 2 o'clock." / "We *have* dinner together *in the evening*.")
3. Show that you can use one or two common sequence markers. ("*Before* class starts we talk." / "We *then* go to bed.")

NATIVE SPEAKER WORDS 英语母语词汇

让我们来学习一些英语母语词汇，这些词汇对于回答该类型的问题非常有用，并且能够帮助你理解下面的答案范例。

Native Speaker Word	Part of Speech	Definition	Example Sentence
routine 惯例，例程	noun	something or a number of things you normally do as a habit	I wake up, clean my teeth, get dressed, then read the morning paper while drinking a cup of coffee – that's my usual morning routine.
schedule 日程表	noun	an organised or personal "list" of things that need or must be done at certain times	You want to have a meeting? Let me look at my schedule for next week...OK, I can fit you in about 3 o'clock.
review 复习	verb	to go over; to revise; to casually look at to refresh one's memory	Flashcards are a great way to review vocabulary and native speaker expressions – you can look at them to refresh your memory of the things you cover in your lessons.
meet up with somebody 跟……见面		to meet friends or colleagues by appointment	I like to meet up with friends for drinks on Friday night after work. We often go to a quiet local bar and play cards.
corridor 走廊	noun	a passage inside a building that people walk along to get to different areas or rooms	I always get lost in my university. There are so many long corridors and so many classrooms – they all look the same!
gossip 说闲话	verb	to talk openly about the lives of other people or to reveal personal or interesting facts about other people	Be careful what you say to Mr. Power. He always gossips about all the people in the office. If you want to keep a secret, don't tell him about it!
regular 定期的，有规律的	adjective	similar, usually the same, with little change	I think my parents' eating habits are too regular; on Mondays they have fish, Tuesdays they have chicken, Wednesday is soup...every week is exactly the same!
sharp 准时地	adverb	exactly at the time said, not later or earlier at all	You ARE late! I told you to be here at 8 o'clock sharp and it's now 8:05.
overtime 超时地 / 加班时间	adverb / noun	extra time spent at work beyond the usual time	Many workers in developed countries refuse to work overtime if it is not paid.
hang out with somebody 与……出去玩		to spend time with somebody, usually friends or family (informal)	I love hanging out with my friends on the weekend. We go shopping, go to the cinema, play badminton and sometimes go dancing.

MODEL ANSWERS 答案范例

阅读雅思考生Alice和David的参考答案。

Interviewer Tell me about your usual daily routine.

Alice Well, usually I wake up around 8 a.m. I always have a cup of coffee while I review my study notes over breakfast. Then I normally ride my bike to school, apart from in winter, when it's way too cold. Before class starts I often meet up with my classmates in the corridor and we gossip a bit about life and school. After school, I always go straight home and then start on my homework while my mum cooks me dinner. I usually go to bed at about 10 p.m.

Interviewer Do you do the same thing at the same time every day?

David During the week, I have a very regular schedule because of my job. I always wake up just after 7 in the morning, then eat my breakfast on the way to the subway station. I get to work at 8 o'clock sharp, and usually work until 5, sometimes I work overtime until 7 or 8. After I get home I normally eat dinner with my wife and after that either hang out with friends or watch TV before going to bed at about 11.

LANGUAGE STEP 1 Adverbs of Frequency 高分语言点1 频率副词

让我们来看一下雅思考生Alice和David是如何使用频率副词的。

Alice Well, *usually* I wake up around 8 a.m. I *always* have a cup of coffee while I review my study notes over breakfast. Then I *normally* ride my bike to school, apart from in winter, when it's way too cold. Before class starts I *often* meet up with my classmates in the corridor and we gossip a bit about life and school. After school, I *always* go straight home and then start on my homework while my mum cooks me dinner. I *usually* go to bed at about 10 p.m.

David …I *always* wake up just after 7 in the morning, then eat my breakfast on the way to the subway station. I get to work at 8 o'clock sharp, and *usually* work until 5, *sometimes* I work overtime until 7 or 8. After I get home I *normally* eat dinner with my wife…

You must use adverbs of frequency well in your test, and if you can master using a variety of <u>different</u> adverbs of frequency it will make your English more interesting and much more like a native speaker.

Let's look at two different kinds of adverbs of frequency.

<u>Adverbs that go after the subject and before the verb</u>

- always

  "I *always* go out partying every night when I'm on holiday."

- often
  "She *often* goes running after class."

- never
  "She *never* rides her bike in winter."

- almost never
  "We *almost never* go out dancing."

- rarely
  "He *rarely* eats rice."

- hardly ever
  "She *hardly ever* exercises."

Adverbs that can go before or after the subject

- usually
  "*Usually* I wake up around 8 a.m."
  "I *usually* ride my bike to school…"

- normally
  "*Normally* I help my mum with the cooking."
  "I *normally* help my mum with the cooking."

- sometimes
  "We *sometimes* go shopping…"
  "*Sometimes* we go shopping…"

小贴士 almost never, hardly ever 和 rarely 这三个词语表达的意思相同。

Exercise 2.1: Word Order

Rewrite the sentences below in the correct order.

1. eat I buns steamed usually

   ____

2. never I almost exercise do

   ____

3. gets hardly ever home early he

   ____

4. she novels never reads

   ____

5. always my bike rides a father

   ____

6. lunch read magazine during I a sometimes

____

7. I parents with watch my TV normally

____

8. play I computer rarely games

____

9. weekend cycling often the go on I

____

LANGUAGE STEP 2 The Present Simple & Times of Day
高分语言点 2 一般现在时和时间的表达方法

让我们再来回顾一下Alice 和David的答案，看看他们是如何使用一般现在时的。

Alice Well, usually I *wake up around 8 a.m.* I always *have* a cup of coffee while I *review* my study notes *over breakfast*. Then I normally *ride* my bike to school, apart from in winter, when it's way too cold. Before class *starts* I often *meet up with* my classmates in the corridor and we *gossip* a bit about life and school. After school, I always *go* straight home and then *start* on my homework while my mum *cooks* me dinner. I usually *go* to bed *at about 10 p.m.*…

David During the week, I *have* a very regular schedule because of my job. I always *wake up* just after *7 in the morning*, then *eat* my breakfast on the way to the subway station. I *get to work at 8 o'clock sharp*, and usually *work* until *5*, sometimes I *work* overtime until *7* or *8*. After I *get* home I normally *eat* dinner with my wife and after that either *hang out with* friends or *watch* TV before going to bed *at about 11*.

The present simple is used to describe what we do every day or very frequently:

"I *get up* at 7:30 in the morning."

"She often *goes* to the movies."

"They *eat* noodles for lunch."

> 小贴士 不要以为一般现在时的使用非常简单，很多英语水平不错的学生往往因为简单的时态错误而失分！

The present simple is often used together with times of day, so make sure you are aware of the following:

- at + hour + o'clock

  "My mum makes me go to bed *at 10 o'clock*."

  "I get up *at 6 o'clock*."

- at + dawn / noon / midnight
  "I never get up *at dawn*."
  "I always eat lunch *at noon*."
- at + hour + a.m. / in the morning
  "I usually wake up *at 8 a.m.*"
  "I usually wake up *at 8 in the morning*."
- at + hour + p.m. / in the afternoon / evening
  "My father often comes home *at 9 p.m.*"
  "My father often comes home *at 9 in the evening*."
- at / on the weekend
  "I normally just relax *at the weekend*."
  "I normally just relax *on the weekend*."

> 小贴士
>
> 掌握正确的时间表达方法很重要，千万不要犯雅思考生中常见的错误，比如 at 8 a.m. o'clock, in noon, on weekend！
>
> 在英语中，我们通常只用数字 1—12 来表达时间，而不使用 24 小时制。因此，23:00 我们可以说 11 o'clock 或者 11 p.m.，但是我们不能说 23 o'clock。

Exercise 2.2: Gap Fill

Write the words below in the correct spaces.

eat	go out	hang out with	have	lie
meet up	play	wake up	watch	watch

Recently I've been very lazy. I ____________ pretty late, around 10 a.m., and take a long time over breakfast. I usually ____________ television while I ____________ my breakfast, then I ____________, ____________ with friends and ____________ football in the street. I go back home and ____________ lunch with my family, then I go out again in the evening and ____________ my mates. After that I normally ____________ in bed till the early hours of the morning and ____________ movies.

Exercise 2.3: Error Correction

Identify the mistakes in the following sentences and write the correct sentences in the spaces provided.

1. I often go to my sister's house for lunch in the weekend.

____

2. On holiday, I usually get up 4 p.m. in the afternoon.

____

3. I always go for a jog on the evening, when it is cool.

____

4. Normally, I go to bed at 11 p.m. o'clock.

____

5. I try to have lunch in noon.

____

6. I leave for work on 6 a.m. o'clock.

____

EXTRA LANGUAGE POINT Sequence Markers
补充语言点次序标志词

首先，让我们来看一下雅思考生Alice和David是如何使用序号标志词的。

Alice Well, usually I wake up around 8 a.m.... *Then* I normally ride my bike to school, apart from in winter, when it's way too cold. *Before* class starts I often meet up with my classmates in the corridor and we gossip a bit about life and school. *After* school, I always go straight home and then start on my homework while my mum cooks me dinner...

David ...I always wake up just *after* 7 in the morning, *then* eat my breakfast on the way to the subway station...*After* I get home I normally eat dinner with my wife and *after* that either hang out with friends or watch TV *before* going to bed at about 11.

To talk about your usual or normal routine, you should use sequence markers. These help you logically link the different activities that you do together and also make things much clearer for the listener.

Remind yourself of the following sequence markers:

- before
- then
- after (activity)
- after that

> 小贴士
> Alice和David并没有在他们做的每件事情后都说then或者after that。他们只是用了一些次序标志词——这就足以使他们听起来像英语母语者。

Exercise 2.4: Gap Fill & Ordering

Write the words below in the correct spaces and then order the sentences 1-4 in the order that they occur.

after the shower after that before then

A. ____________ I have something to eat. I rarely have a very big breakfast.

B. ____________, I come home and take a quick shower.

C. On Sundays I normally get up fairly early and have a run in the local park ____________ doing anything else.

D. ____________ I throw some really comfortable clothes on.

For more practice, please go to: www.EQEnglish.com

Formula 3: What do you like to do (in your spare time)?

AIMS 学习目标

In this lesson you'll master the Formula for
"What do you like to do (in your spare time)?" type questions.
本课的高分公式将教会你如何回答下列同类型的问题，比如：

- What do you like to do in your spare time?
- What do you like to do when you are on holidays?
- What do you like to do when you are not working?

THE FORMULA 高分公式

When the examiner asks you "What do you like to do (in your spare time)?" type questions, you must:

Answer Order

- Identify a couple of things you like doing.
- Describe why you like them.

Language Steps

1. Use either enjoy / like + verb-ing or like to + verb. ("I *like studying* English." / "I *like to study* English.")
2. Use one or two native speaker phrasal verbs to say "I like". ("I'm *quite* into playing guitar." / "I'm *really* keen on studying English.")
3. Use some adjectives of positive feeling to show the degree of your interest. ("I like playing football. It's *exciting*." / "I'm quite into learning new languages. I find it *fascinating*.")

NATIVE SPEAKER WORDS 英语母语词汇

让我们来学习一些英语母语词汇，这些词汇对于回答该类型的问题非常有用，并且能够帮助你理解下面的答案范例。

Native Speaker Word	Part of Speech	Definition	Example Sentence
be quite into something 热衷于做某事		to be keen on something ("Quite into" is a way of expressing that you have a strong interest in something.)	He goes to concerts all the time. He's quite into music.
movie / film 电影	noun	a story told by using sound and moving pictures, shown at a cinema (film = British English, movie = American English)	The film *Titanic* is extremely popular with some people, but I don't really like romantic movies.
hip-hop 街舞	noun	a type of music with a strong beat that usually involves rapping, not singing to music	Eminem is one of the most famous hip-hop stars.
gig 演奏会，演唱会	noun	informal – a single musical performance by an individual or band	For me, gigs aren't worth going to; you have to buy expensive tickets, spend a long time getting there and the performance is usually worse than the band's CD.
be keen on something 对……着迷，喜爱		to be very interested in something	My father's recently become keen on photography, so he's bought an expensive digital camera and spends a lot of time taking photos of everything.
novel 小说	noun	a long story about imaginary people and events	I think the "Harry Potter" novels are fantastic.
short story 短篇小说		a short story about imaginary people and events	I often buy those small magazines with short stories in them and read them on the subway on my way to work.
every so often 偶尔，不时		sometimes, not very often	Although I come from Chongqing I only eat spicy food every so often.
stimulating 令人兴奋的，刺激的	adjective	to describe something that makes you feel enthusiastic and full of ideas	Students only need to talk to Professor Smith for a while and then they're suddenly bursting with ideas – he's so stimulating.

MODEL ANSWERS 答案范例

阅读雅思考生Alice和David的参考答案。

Interviewer What do you like to do in your spare time?

Alice Well, I have lots of hobbies I like to do in my spare time. I'm very interested in studying English and I'm also quite into movies – sometimes I combine these two interests by watching British or American films. What I particularly enjoy doing, though, is playing football – it's so exciting!

Interviewer What do you like to do in the evening?

David I work really hard during the day so in the evening I like to relax and unwind. I'm a big fan of hip-hop and rock music, and I like hanging out with friends and watching gigs. I'm also keen on reading novels and short stories. I'm involved in a reading group at my university and every so often we get together and discuss the latest books we've read over dinner – it's so stimulating to talk and hear different views about the books we've all read.

LANGUAGE STEP 1 Like & Enjoy 高分语言点 1 Like & Enjoy 的用法

首先，让我们来看一下雅思考生Alice和David是如何使用动词like和enjoy的。

Alice Well, I have lots of hobbies I *like to do* in my spare time. I'm very interested in studying English and I'm also quite into movies – sometimes I combine these two interests by watching British or American films. What I particularly *enjoy doing*, though, is playing football – it's so exciting!

David I work really hard during the day so in the evening I *like to relax and unwind*. I'm a big fan of hip-hop and rock music, and I *like hanging out* with friends and watching gigs…

Like and enjoy are two very common verbs that you need to master to do well in your IELTS test.

Like

Notice that David uses "like" in two different ways to say the same thing.

- like + to verb
  "I *like to relax*."

- like + verb-ing
  "I *like hanging out* with friends."

Enjoy

- enjoy + verb-ing
  "I really *enjoy playing* tennis."

小贴士 enjoy 后面只能接动词的 ing 形式，比如可以说“I *enjoy practising* the guitar for a couple of hours every day.”，而不能说“I enjoy to practise.”

If you or the interviewer has already mentioned an activity, and you continue to discuss that activity, you can refer to that activity as “it”.

For example:

“I really enjoy studying English. *It* is fun.”

In the second sentence, “it” refers back to “studying English”. Use “it” when you are sure that both you and the person you are speaking to are talking about the same thing. Remember, if what you were talking about before was plural, you must say “they” instead of “it”.

For example:

“I like watching football matches – *they* are so exiting.”

Exercise 3.1: Error Correction

Each of the sentences below has at least one mistake. Identify the mistakes and write the correct sentences in the spaces provided.

1. When I'm not working I really enjoy to cycle in the countryside outside my city. They are a very healthy and exciting pastime.

   ____

2. I really like to getting involved in team sports. It is particularly good for building up cooperative skills and healthy competition.

   ____

3. I especially liking to spend my free time sleeping and being lazy in my dormitory.

   ____

4. My friends and I are really keen on play computer games. It is a really good way to spend an evening.

   ____

5. I enjoy to take part in martial arts like Kungfu; it can keep you fit and make you strong!

   ____

6. She enjoys go out to bars on weekends and hang out with friends.

   ____

LANGUAGE STEP 2 Native Speaker Ways to Say “I Like”
高分语言点 2 用英语母语者的方式表达 I Like

让我们再回顾一下雅思考生Alice和David是如何表达I Like的。

Alice Well, I have lots of hobbies I like to do in my spare time. I'm very interested in studying English and I'*m also quite into* movies – sometimes I combine these two interests by watching British or American films…

David I work really hard during the day so in the evening I like to relax and unwind. *I'm a big fan of* hip-hop and rock music, and I like hanging out with friends and watching gigs. I*'m* also *keen on* reading novels and short stories...

Let's look at the structures for these native speaker ways to say you "like" something:

- I'm quite into + activity / hobby
  "*I'm quite into playing tennis* – I get very excited about it."
- I'm a fan of + activity / hobby
  "*I'm a big fan of guitar music* – I often go to concerts."
- I'm keen on + activity / hobby
  "*I'm really keen on going to eat* in Thai restaurants. I love Thai food."
- I'm interested in + activity / hobby
  "*I'm very interested in law*; I'm always reading about the latest laws and legal cases."

> 小贴士
> 在使用这些英语母语者常用的动词短语时，要注意其中不同介词的搭配，比如 quite into，a fan of，keen on，interested in。

Exercise 3.2: Word Order

Rewrite the words below in the correct order.

1. quite on detective into stories I'm TV watching

____

2. of fan comedies huge a romantic She's

____

3. interested I'm latest in fashions extremely the

____

4. very dancing He's with at clubs on friends keen

____

LANGUAGE STEP 3 Adjectives of Positive Feeling
高分语言点 3 表达正面感觉的形容词

让我们来看看雅思考生Alice和David用了哪些形容词来表达自己的感觉。

Alice Well, I have lots of hobbies I like to do in my spare time. I'm very *interested* in studying English and I'm also quite into movies – sometimes I combine these two interests by watching British or American films. What I particularly enjoy doing, though, is playing football – it's so *exciting*!

David ...I'm involved in a reading group at my university and every so often we get together and discuss the latest books we've read over dinner – it's so *stimulating* to talk and hear different views about the books we've all read.

To explain why you like doing something, you should use adjectives of positive feeling. It is often difficult for non-native speakers to use these correctly, and candidates frequently lose marks in the IELTS test because of this type of mistake.

Adjectives of positive feeling come from action verbs such as "satisfy", "bore" and "excite". There are two ways to turn these types of verbs into adjectives of positive feeling.

- Use to be + verb-ed when talking about the person who is experiencing the emotion:
  "He *is bored* when he has nothing to do."
  "She *is fascinated* by music."
  "They *are interested* in playing football."
  "I *am satisfied* with my lessons."
  "The dog *is excited* when I give him food."
- Use to be + verb-ing when talking about the thing that is causing the emotion:
  "Football is *boring*."
  "Music is *fascinating*."
  "Studying English is *interesting*."
  "Seeing a concert is *exciting*."
  "Eating a big dinner is *satisfying*."

Exercise 3.3: Sentence Completion

Complete the sentences below by writing the correct forms of the words in brackets.

1. I really enjoy reading; a good book is so ____________ (satisfy).
2. I think movies are ____________ (bore).
3. My friends are all ____________ (excite) about the concert on Sunday.
4. I love studying English. I'm ____________ (fascinate) by the grammar.
5. I'm really ____________ (interest) in learning more about other countries.
6. Julia finds her art classes incredibly ____________ (satisfy).

For more practice, please go to: www.EQEnglish.com

Formula 4: What do you dislike about X?

AIMS 学习目标

In this lesson you'll master the Formula for
"What do you dislike about X?" type questions.
本课的高分公式将教会你如何回答下列同类型的问题，比如：

- What do you dislike about parties?
- What don't you like about your job?
- What do you dislike about eating in restaurants?

THE FORMULA 高分公式

When the examiner asks you "What do you dislike about X?" type questions, you must:

Answer Order

- Identify which aspects of the topic you don't like – name just one or two things.
- Describe the degree of dislike you have for them.
- Give examples why you don't like them.

Language Steps

1. Use native speaker expressions of dislike. ("I'*m not keen on* sports.")
2. Use native speaker degrees of dislike words and phrases. ("I *absolutely* hate going to the cinema.")
3. Use very much correctly to express dislike. ("I don't like basketball *very much*.")

NATIVE SPEAKER WORDS 英语母语词汇

让我们来学习一些英语母语词汇，这些词汇对于回答该类型的问题非常有用，并且能够帮助你理解下面的答案范例。

Native Speaker Word	Part of Speech	Definition	Example Sentence
stranger 陌生人	noun	a person you don't know	Parents often tell small children not to talk to strangers as it can be dangerous.

续表

Native Speaker Word	Part of Speech	Definition	Example Sentence
find oneself doing something 突然意识到自己在做某事		to suddenly realise that you are doing something unintentionally	Tom says he hates rock music, but whenever his son plays a Rolling Stones song he finds himself singing along.
superficial 表面的，肤浅的	adjective	not deep or meaningful, very shallow, without much meaning	People who judge others by their clothes are very superficial.
field 领域，范围	noun	an area of an activity, job or interest	Although lots of university graduates would like to get into marketing, it's a very competitive field and only the very best candidates succeed.
line manager 直线经理，直接主管		one's line manager is a manager more senior than you to who you are responsible for your work on a day-to-day basis	Sometimes, workers have to make complaints about their line managers to the manager of the line manager, which can be very awkward.
commute 通勤，来回往返于	noun / verb	the journey between one's workplace and home; to make that journey	I would rather live in a smaller city so that I didn't have to spend so much time commuting to work every day.
rush hour 高峰期		the time in the mornings and evenings when the roads and pavements are busy because most people are travelling to or from work	I never get the bus during rush hour, because the traffic is so bad. If I need to go somewhere in the city, I do it between about 10 a.m. and 4 p.m.
jam-packed 拥挤不堪的	adjective	full of things or people, very close together	Beautiful beaches are often ruined during the summer because they are jam-packed with tourists.

MODEL ANSWERS 答案范例

阅读雅思考生Alice和David的参考答案。

Interviewer What do you dislike about parties?

Alice Well, I generally enjoy the parties I go to, but there are a few things I don't like. I don't like all the drinking that usually happens and I'm not keen on meeting lots of new people at parties. If there are too many strangers at a party I find myself having the same conversation again and again: Where are you from?

What's your major? What's your job? I can't stand repeating myself and this kind of conversation is very superficial; you don't really get to know the person at all.

Interviewer What don't you like about your job?

David I don't particularly like my job. I'm not interested in the field I work in, and I don't like my line manager or many of my colleagues very much – they're all so boring. But what I absolutely hate about my job is the commute. It takes me about two hours to get to work; I have to travel during the rush hour on the subway and public buses which are always jam-packed with people – it's terrible!

LANGUAGE STEP 1 Expressing Dislike
高分语言点 1 表达厌恶

让我们来看一下雅思考生Alice和David是如何表达厌恶的。

Alice Well, I generally enjoy the parties I go to, but there are a few things I *don't like*. I *don't like* all the drinking that usually happens and I*'m not keen on* meeting lots of new people at parties…I *can't stand* repeating myself and this kind of conversation is very superficial…

David I *don't particularly like* my job. I*'m not interested in* the field I work in, and I *don't like* my line manager or many of my colleagues very much – they're all so boring. But what I *absolutely hate* about my job is the commute…

Notice that Alice and David use a variety of phrases to talk naturally about things they don't like. You should also try to use a varied range of ways to say you dislike something. Here are some more expressions you should try to use:

- expression + noun

  "I *don't like parties*."

  "I *don't enjoy music concerts*."

  "I*'m not keen on fashion*."

  "I*'m not really a fan of music*."

  "I*'m not interested in history*."

  "I *hate TV documentaries*."

  "I *can't stand supermarkets*."

- expression + verb-ing

  "I *don't like living* in a big city."

  "I *don't enjoy watching* television."

  "I*'m not keen on reading* about fashion."

  "I*'m not really a fan of listening* to live music."

"I'*m not interested in learning* about history."
"I *hate watching* TV documentaries."
"I *can't stand going* to the supermarket."

Exercise 4.1: Rephrasing

Look at the sentences below and rewrite them in the spaces provided using the phrases in brackets.

1. I don't like to travel a lot for work, but my boss makes me. (hate)

   ____

2. I dislike formal parties where you have to look very smart and behave very well. (not keen on)

   ____

3. I don't enjoy it when my manager criticises me in front of all my colleagues. (can't stand)

   ____

4. Susan doesn't like English at all and thinks it's a complete waste of time. (not interested in)

   ____

5. I don't like to go to expensive restaurants. (not really a fan of)

   ____

6. I don't like to watch TV soap operas. (don't enjoy)

   ____

LANGUAGE STEP 2 Expressing Degrees of Dislike
高分语言点2表达不同程度的厌恶

让我们再回顾一下Alice 和David是如何表达厌恶的。

Alice I *can't stand* repeating myself and this kind of conversation is very superficial; you don't really get to know the person at all...

David I *don't particularly like* my job...But what *I absolutely hate* about my job is the commute...

There are many ways of saying you don't like something in English. Just saying "I don't like..." all the time is boring for you and for your listener!

Let's look at some ways to express the degree of dislike:

- I *absolutely* hate...
- I don't *really* like...
- I *thoroughly* dislike...
- I don't *really* enjoy...
- I *can't stand*...

- I *really* don't like...
- I *strongly* dislike...

Exercise 4.2: Gap Fill

Write the words below in the correct spaces.

thoroughly dislike	can't stand	really don't like
absolutely	don't really	strongly

1. I ___________ like Jerry's parties. He always invites boring people.
2. Margaret ___________ dislikes office parties because she has to pretend to like all of her colleagues and her job. She finds it quite annoying.
3. I ___________ our seminar classes at university because none of my classmates prepare for the classes and everyone is too nervous to discuss the topic. It's a waste of time.
4. My wife ___________ hates her job because the work is boring, her boss is an idiot and her salary is terrible!
5. Many parents ___________ bringing their children to parties because they have to spend all of their time looking after the kids rather than relaxing and having a good time themselves.
6. My mother ___________ travelling to work by bus; it's always so crowded, the journey takes a long time and she hates the TVs they have now.

LANGUAGE STEP 3 Very Much 高分语言点 3 Very Much 的用法

我们来看一下雅思考生David是如何使用very much的。

David ...I don't like my line manager or many of my colleagues *very much* – they're all so boring...

Many students make the terrible mistake of saying the following types of sentences in the IELTS test:

"I *very like* playing tennis." (×)

"I *don't like very much* going shopping." (×)

This is very bad English and does <u>not</u> sound like a native.

Look at the following <u>correct</u> native speaker sentences and see if you can see the correct word order patterns:

"I like playing tennis *very much*."

"I don't like going shopping *very much*."

There are three rules you must remember:

- You cannot use "very" before a verb.
- You cannot use "very much" before a verb.
- You can use "very much" after the activity.

Examples:

"I like reading romantic novels *very much*."

"I *really* like reading romantic novels."

"I don't like going climbing in the mountains *very much*."

"I *really* don't like going climbing in the mountains."

If you want to sound like a native, we advise you to only use very much with short sentences.

小贴士 very much 和 very 的用法与 really 的用法是不同的。

Exercise 4.3: Error Correction

Some of the sentences below are incorrect, some are correct. Identify the incorrect sentences and write the correct sentences in the space provided.

1. I very enjoy studying English.

 ____

2. I very much like going to the seaside and swimming in the sea.

 ____

3. I don't very much enjoy going to parties.

 ____

4. I very like all parts of my job.

 ____

5. I enjoy my job very much.

 ____

For more practice, please go to: www.EQEnglish.com

Formula 5: How often do you do X?

AIMS 学习目标

In this lesson you'll master the Formula for
"How often do you do X?" type questions.
本课的高分公式将教会你如何回答下列同类型的问题，比如：

- How often do you read books?
- How often do visitors come to your home?
- How often do you go out to dinner with friends?

THE FORMULA 高分公式

When the examiner asks you "How often do you do X?" type questions, you must:

Answer Order

- Say how frequently you do the activity the examiner asks you about.
- Explain why you do it that frequently.

Language Steps

1. Use a range of different adverbs of frequency correctly. ("I *never* go to the cinema." / "I *regularly* watch DVDs.")
2. Use a variety of adverbs of infrequency to describe something you don't do often. ("I *don't always* eat at home." / "*Every once in a while* I play sports.")

NATIVE SPEAKER WORDS 英语母语词汇

让我们来学习一些英语母语词汇，这些词汇对于回答该类型的问题非常有用，并且能够帮助你理解下面的答案范例。

Native Speaker Word	Part of Speech	Definition	Example Sentence
once in a blue moon 极少地，难得		rarely (Native speakers use this phrase to show that an action happens very, very rarely.)	I am always very good about staying on a diet; it's only once in a blue moon that I might eat a piece of cake.
used to 过去常常		to show that something usually occurred or was true in the past	Clare used to be a really good student, but lately she's become really lazy.

续表

Native Speaker Word	Part of Speech	Definition	Example Sentence
have somebody over 邀请某人来		invite (when you invited somebody to your home, usually for a meal or drinks)	Last night I had some friends over to my house and cooked dinner for them.
socialise 社交	verb	to spend time with other people for enjoyment	I love parties because I like to socialise – they are a great opportunity to hang out with friends and meet new people.
bookworm 书虫，书迷	noun	somebody who reads all the time	I don't understand how Jane can date a bookworm like John; he's so boring, always reading and hardly ever going out with friends.
mix something up 把……混合起来		to change or vary things from the normal pattern, for fun or to make them more interesting	I've been working on the same project at work for six months and I'm completely bored. I wish our manager would mix the work up and give us some new tasks.
poetry 诗歌	noun	a type of writing where the text is arranged in lines, which may or may not rhyme (Many students confuse this word with "poet" and "poem".)	Li Bai (李白) was a Chinese poet, whose poetry is very famous. One poem he wrote was called "Drinking Alone by Moonlight" (《月下独酌》).
be in the mood 想要做某事		to feel like doing something	Helen just asked me to go and play tennis with her, but I'm not in the mood; I just feel like sitting on the sofa and reading a book.

MODEL ANSWERS 答案范例

阅读雅思考生Alice和David的参考答案。

Interviewer How often do you socialise with friends?

Alice I used to go out to dinner with my friends all the time, but I'm in my last year of university now and I'm really busy – I don't often have the chance to take a break and spend time with my friends. Once in a blue moon I'll have someone over for coffee, or I'll go to a friend's house and hang out. I hope I'll have more time to socialise after I graduate!

Interviewer How often do you read books?

David To be honest, I'm always reading books; I'm a complete bookworm! I usually read novels, but sometimes I mix it up slightly and read books about history or nature. I prefer reading novels because they are a great way to relax and escape from daily life, but I also enjoy history and nature books because they help me learn more about the world we live in. From time to time I might read some poetry, but I have to be in the right mood.

LANGUAGE STEP 1 Adverbs of Frequency 高分语言点 1 频率副词

让我们来看一下雅思考生Alice和David是如何使用频率副词的。

Alice I used to go out to dinner with my friends *all the time*, but I'm in my last year of university now and I'm really busy…

David To be honest, I'm *always* reading books; I'm a complete bookworm! I *usually* read novels, but *sometimes* I mix it up slightly and read books about history or nature…

Remind yourself of the following groups of adverbs of frequency:

Adverbs of Frequency that go before the verb

- always
  "I *always* read the Sunday papers."
- seldom / rarely
  "Jonathan *rarely* goes to fast-food restaurants."
- never
  "I *never* read the Sunday papers."

Adverbs of Frequency that can go before the verb or at the end of the sentence

- often
  "I *often* listen to music."
  "I listen to music *often*."
- frequently
  "I *frequently* go to bars with my friends."
  "I go to bars with my friends *frequently*."

Adverbs of Frequency that can go at the beginning of the sentence or before the verb or at the end of the sentence

- usually
  "*Usually* I play football on Sunday."
  "I *usually* play football on Sunday."
  "I play football on Sunday *usually*."
- sometimes
  "*Sometimes* I go to nightclubs."
  "I *sometimes* go to nightclubs."
  "I go to nightclubs *sometimes*."

- occasionally

  "*Occasionally* Lee reads a newspaper."

  "Lee *occasionally* reads a newspaper."

  "Lee reads a newspaper *occasionally*."

Adverbs of Frequency that can only go at the end of the sentence

- all the time

  "I listen to my MP3 *all the time*."

小贴士 always 和 never 都是表示极端的频率副词。它们只适用于一直做某事或者从来没有做过某事。因此，尝试用一些使用范围更广的频率副词来描述你做某事的频率——这样可以使你听起来更像一个英语母语者。

Exercise 5.1: Word Placement

Circle the letters that represents the appropriate position for the adverbs of frequency in brackets.

1. A I B go cycling with my friends C. (sometimes)

2. A she B smokes cigarettes C. (never)

3. A I B go to concerts C. (often)

4. A she B goes swimming on Thursday nights C. (usually)

5. A he B invites me to his house for dinner C. (occasionally)

6. A I B read the newspaper each morning while I eat breakfast C. (always)

7. A my mother B cooks dinner or lunch for her friends and neighbours C. (frequently)

8. A I B watch TV C. (all the time)

9. A he B listens to the radio C. (seldom)

LANGUAGE STEP 2 Adverbs of Infrequency
高分语言点 2 用于形容很少做某事的副词

让我们来看一下雅思考生Alice和David用了哪些副词描述自己很少做某事。

Alice …I *don't often* have the chance to take a break and spend time with my friends. *Once in a blue moon* I'll have someone over for coffee, or I'll go to a friend's house and hang out…

David …*From time to time* I might read some poetry, but I have to be in the right mood.

When you do not do the activity the examiner asks you about frequently, you should use a varied range of adverbs of infrequency.

Colloquial expressions

In addition to "never", "seldom" and "rarely" (see Language Step 1), you can also use the following colloquial expressions to sound more like a native:

- every once in a while (= sometimes)
  "I play football on Sunday morning *every once in a while*."
- from time to time (= occasionally)
  "I have friends over *from time to time*."
- once in a blue moon (= rarely)
  "I drink alcohol *once in a blue moon*."
- hardly ever (= almost never)
  "I *hardly ever* play video games."

小贴士 以上习惯用语，除了 hardly ever 只能放在动词的前面之外，其他短语都既可以放在句首又可以放在句尾。

Using "don't"

It's also often useful to form adverbs of infrequency by adding "don't" before an adverb of frequency. "Don't" can be used with the following adverbs:

- always
  "I *don't always* go to the university canteen to eat."
- usually
  "She *doesn't usually* have guests to dinner."
- often
  "He *doesn't often* socialise with friends."

- all the time

  "I *don't* go to expensive restaurants with friends *all the time*; just occasionally."

> 小贴士
>
> 我们不能把 don't 放在 sometimes, rarely, occasionally 和 never 的前面。因此，我们不可以说 "Don't sometimes…"，"Don't rarely…"，"Don't occasionally…" 和 "Don't never…"。
>
> 英语母语者也用 don't really + verb + much 的结构来描述他们很少做某事。比如："I *don't really* read *much*."

Exercise 5.2: Practice with a Friend

On your own or with a partner, try answering the following questions using the adverbs of infrequency below.

• every once in a while	• don't always
• from time to time	• don't usually
• once in a blue moon	• don't often
• hardly ever	• don't…all the time

1. How often do you read books in English?
2. How often do you go to expensive restaurants?
3. How often do you cook dinner for guests?
4. How often do you go to music concerts?
5. How often do you watch Chinese operas?
6. How often do you go on holiday with your friends?
7. How often do you read science magazines?
8. How often do you watch American soap operas?

EXTRA LANGUAGE POINT Explaining Frequency
补充语言点 解释经常或不经常做某事的原因

让我们来看一下Alice和David是如何解释自己为什么经常或不经常做某事。

Alice I used to go out to dinner with my friends all the time, *but I'm in my last year of university now and I'm really busy – I don't often have the chance* to take a break and spend time with my friends…

David …I prefer reading novels *because they are a great way to relax and escape from daily life*, but I also enjoy history and nature books *because they help me learn more about the world we live in*. From time to time I might read some poetry, but I have to be in the right mood.

Remember that the second thing you should say to the examiner when answering "How often do you do X?" type questions is why you do the action frequently or infrequently.

Practise using the following phrases:

- *I* [adverb of (in)frequency] do (it) because...
  "*I always play* basketball after work *because* I can keep fit and socialise with my colleagues."
  "*I don't often go* to the cinema *because* it's too expensive."
- *I* can't do (it) because...
  "*I can't socialise* with my friends very often *because* I live in a completely different part of the city."
  "*I* would like to read more books but I *can't because* I don't have the time."
- *I* (adverb of infrequency) have the chance to...
  "*I don't usually have the chance to hang out* with my old friends because I recently moved to a new city."
  "*I don't often have the chance to read* long novels because I am so busy at work."

Exercise 5.3: Matching

Match sentences halves 1-5 with sentence halves A-E.

1. I don't often wake up later than 8 a.m....
2. I can't drink coffee with breakfast...
3. I sometimes have the chance to go to the theatre in the evenings...
4. I rarely have the chance...
5. I usually hang out with my friends on the weekend...

A. ...because it helps me relax after the working week.
B. ...because my girlfriend can occasionally get free tickets.
C. ...because it makes me nervous and it isn't good for the stomach.
D. ...because I don't like to lie in bed late in the morning.
E. ...to have people over for dinner.

For more practice, please go to: www.EQEnglish.com

Formula 6: What do you like most about X?

AIMS 学习目标

In this lesson you'll master the Formula for
"What do you like most about X?" type questions.
本课的高分公式将教会你如何回答下列同类型的问题，比如：

- What do you like most about student life?
- What do you like most about your job?
- What is the best thing about your city?
- What is your favourite type of weather?

THE FORMULA 高分公式

When the examiner asks you "What do you like most about X?" type questions, you must:

Answer Order

- Say which aspect of X you like the most.
- Explain why.

Language Steps

1. Use adverbs modifying verbs to express degrees of like. ("I *especially* like playing the piano." / "Students *particularly enjoy* going to bars and restaurants.")
2. Use parallel structure correctly. ("I like going to the cinema, *watching* TV and *playing* video games.")
3. Use simple linking words accurately. ("*Although* Beijing has developed very fast, it's still not very expensive." / "I don't like travelling to work, *but* I enjoy my job.")

NATIVE SPEAKER WORDS 英语母语词汇

让我们来学习一些英语母语词汇，这些词汇对于回答该类型的问题非常有用，并且能够帮助你理解下面的答案范例。

Native Speaker Word	Part of Speech	Definition	Example Sentence
golden opportunity 绝好的机会		a very good opportunity or chance to do something	Getting a scholarship to study at Harvard University was a golden opportunity for David.
expand / broaden / widen (somebody's) horizons 开阔视野		to increase somebody's knowledge so that they think about or consider things they didn't before	My father always told me that I should go travelling and see the world as it would help expand my horizons.
Salsa (dancing) 萨尔萨（舞蹈）	noun	a type of dance from South America, where couples dance together	I've also wanted to try Salsa dancing because it looks like a lot of fun and the men seem so sexy!
yoga 瑜伽	noun	a type of exercise originally from India which exercises the body through stretching and breathing exercises	Although I don't play any sports I'm quite fit because I do yoga frequently.
coast 海滨，海岸	noun	the area of land next to the sea	Susan wanted to move nearer the coast so she could go swimming and sailing whenever she wanted.
the odd 很少的		not often, rarely	I don't like my current company; I work really hard and although I get the odd "well done" from my manager, I don't feel my work is appreciated at all.
typhoon 台风	noun	a very strong, violent and dangerous type of wind	Pete was sailing in the Pacific Ocean when his yacht was caught in a typhoon. The storm blew his boat about 500 kilometres, but he was lucky and survived.
breeze 微风	noun	a very soft and gentle wind	We had a lovely afternoon together, drinking tea and chatting in the garden with lots of sunshine and a gentle breeze.
value 重视	verb	to think that something is important or valuable	Most companies value experience over education qualifications.
all year round 全年，整年		all year, at all times of the year	I could tell my grandmother's health wasn't very good because she felt cold all year round.

MODEL ANSWERS 答案范例

阅读雅思考生Alice和David的参考答案。

Interviewer What do you like most about student life?

Alice What I particularly like about student life is the golden opportunity it gives me to expand my horizons. At university I can not only increase my knowledge about my major and learn new things like Salsa and yoga, but I can also meet lots of new people.

Interviewer What is the best thing about your hometown?

David My hometown is Xiamen, in Fujian Province. The best thing about my hometown is its location. It's right on the coast, and from most places in the city there are beautiful views of the sea. Although we get the odd typhoon every year because we are by the seaside, we also enjoy light sea breezes during the summer. But what I especially value about Xiamen's location is the fresh seafood we can eat all year round.

LANGUAGE STEP 1 Expressing Degrees of Like
高分语言点 1 表达喜爱的程度

让我们来看一下雅思考生Alice和David是如何表达不同的喜爱程度的。

Alice What I *particularly* like about student life is the golden opportunity it gives me to expand my horizons...

David ...But what I *especially* value about Xiamen's location is the fresh seafood we can eat all year round.

As you can see, Alice and David use different ways to express how much they like different aspects of X. Let's look at some more native speaker ways to express degrees of like:

	Adverb	Verb	Activity / Place
I	really especially particularly	like enjoy love	verb-ing noun

Examples:

"I *really enjoy watching* the trees by the lake bend in the wind."

"I *particularly like* my hometown's *food*."

"I *especially love attending* my Psychology lectures."

Any of the above combinations are fine, and using some varied language will make you sound more like a native speaker.

Notice that "like", "love" and "enjoy" must be followed by either "verb-ing" or a noun, so:
"I especially like / enjoy / love *walking* in the countryside."
"I especially like / enjoy / love *the countryside*."

You cannot say: "I like / enjoy / love *to walking*."

小贴士 与中文不同的是，very 不可以放在 like, enjoy 和 love 这些词的前面。因此，"I very like walking in the countryside." 这种表达是错误的。你应该说 "I *really* / *particularly* / *especially like* walking in the countryside."。

Exercise 6.1: Error Correction

Some of the sentences below are incorrect, some are correct. Identify the incorrect sentences and write the correct sentences in the spaces provided.

1. I really liking meeting new people.

   ____

2. I particularly to love travelling as part of my job.

   ____

3. She especially enjoys visit the famous sights in my hometown.

   ____

4. I enjoy to taking photographs and sending postcards home.

   ____

5. I very like living with my classmates in our dormitory.

   ____

6. I really love snowy weather.

   ____

LANGUAGE STEP 2 Parallel Structure 高分语言点 2 平行结构

让我们再来回顾一下雅思考生Alice和David是如何使用平行结构的。

Alice …At university I can not only *increase* my knowledge about my major and *learn* new things like Salsa and yoga, but I can also *meet* lots of new people.

David …Although we *get* the odd typhoon every year because we *are* by the seaside, we also *enjoy* light sea breezes during the summer…

Parallel structure means making sure that the series of words in a sentence are "in agreement" or "in line" with each other. The best way to understand this is by looking at some examples:

"I really enjoy *watching* plays, *writing* papers and *listening* to the school band."

"My mother particularly likes *to dance*, *go out* to restaurants and *spend* time with the family."

As you will notice, all of the verbs in the above sentences have the same form, and so can be said to "agree" with each other. Many students lose points in the IELTS test because of simple "agreement" errors, such as the following:

"I especially like *reading* scientific journals, *have fun* with my study mates and *relaxing* on campus." (×)

"I like to read scientific journals, *have fun* with my study mates and *relaxing* on campus." (×)

Exercise 6.2: Multiple Choice

Choose the appropriate words from the choices below to complete the sentences.

1. There are many things that I like about Spring Festival. We all watch television, light fireworks outside the door, and ____________ songs together.
   A. sing　　B. singing
2. He especially loves whistling whilst ____________ his bike through the hutongs of Beijing.
   A. ride　　B. riding
3. I really love to hike, swim, and ____________ my bicycle.
   A. ride　　B. riding
4. Wow, there are so many things I love about my job. My workmates are great. We do a lot together in our free time. We often go drinking in bars, ____________ in clubs and singing at karaoke bars during the weekend!
   A. dance　　B. dancing
5. As a student I enjoy learning new things, ____________ my friends on campus and studying in the library.
   A. to meet　　B. meeting
6. My study mates like ____________ every day, play sports together and study in the park.
   A. to exercise　　B. exercising

LANGUAGE STEP 3 Linking Words 高分语言点 3 连接词

让我们来看一下雅思考生Alice和David的回答中使用了哪些连接词。

Alice ...At university I can *not only* increase my knowledge about my major and learn new things like Salsa and yoga, *but* I can *also* meet lots of new people.

David ...*Although* we get the odd typhoon every year *because* we are by the seaside, we also enjoy light sea breezes during the summer. *But* what I especially value about Xiamen's location is the fresh seafood we can eat all year round.

To sound like a native and to improve your score on your speaking test, it's good to show slight comparison, contrast and consequence between ideas and feelings using transitional or linking words.

Take a look at the following linking words, and how they are used:

- but
  "I really like my maths teacher, *but* I like my science teacher more."
- however
  "My major is history, *however*, I find art class more exciting."
- although
  "*Although* I study hard most of the time, I always find time for fun on the weekends."
  "I always find time for fun on the weekends, *although* I study hard most of the time."
- though
  "I enjoy learning to play the violin, *though* it is difficult at times."
  "*Though* it is difficult at times, I enjoy learning to play the violin."
- as opposed to
  "Students discuss ideas, *as opposed to* just copying from books."
- besides
  "*Besides* cooking and painting, I often do other activities like singing and hanging out with my friends."
  "I often do other activities like singing and hanging out with my friends *besides* cooking and painting."
- as well as
  "She is my classmate *as well as* my best friend."
  "*As well as* being my best friend she is my classmate."
- also
  "I love running in the park. I *also* run in the gym."

> 小贴士
>
> 与中文不同的是，在英语中 although 和 but 不能在同一个句子中使用。因此，你不可以说 "*Although* I live near the coast, *but* I don't like the sea."，你应该说 "*Although* I live near the coast, I don't like the sea."。

Exercise 6.3: Matching

Match the sentence halves 1-8 with sentence halves A-H.

1. I am really happy with my university's appearance, the sports facilities and the sculptures, ...
2. I enjoy a lot of things about being a student,...
3. I like my city because it is old, historical and...
4. I love the winters in Beijing because of the snow, ice and clear skies;...
5. As well as being a modern, clean and fashionable place to live,...
6. Although I am generally not a very social person,...
7. My job offers me lots of opportunities to be creative and work in a team...
8. When I go travelling I enjoy going for long walks...

A. ...however, I don't really like going too far into unknown territory – I'm afraid of getting lost!
B. ...I really like my hometown because it's so interesting.
C. ...the thing about working life I enjoy the most is going out to lunch and dinner with my workmates.
D. ...though my favourite thing is most certainly the new restaurant on campus – it's great!
E. ...besides having flexible working hours.
F. ...also a friendly place to live.
G. ...but the thing I like most is the opportunity to meet lots of clever, thoughtful people.
H. ...as opposed to the awful summers with hot, dry air.

For more practice, please go to: www.EQEnglish.com

Formula 7: Is X popular (in your country)?

AIMS 学习目标

In this lesson you'll master the Formula for
"Is X popular (in your country)?" type questions.
本课的高分公式将教会你如何回答下列同类型的问题，比如：

- Are bikes popular in your country?
- Is watching team sports popular where you live?
- Is playing sports popular in your university?
- Is music popular in China?

THE FORMULA 高分公式

When the examiner asks you "Is X popular (in your country)?" type questions, you must:

Answer Order

- Show you understand the question which is asking about PEOPLE IN GENERAL and not YOU.
- Talk about TYPES of people in society like a native.
- Talk about how MANY people like to do X.

Language Steps

1. Talk about types of people. ("*People of all ages* like to ride bikes." / "Most *businessmen* own cars.")
2. Use quantity words to talk about how many people like X. ("I think *most people* ride the subway." / "*The majority* of British people drink milk with their tea.")
3. Use one or two expressions of habit like a native. ("*In general*, Sichuan people enjoy spicy food." / "*As a rule*, older generations are more traditional.")

NATIVE SPEAKER WORDS 英语母语词汇

让我们来学习一些英语母语词汇，这些词汇对于回答该类型的问题非常有用，并且能够帮助你理解下面的答案范例。

Native Speaker Word	Part of Speech	Definition	Example Sentence
generally speaking 一般说来		in most situations, usually, ordinarily	Generally speaking, I don't eat fast food but sometimes – perhaps just a few times a year – I might go to McDonald's.
regularly 定期地，有规律地	adverb	frequently, often	Steve is so fit and strong because he exercises regularly.
as for 至于，关于		used to change the topic of what you are talking about	I love playing golf and tennis. As for cooking, I have no real interest in it.
sexist 歧视妇女（的）；与性别歧视有关的	adjective	describing somebody or something that says men are better than women or women are better than men	In the past, most men were sexist; they didn't believe women could be trusted with money, power of responsibilities.
depend on 取决于，依靠		whether something is true or not is determined by something else	Is Italy a good place to go on holiday? It depends on what kind of holiday you want – if you want to see ancient buildings, eat pizza and drink red wine, it'll be great.
as a rule 通常，一般而言		usually, generally true	As a rule, I'm a very calm person but sometimes I get really annoyed.
pop (music) 流行音乐	noun	the most popular music in a society, usually uncomplicated and easy to remember	Some modern pop music is fantastic – like Coldplay and U2 – but most of it is pretty terrible.
tend 倾向于	verb	to be likely to happen, to usually do something	Bikes tend to be popular with older people and students.
folk music 民间音乐		a traditional style of music, often from the countryside	I don't think anyone listens to English folk music anymore; it's too old-fashioned.
concert 音乐会	noun	an event where musicians play music to a very large audience	I love going to concerts; it's so exciting to see my favourite stars singing and dancing on the stage and the atmosphere is fantastic because there's thousands of people.

MODEL ANSWERS 答案范例

阅读雅思考生Alice和David的参考答案。

Interviewer Is basketball popular in your country?

Alice Yes, basketball is extremely popular in China. Generally speaking, I would say that the majority of high school and university male students regularly play basketball. As for watching basketball, I think most Chinese men under the age of, say 30, frequently watch NBA matches. Although it sounds a bit sexist, I don't believe basketball is very popular with many Chinese women.

Interviewer Is music popular in China?

David I think it depends on what kind of music you are talking about. Most people in China listen to music every day. As a rule, the younger generation usually listens to pop, rock or hip-hop music, whereas older people tend to listen to older Chinese songs or folk music. I think many wealthy people listen to classical music, sometimes going to live concerts.

LANGUAGE STEP 1 Types of People 高分语言点 1 不同类型的人

让我们来看一下雅思考生Alice和David是如何描述不同类型的人的。

Alice ...Generally speaking, I would say that the majority of *high school and university male students* regularly play basketball. As for watching basketball, I think most Chinese men under the age of, say 30, frequently watch NBA matches...I don't believe basketball is very popular with many *Chinese women*.

David ...As a rule, *the younger generation* usually listens to pop, rock or hip-hop music, whereas *older people* tend to listen to older Chinese songs or folk music. I think many *wealthy people* listen to classical music, sometimes going to live concerts.

Notice that both Alice and David say what types of people X is popular with. Talking about types of people is a great way to sound like a native speaker when answering "Is X popular (in your country)?" type questions.

Remember:

- A country is made up of different types of people, different groups.
- These different groups have different interests and likes and dislikes.

So, don't just speak for the whole nation and say:
"Chinese people like to drink tea."

A native speaker will talk about the types of people that X is popular with, rather than saying that all people like it. So, a better answer – that does not generalise – would be:

"In general, *a lot of elderly Chinese people* like drinking tea, though there are some who do not like tea."

Now let's look at some more words and expressions to talk about the different types of people that make up a society:

Age Groups & Generations	Work-Related Groups	Social Classes
the older generation	retired people	poor people
the elderly	office workers	rich people
younger people	white-collar workers	the working classes
school kids	unemployed people	the middle classes
the younger generation	housewives	the upper classes
adolescents	job seekers	

Exercise 7.1: Matching

Match the words on the left with the words on the right that have a similar meaning.

1. elderly people
2. office workers
3. lower classes
4. teenagers
5. the upper classes
6. job seekers

A. the unemployed
B. very wealthy people
C. adolescents
D. the older generation
E. poorer people
F. white-collar workers

Exercise 7.2: Gap fill

Write the words below in the correct spaces.

adolescents　　white-collar workers　　the unemployed
elderly people　　wealthy people

1. Traditional Chinese activities such as playing Chinese chess and *tai chi* (太极拳) are still very popular with ____________ in China.
2. Bikes are not as popular as they were a few years ago. Now, bikes are mostly ridden by poor people (such as ____________) and ____________at school and college.
3. The bus is mainly popular with students and ____________ travelling to and from work; most ____________ tend to have their own car and take taxis everywhere.

LANGUAGE STEP 2 Quantity Words 高分语言点 2 数量词

让我们来回顾一下雅思考生Alice和David使用了哪些词语描述数量。

Alice ...Generally speaking, I would say that *the majority of* high school and university male students regularly play basketball...I think *most* Chinese men under the age of, say 30, frequently watch NBA matches...I don't believe basketball is very popular with *many* Chinese women.

David ...*Most* people in China listen to music every day...I think *many* wealthy people listen to classical music, sometimes going to live concerts.

Again, you will have noticed that David and Alice use quantity words in their answers so that they do not make absolute statements.

Look at the following quantity words which you should master so that you also don't generalise about people:

- most people
  "I think *most people* like to occasionally watch and play sports."
- the majority of people
  "*The majority of* teenagers listen to pop music at least once a week."
- a lot of people
  "I believe *a lot of people* will decide to study abroad in the future."
- (not) many people
  "*Not many elderly people* are interested in basketball."
- a small percentage of people
  "Only *a small percentage of students* have their own cars."
- very few people
  "In my opinion, *very few poor people* have the chance to study English."

Exercise 7.3: Rephrasing

Rephrase the sentences below using the words in brackets.

1. All Chinese people regularly play badminton when they are young. (a lot)

____

2. No women play golf in China. (not many)

____

3. Every single Chinese person likes to listen to music. (the majority of)

____

4. Nobody at my university play table tennis. (very few)

____

5. Everyone watched the 2008 Olympics Opening Ceremony. (most)

____

6. No rich people ever ride a bike. (a small percentage of)

____

LANGUAGE STEP 3 Expressions of Habit
高分语言点 3 描述习惯性行为

我们来看一下雅思考生Alice和David是如何描述习惯性行为的。

Alice ...*Generally speaking*, I would say that the majority of high school and university male students regularly play basketball...

David ...*As a rule*, the younger generation usually listens to pop, rock or hip-hop music, whereas older people *tend to* listen to older Chinese songs or folk music...

When you are trying to talk about a lot of people you should also use different expressions of habit to express that something is general and not true to everyone in that group.

Look at the following expressions to say what people "usually" or "normally" do:

- in general
  "*In general*, people in India like to eat spicy food."

- generally speaking
  "*Generally speaking*, English people don't really learn many other languages."

- as a rule
  This expression simply means "generally", and has nothing to do with rules.
  "*As a rule*, the older generation tends to be more traditional than the younger generation."

- more often than not
  "Businessmen drive cars to work *more often than not*."

- tend to
  "Most people in China *tend to* enjoy playing mah-jong (麻将)."

Exercise 7.4: Word Order

Rewrite the words below in the correct order.

1. football more as boys a rule is with popular

____

2. eat southern speaking rice Chinese a lot of generally

____

3. regularly more than university often sports students play not very

____

4. together sport watching to like tend men

____

5. like rich drive general to cars in people

____

For more practice, please go to: www.EQEnglish.com

Formula 8: What is the best time (of year) to do X?

AIMS 学习目标

In this lesson you'll master the Formula for
"What is the best time (of year) to do X?" type questions.
本课的高分公式将教会你如何回答下列同类型的问题，比如：

- What time of year is best for outdoor activities where you live?
- What is the best time of day for studying?
- What time of year is best for travelling in your country?

THE FORMULA 高分公式

When the examiner asks you "What is the best time (of year) to do X?" type questions, you must:

Answer Order

- Tell the examiner which time is best for X.
- Describe what the conditions at that time are (i.e. weather, social conditions).
- Explain WHY that's the best time.

Language Steps

1. Use superlatives correctly. ("Guilin is *the most beautiful* place in China." / "This is *the best* time to travel.")
2. Use prepositions of time correctly for times of day, month and year. ("Beijing is beautiful *in* the late fall." / "Beijing is beautiful *at* any time *of* the year.")
3. Use a few colloquial expressions for conditions. ("The winter months are *ideal for* skiing." / "The Summer is *perfect for* cycling in the mountains.")

NATIVE SPEAKER WORDS 英语母语词汇

让我们来学习一些英语母语词汇，这些词汇对于回答该类型的问题非常有用，并且能够帮助你理解下面的答案范例。

Native Speaker Word	Part of Speech	Definition	Example Sentence
outdoor 户外的，野外的	adjective	done outside (It is usually used to describe activities that take place in the open air, away from buildings.)	I don't want an office job; I want a job that involves lots of outdoor tasks so that I'm not stuck in an office all day.
depend on 取决于，依靠		to be determined by, changeable according to a particular circumstance or situation	Whether or not you like Sichuan food depends on if you like a lot of spice.
provide 提供，供应	verb	to give somebody something, to supply	Many companies have a bonus scheme to reward staff that work hard. This obviously provides an incentive for the staff to do a good job.
rock climbing 攀岩		an activity where you use your arms and legs to climb up very steep rocks / mountain sides	I've never been good at rock climbing; I think it's because my arms aren't strong enough.
hiking 远足，徒步旅行	noun	a long walk in the countryside, often including hills and mountains	I absolutely love hiking; it's great to walk through green fields, meadows, up hills and through valleys.
be into something 对某事很有兴趣		to be interested in something	My little nephew Daniel is really into aeroplanes; he's always running around the house with a toy aeroplane in his hand and making engine noises.
sledging 滑雪橇	noun	an activity where one sits on a wooden "sledge" and slides down snowy hills, usually popular with children	A few years ago my sister broke her leg when she tried sledging – the hill she went down was far too big.
snowboarding 滑雪板	noun	an activity where one stands with both legs on one "board" and in this way slide down a mountain; much the same as to skateboard, but on snow	Although snowboarding is really fashionable, I'm too frightened of hurting myself to try it.
depth of winter 隆冬，深冬		the coldest part of winter, usually around the middle of winter	My favourite time of the year is the depth of winter. Then, there's usually lots of snow, people are on holiday from work and I can enjoy sitting in front of the fire with a good book.

续表

Native Speaker Word	Part of Speech	Definition	Example Sentence
dawn 黎明，晨曦	noun	the very early time in the morning when the sun first rises	I've only seen the dawn once or twice in my life; I'm far too lazy to get up so early!
get into something 投入做某事		to be able to concentrate on something	This weekend Adam's family is going away and he'll be in the house by himself. He hopes he'll finally be able to get into that big history book he bought recently.
distract 分心，转移注意力	verb	to stop somebody concentrating on something	Whenever I write papers or revise for exams, I must be alone – otherwise I get distracted by the other person and I can't concentrate.
productive 多产的	adjective	producing a lot, providing a large amount of something	Many firms have far too many meetings; often they do not have a clear focus and are not very productive. The company would be better off if the staff kept working.

MODEL ANSWERS 答案范例

阅读雅思考生Alice和David的参考答案。

Interviewer What time of year is best for outdoor activities where you live?

Alice I think the best time of year to do outdoor activities is either in the summer or in the winter, because it depends on what activities you would like to do. The weather between June and early September provides the best conditions for rock climbing, hiking, mountain biking or playing sports like tennis and football because it is warm, sunny and bright. However, if you are into winter activities like ice-skating, sledging and snowboarding then the depth of winter is the best time to do them.

Interviewer What is the best time of day to study?

David I think the best time of day to study is in the very early morning, just after dawn. This is the quietest time of the day, when there is no one else around and everywhere is completely silent. This means I am able to really get into what I'm studying and not be distracted by friends or family. It's definitely the most productive time of day for me, I just find it difficult to get up so early!

LANGUAGE STEP 1 Superlatives 高分语言点1最高级

让我们来看一下雅思考生Alice 和David是如何使用最高级的。

Alice I think *the best* time of year to do outdoor activities is either in the summer or in the winter…The weather between June and early September provides *the best* conditions for rock climbing, hiking, mountain biking or playing sports like tennis…

David I think *the best* time of day to study is in the very early morning, just after dawn. This is *the quietest* time of the day…It's definitely *the most productive* time of day for me, I just find it difficult to get up so early!

Notice that Alice and David both use a number of different superlatives in their model answers. This is also something you should master so that you can answer this type of question correctly.

Let's review some rules about correctly changing adjectives into superlatives.

Adjectives with one syllable

Adjective	Comparative	Superlative
hot	hotter	the hottest
small	smaller	the smallest
light	lighter	the lightest
big	bigger	the biggest

Adjectives with more than one syllable

Adjective	Comparative	Superlative
beautiful	more beautiful	the most beautiful
interesting	more interesting	the most interesting
exciting	more exciting	the most exciting
enjoyable	more enjoyable	the most enjoyable

Remember these exceptions

Adjective	Comparative	Superlative
good	better	the best
bad	worse	the worst
fun	more fun	the most fun

小贴士 最高级似乎是一个大家很熟悉的高分语言点，但重要的是，你一定要在口语考试中恰当地使用它们。

Exercise 8.1: Sentence Completion

Complete the following sentences by writing the appropriate comparative or superlative forms of the adjectives in brackets.

1. Winter is probably ____________ (bad) time of year to travel to Beijing; there are no leaves on the trees, the weather is freezing cold and the people are not happy!
2. Spring is ____________ (beautiful) time of year to go to Guilin. It's lovely and warm and the flowers are all in bloom.
3. Summer is a ____________ (suitable) time of year to visit Harbin than any other seasons. It's the only time when the weather is not cold, but actually quite warm.
4. ____________ (pleasant) season in which to visit Thailand is most certainly Spring, in late March and early April.
5. Winter is ____________ (good) time to go skiing in Beijing.
6. The spring is ____________ (fun) time of year to go climbing in the mountains because it's not too hot and not too cold.
7. Flying a kite is ____________ (enjoyable) thing to do in spring in Shanghai.
8. The height of summer is ____________ (warm) season of the year to go camping.
9. Beijing is undoubtedly much ____________ (hot) than Xi'an in the summer months. It's almost unbearable. I would advise tourists to avoid Beijing at the peak of summer.

LANGUAGE STEP 2 Prepositions of Time 高分语言点2时间介词

让我们来回顾一下雅思考生Alice和David的回答中使用了哪些时间介词。

Alice I think the best time of year to do outdoor activities is either *in* the summer or *in* the winter...The weather *between* June and early September provides the best conditions for...

David I think the best time *of* day to study is *in* the very early morning, just *after* dawn...

To get a good score you must use prepositions of time correctly.

- "At" is used with festivals, the time of day, and with dawn, noon, night, midnight, dusk.
  "The train will arrive *at* 9 p.m."
  "The streets are always busy *at* Christmas."
- "On" is used with a particular day or date.
  "I'm often late to work *on* Mondays."
  "Peter gave Helen a call *on* Friday."
- "In" is used with years, seasons, months, and other parts of the day.
  "She said she would give you a call *in* the evening."
  "For me, Australia is far too hot *in* the summer."

- "By" is used to show that an activity will be completed or end by a certain time or point (and no later).
  "I usually start to feel tired *by* 10 p.m."
  "All the leaves on the trees will have fallen *by* November."
- "During" is used to talk about something that happens at a certain period of time, and can be used with parts of the day, seasons and festivals (<u>not</u> a point in time like "noon").
  "The best time to do exercise is *during* the morning break."
  "Not many people like to visit Xinjiang *during* the summer months."
- "Until" is used to talk about something which will continue to happen until a certain time or particular event occurs.
  "The park is a really quiet place to study *until* about 5 o'clock, when everybody finishes work."
  "I like swimming in the sea *until* late September, after that it gets cold."

小贴士

in 或者 the middle of 后面可以接月份、年份、季节、城市和乡镇。on 后面接星期、the weekend 或者节假日。at 后面接 Christmas, the weekend, the New Year 或者 the beginning of。during 后面接一段时间：the month of January, the weeks, the summer, the spring festival 或者 the holidays。

Exercise 8.2: Gap Fill

Write the words and phrases below in the correct spaces.

on　　in　　at the beginning of　　during　　at　　in the middle of winter

1. The most exciting time to go skiing is ____________ when the snow is really thick and fluffy.
2. The best time of year to climb mountains is certainly ____________ Spring when the air is fresh and cool – not too hot, not too cold.
3. When it is really hot, ____________ the summer months, it is a great time to go swimming in the sea.
4. In Scotland, in March, I like to go walking in the hills. This is the best time for this kind of sport. It's not fun ____________ January or February because of the rain.
5. The time when people give presents the most is certainly ____________ Christmas.
6. However, in China, I think most people give gifts or presents ____________ people's birthdays.

LANGUAGE STEP 3 Colloquial Expressions for Advantageous Conditions
高分语言点 3 对……有利的口头表达

让我们来看一下雅思考生Alice是如何表达对……有利的。

Alice ...The weather between June and early September *provides the best conditions for* rock climbing, hiking, mountain biking or playing sports...

There are many ways to explain the idea that something is "the best" or "the most suitable". We've already looked at superlatives as one way of doing this, but now let's look at some alternative native speaker expressions for this.

- good / great for
  "The cold weather in Harbin is *good for* making ice sculptures."
  "Evenings at home are *great for* relaxing and listening to music."
- ideal for
  "Spring in Beijing is *ideal for* hiking along the Great Wall."
  "The day before a big national holiday is *ideal for* throwing a party."
- provides the perfect conditions for
  "The combination of mountains and lakes near my hometown *provides the perfect conditions* for camping in the summer."
  "The karst stones and dry weather of the summer in Yangshuo *provide the perfect conditions* for rock climbing and mountain biking."

Exercise 8.3: Matching

Match the sentence halves below.

1. Summer is ideal for...
2. The snow in Harbin...
3. Fall is good for...
4. The mountains and rocks in Guilin...
5. The weather in Hainan is...

A. ...provide the perfect conditions for rock climbing.
B. ...swimming in the lake near my town.
C. ...ideal for beach volleyball.
D. ...hiking in the hills and looking at the red leaves.
E. ...provides the perfect conditions for skiing and snowboarding.

EXTRA LANGUAGE POINT Depend On
补充语言点 Depend On 的用法

我们来看一下雅思考生Alice是如何使用depend on这个短语的。

Alice I think the best time of year to do outdoor activities is either in the summer or in the winter, because it *depends on* what activities you would like to do…

When answering "What's the best time (of year) to do X?" type questions, it would be easy to say things such as "Winter in Beijing is always relaxing." or "The morning is the best time of day to study." However, such statements are not always true because situations change according to different circumstances and according to people's preferences. The verb phrase "depends on" helps us qualify what we say.

- "Depend on" can be used by itself.
  "The availability of train tickets during the Spring Festival *depends on* the amount of people travelling."
  "The best time to do exercise *depends on* people's lifestyles."
- Or "depend on" can be used with gerunds (the -ing form of the verb).
  "Finding a good job *depends on having* good qualifications."
  "Being happy doesn't necessarily *depend on being* very rich."

You should practise using this verb phrase. You will sound more like a native English speaker and be able to give more accurate answers if you can use it well.

For more practice, please go to: www.EQEnglish.com

Formula 9: Why do some people like X?

AIMS 学习目标

In this lesson you'll master the Formula for
"Why do some people like X?" type questions.
本课的高分公式将教会你如何回答下列同类型的问题，比如：

- Why do some people like cooking?
- Why do some people enjoy reading?
- Why do some people like gardening?

THE FORMULA 高分公式

When the examiner asks you "Why do some people like X?" type questions, you must:

Answer Order

- Describe why some people enjoy X or doing X.
- Say which types of people or personality enjoy it.
- Explain why it's good for them and why they might like it.

Language Steps

1. Use native words to talk about types of people. ("Most *teenagers* enjoy listening to pop music.")
2. Use native personality adjectives. ("*Creative* people tend to enjoy going to the theatre and art museums.")
3. Use native activity adjectives. ("Volunteering at the hospital is very *rewarding*.")

NATIVE SPEAKER WORDS 英语母语词汇

让我们来学习一些英语母语词汇，这些词汇对于回答该类型的问题非常有用，并且能够帮助你理解下面的答案范例。

Native Speaker Word	Part of Speech	Definition	Example Sentence
creative （人）有创造力的，创新的	adjective	producing or using new and effective ideas, results etc	Working in a bank is not very creative – you just do the same things again and again every day.

续表

Native Speaker Word	Part of Speech	Definition	Example Sentence
express oneself 表达自己的思想		to use something as a way to communicate what you think or feel	I love playing the piano: although I play the music somebody else wrote, I can express myself through the piano – so each time I play it's different.
conservative 保守的，守旧的	adjective	not liking changes or new ideas	Travelling in Asia and Africa is really not suited for conservative people – only open-minded people willing to try and learn new things should go.
from scratch 从头开始，白手起家		to make something from the beginning without using things that already exist	I don't like working at this language school – because it's so new, there aren't any lesson plans or teaching materials. I have to make every lesson plan from scratch.
satisfying 令人满意的	adjective	making you feel pleased – usually because you have achieved something	Stephanie doesn't think her job is very satisfying as she doesn't get a chance to try anything new and she just does whatever her boss tells her to.
therapeutic 治疗的，有疗效的	adjective	making you feel relaxed or happier	When I want to relax, I never go to a bar or club – they're always so noisy and smelly; going to a bar is not therapeutic at all.
patient 有耐心的	adjective	describing a person who can wait or continue doing something unpleasant without complaining	I wish my German teacher was more patient; as soon as I make one little mistake she gets annoyed with me and she only explains things once.
energetic 精力充沛的，有活力的	adjective	describing a person who has a lot of energy or an activity that requires a lot of energy	To lose weight you should be more careful what you eat and start doing some kind of energetic activity like playing badminton or rugby.
unwind 放松，展开	verb	to relax after being very busy, tense or worried	Rachel should take the time to unwind after work; being so anxious all the time can't be good for her health.

MODEL ANSWERS 答案范例

阅读雅思考生Alice和David的参考答案。

Interviewer Why do some people like cooking?

Alice I think people of all ages enjoy cooking, especially creative people. For those who love to create new things, cooking provides a great way to express themselves as they can experiment with different dishes and ingredients. Even quite conservative people like cooking; as everything needs to be created from scratch, it can be very satisfying to successfully cook a whole meal from start to finish.

Interviewer Why do some people like gardening?

David Gardening is most popular with middle-aged and elderly people, probably because gardening is a very therapeutic and relaxing activity. Members of the older generation are generally more patient and often prefer less energetic activities – gardening is a good way to unwind whilst making their home more beautiful.

LANGUAGE STEP 1 Types of People 高分语言点 1 不同类型的人

我们来看一下雅思考生Alice和David是如何描述各种不同类型的人的。

Alice I think *people of all ages* enjoy cooking, especially creative people…

David Gardening is most popular with *middle-aged* and *elderly people*, probably because gardening is a very therapeutic and relaxing activity. *Members of the older generation* are generally more patient and often prefer less energetic activities…

Notice that Alice and David do <u>not</u> talk about <u>themselves</u> and whether they like cooking, but talk about the different types of people in society and say whether they like cooking.

Remind yourself of some useful words to talk about types of people:

- married couples
- single parents
- teenagers
- adolescents
- the elderly
- the older generation
- retired people
- rich people
- poor people

Exercise 9.1: Table Completion

Complete the table below by writing the following words in the appropriate column. Some have been done for you.

grandparents	~~retired people~~	married couples
~~single parents~~	the elderly	office workers
housewives	~~rich people~~	white-collar workers
~~younger people~~	teenagers	~~parents~~
the older generation	job seekers	the younger generation
~~unemployed people~~	people in a relationship	the working classes
the upper classes	couples	~~poor people~~

school kids
property owners
the middle classes
single people
adolescents
the homeless

Age Groups & Generations	Family / Relationship Groups	Work-Related Groups	Social Classes
younger people	parents	retired people	poor people
	single parents	unemployed people	rich people

LANGUAGE STEP 2 Personality Adjectives
高分语言点 2 描述人物性格的形容词

我们来看一下雅思考生Alice和David用了哪些形容词描述人物的性格。

Alice I think people of all ages enjoy cooking, especially *creative* people...Even quite *conservative* people like cooking...

David ...Members of the older generation are generally more *patient* and often prefer less *energetic* activities...

Notice that Alice and David use different personality adjectives to help them say why different groups of people enjoy doing X – you should too.

Look at the following useful native personality adjectives:

- energetic
- apathetic
- curious
- studious
- social
- family-oriented
- patient
- creative

Exercise 9.2: Matching

Match the personality adjectives on the left with their definitions on the right.

1. creative
2. social
3. energetic
4. family-oriented
5. studious
6. apathetic
7. curious

A. somebody who is not interested or concerned about anything
B. somebody who studies a lot, even in their free time
C. somebody who is interested in new things and learning about different ideas and opinions
D. somebody who is outgoing and enjoys talking to others a lot and meeting new people
E. somebody who is very active and enjoys doing physical things
F. somebody who prefers spending time with their family
G. somebody who enjoys making new things

Exercise 9.3: Gap Fill

Write the words below in the correct spaces.

family-oriented   energetic   curious   studious   apathetic   social

1. He is a very ____________ young man – he loves all kinds of sports that involve running around or doing adventurous outdoor pursuits.
2. Alice is very ____________. She spends a lot of free time going to dinners with friends, hanging out in the bar near campus and meeting new people..
3. ____________ people tend to be quite lazy about life, and like sitting around for long hours watching soap operas on television and doing things that do not require much thought or energy.
4. I am a very ____________ person. I am very intrigued to learn about different cultures and different opinions. I like to read about world philosophy and religion sometimes.
5. Daisy is very ____________. She spends nearly every weekend visiting her family and seems to prefer that than going out with friends.
6. He is a very ____________ person – he sits in the classroom till the early hours of the morning just reading and taking notes from his textbooks.

LANGUAGE STEP 3 Activity Adjectives
高分语言点 3 描述人物活动的形容词

让我们来看一下雅思考生Alice 和David是如何描述人物活动的。

Alice ...For those who love to create new things, cooking provides a great way to express themselves as they can experiment with different dishes and ingredients...it can be very *satisfying* to successfully cook a whole meal from start to finish.

David Gardening is most popular with middle-aged and elderly people, probably because gardening is a very *therapeutic* and *relaxing* activity. Members of the older generation are generally more patient and often prefer less *energetic* activities – gardening is a good way to unwind whilst making their home more beautiful.

Notice that Alice and David talk about the benefits people get from doing cooking and gardening – this helps them explain why people like to do these activities.

Look at the following useful native speaker activity adjectives and the types of activity they can be used to describe:

- therapeutic – gardening, cooking, yoga, *tai chi*, meditation
- relaxing – gardening, watching TV, listening to the radio, knitting, reading
- healthy – going to the gym, doing physical exercise, running
- good (for the mind) – crosswords, puzzles, detective stories, studying
- informative – the news, blogs, reading books
- inspiring – looking at art, watching live music, going to the theatre or cinema
- rewarding – doing charity work, studying, raising money for a cause
- fun – sports, games, card games, travelling
- satisfying – painting, drawing, cooking, gardening

Exercise 9.4: Multiple Choice

Choose the appropriate words from the choices below to complete the sentences.

1. I think gardening is a very ____________ activity. Being outdoors helps people relax and feel good.
   A. inspiring B. therapeutic C. healthy
2. I think cycling is a very ____________ pastime. It's better for you than running.
   A. healthy B. good for the mind C. rewarding
3. Reading about history from many different sources is very ____________.
   A. fun B. relaxing C. informative
4. For me, going to the gym everyday, feeling fitter and looking better all the time is truly ____________.
   A. satisfying B. healthy C. inspiring

5. Going to see live music is a really fun and ____________ thing to do on weekends.
   A. therapeutic   B. informative   C. inspiring
6. Doing volunteer or charity work is a ____________ way to help others.
   A. healthy   B. rewarding   C. fun
7. For many married couples, going to expensive restaurants for a romantic dinner is really ____________.
   A. healthy   B. rewarding   C. fun
8. Most people agree that everybody should go to university because studying is ____________ – studying helps broaden our horizons and stretches our brains.
   A. good for the mind   B. therapeutic   C. inspiring

For more practice, please go to: www.EQEnglish.com

Formula 10: When was the first / last time you did X?

AIMS 学习目标

In this lesson you'll master the Formula for "When was the first / last time you did X?" type questions.

本课的高分公式将教会你如何回答下列同类型的问题，比如：

- When was the first time you used a computer?
- When was the last time you went on holiday?
- When was the last time visitors came to your house?

THE FORMULA 高分公式

When the examiner asks you "When was the first / last time you did X?" type questions, you must:

Answer Order

- Say WHEN you first / last did it.
- Say WHY you did it.
- Describe what the experience was LIKE.

Language Steps

1. Use prepositions and adverbs of time correctly. ("*The last time* I went fishing was *about* three years ago." / "*The first time* I used a computer was *in* high school *in* 1984.")
2. Have great control of the past simple to talk about completed events. ("I *went* on holiday last May." / "My father *bought* me a computer when I *was* 10.")
3. Use varied adjectives of experience to sound more like a native. ("Camping in the USA was so *boring*." / "I thought acting was so *intriguing*.")

NATIVE SPEAKER WORDS 英语母语词汇

让我们来学习一些英语母语词汇，这些词汇对于回答该类型的问题非常有用，并且能够帮助你理解下面的答案范例。

Native Speaker Word	Part of Speech	Definition	Example Sentence
intriguing 吸引人的，有趣的	adjective	describing something or someone which is very interesting; perhaps because it is / they are strange or odd	I found my trip to Tibet (西藏) intriguing because the culture was so different to ours; sometimes I felt that the more I learnt about it the less I understood it.
minority 少数民族	noun	a group of people in society who all have the same culture / historical background	The PRC contains 56 different minorities.
trek 艰苦跋涉，徒步旅行	verb / noun	to walk a long way, usually in a natural setting such as in mountains, next to rivers etc	Northern Thailand is a great place for going on mountain treks.
scuba dive / diving 潜水		an activity where people swim deep under the sea using special breathing equipment	The first time I went scuba diving was two years ago, it was great to see all the fish, turtles and shellfish in their natural environment.
reserve 保护区	noun	an area that is protected by the government for environmental reasons (Common collocations are "nature reserve", "forest reserve", "wildlife reserve".)	Kenya is famous for its excellent wildlife reserves, where visitors can see elephants, zebras, lions and tigers in the wild.
come over 过来		to come this place / area from another place (often used with the meaning of "come to my / our house")	Ever since my boyfriend argued with my father, he's been unwilling to come over to our house.
keep somebody from doing something 阻止某人做某事		to prevent, stop somebody from doing something	Most teachers know it's almost impossible to keep students from behaving badly and talking in class.
go to plan 照计划进行		the same as "to go according to plan"; for things to happen in the way you want or expect	I intended to get to the job interview really early and spend some time thinking about the questions I would be asked. But the interview didn't really go to plan; I was late and as soon as I arrived I had to go and have the interview.
certainly 当然	adverb	used to show that there is no doubt about something	It is certainly a huge responsibility and certainly expensive for a country to host the Olympic Games.

MODEL ANSWERS 答案范例

阅读雅思考生Alice和David的参考答案。

Interviewer When was the last time you went on holiday?

Alice The last time I went on holiday was about three years ago…in February 2006. My family and I went to Hainan for two weeks during the Spring Festival. Hainan is an intriguing place to visit because of the Li and Miao minority culture in the west of the island – my family and I drove out to the mountains there, trekked in the Forest Reserve and then learnt how to scuba dive. I really can't wait to go back there!

Interviewer When was the last time visitors came to your house?

David The last time visitors came to my house was just last week. It was my wife's birthday, and so I secretly arranged for a few close friends to come over for dinner and drinks. Although it was difficult to keep my wife from finding out, it was quite exciting in a way and certainly a bit of a challenge! In the end, everything went to plan and we all had a great time – it was definitely a really enjoyable evening.

LANGUAGE STEP 1 Prepositions and Adverbs of Time
高分语言点 1 介词和时间副词

我们来看一下雅思考生Alice和David是如何使用介词和时间副词的。

Alice *The last time* I went on holiday was *about* three years *ago…in* February 2006…

David *The last time* visitors came to my house was just *last* week…

When talking about something that happened in the past, you need to use prepositions and adverbs of time to say <u>when</u> it happened.

Look at the following prepositions and adverbs of time, and how they are used:

- around (months, occasions, festivals, special days)
  "…*around* Christmas…"
  "…*around* my 10th birthday…"

- last (weeks, weekends, months, years, festivals)
  "…*last* weekend…"
  "…*last* month…"

- in (months, seasons, years)
  "…*in* December…"
  "…*in* 1979…"

- during (months, seasons, long festivals)
  "...*during* the Spring Festival..."
  "...*during* the spring..."
- on (days, special days)
  "...*on* the 5th of November 2005..."
  "...*on* my parents' 25th wedding anniversary..."

You should also master using the following useful expressions:

- about + time period + ago
  "I last played a computer game *about two years ago*."
  "They visited the Summer Palace *about three days ago*."
- the last / first time I + past verb + was...
  "*The last time I went* swimming *was* a few hours ago."
  "*The first time I ate* insects *was* in the summer of 2007."

Exercise 10.1: Error Correction

Some of the sentences below are incorrect, some are correct. Identify the incorrect sentences and write the correct sentences in the spaces provided.

1. The last times I play basketball were when I was at school.

   ____

2. In my 25th birthday I go to a Japanese restaurant with my friends and colleagues.

   ____

3. I think my boyfriend's parents coming to visit in Tomb Sweeping Day.

   ____

4. My grandmother give me the computer as a present the before Christmas, so it's still really new.

   ____

5. I went to Thailand on vacation about two years before.

   ____

6. My parents often go abroad during the summer.

   ____

7. I finally passed my driving test on 1997.

   ____

LANGUAGE STEP 2 The Past Simple 高分语言点 2 一般过去时

我们来看一下雅思考生Alice 和David是如何使用一般过去时的。

Alice The last time I *went* on holiday *was* about three years ago…in February 2006. My family and I *went* to Hainan for two weeks during the Spring Festival…my family and I *drove* out to the mountains there, *trekked* in the Forest Reserve and then *learnt* how to scuba dive…

David The last time visitors *came* to my house *was* just last week. It *was* my wife's birthday, and so I secretly *arranged* for a few close friends to come over for dinner and drinks. Although it *was* difficult to keep my wife from finding out, it *was* quite exciting in a way and certainly a bit of a challenge! In the end, everything *went* to plan and we all *had* a great time – it *was* definitely a really enjoyable evening.

小贴士 不要以为一般过去时非常简单，很多英语水平不错的学生往往因为简单的时态错误而失分。

A lot of students, especially when they are nervous in speaking tests, forget to get their past tenses right, especially for irregular verbs. The only way to get it right is to practise.

Look at the table below to remind yourself of the past tense form of some commonly used irregular verbs:

Base Form	Past Tense Form	Base Form	Past Tense Form
come	came	do	did
drink	drank	eat	ate
get	got	give	gave
go	went	read	read

Test yourself by completing the following exercise. You can find the correct answers in the Answer Key section – but don't look until you have completed the table!

Exercise 10.2: Table Completion

Complete the table below with the correct forms of the verbs shown.

Base Form	Past Tense Form	Base Form	Past Tense Form
become		lay	
begin		leave	
break		let	
bring		lose	
build		make	
buy		mean	
catch		meet	
choose		pay	
come		put	
cut		read	
do		ride	
draw		run	
drink		say	
drive		see	
eat		sell	
fall		send	
feed		sleep	
find		stand	
fly		swim	
forget		take	
get		teach	
give		tell	
go		think	
have		try	
hear		understand	
hide		wake	
hit		wear	
keep		welcome	
know		write	

LANGUAGE STEP 3 Adjectives of Experience
高分语言点 3 描述经历的形容词

我们来看一下雅思考生Alice和David用了哪些形容词描述自己的经历。

Alice …Hainan is an *intriguing* place to visit because of the Li and Miao minority culture in the west of the island…

David …Although it was difficult to keep my wife from finding out, it was quite *exciting* in a way and certainly a bit of a challenge! In the end, everything went to plan and we all had a great time – it was definitely a really *enjoyable* evening.

After saying when you last did X, and using prepositions and past simple verbs correctly, you should add a few details to describe what the activity was like.

Here are some useful adjectives of experience:

- difficult, challenging – for things you learned to do that were not easy but you enjoyed learning
- exciting, thrilling, exhilarating, stimulating, enjoyable – for things that you really enjoyed and that were a lot of fun as well as being interesting
- fascinating, intriguing, surprising – for things or experiences that were new and you felt very curious about them before / while doing them
- depressing, upsetting, unpleasant – for things that happened that made you feel sad, very uncomfortable
- embarrassing, humiliating – for things that made you feel very uncomfortable because other people were watching or because you felt silly
- irritating, annoying, frustrating – for things that you did not enjoy because you thought they were stupid, a waste of time or far too difficult

Look at some examples of these words in context:

"The party I attended was really *exciting*. I am not used to going to parties with people from lots of different countries, so it was *fascinating* to see how everyone behaved. It was *surprising* to see so many people having different conversations at the same time!"

"The last time I went on holiday was really *depressing*, if I am honest. It rained the whole time and my mother got sick. It was *upsetting* and *frustrating* because I don't have much time off work and rarely get holidays."

"I used a computer for the first time when I was in middle school. I found it really *embarrassing* because my classmates all knew how to use one but I didn't!"

Notice that Alice and David don't just say simple sentences such as "I found it fun." In the above examples the candidates use adjectives of experience to describe their experiences in a more interesting way and explain why the experience felt like that.

Exercise 10.3: Gap Fill

Write the words below in the correct spaces.

annoying	intriguing	stimulating	enjoyable
thrilling	exhilarating	frustrating	

1. The last time I went to the cinema was about three months ago. My friend and I were really excited about watching the new Zhang Yimou movie but in the end it was really ____________ because we had to queue up for a long time to buy the tickets and the film wasn't that great anyway.
2. The first time I visited an art gallery was in 2005. My family all went together, and whilst my parents were not impressed with modern art, for me it was ____________ because it was all so new, and it made me consider things I had never really thought deeply about before.
3. I last had visitors to my home just a few days ago. They were my and my husband's university classmates, and it was great because their conversation is so ____________ and their company is really ____________. We talk about everything and anything and we always have so much fun.
4. The first time I used a computer was on my 12th birthday, when my uncle gave me a laptop as a present. It was so ____________ to be able to use this brand-new technology to surf the Web, play computer games and chat to my friends!
5. The last time I went to a party was last week. There were lots of foreigners there who I didn't know. Although the atmosphere of meeting lots of new people was ____________, it was really quite ____________ because I felt that I couldn't express myself in English very well.

For more practice, please go to: www.EQEnglish.com

Formula 11: Did you ever learn to do X?

AIMS 学习目标

In this lesson you'll master the Formula for
"Did you ever learn to do X?" type questions.
本课的高分公式将教会你如何回答下列同类型的问题，比如：

- Did you learn how to ride a bike when you were a child?
- Did you learn to play a musical instrument in school?
- Did you learn how to swim when you were young?

THE FORMULA 高分公式

When the examiner asks you "Did you ever learn to do X?" type questions, you must:

Answer Order

- Say if you did learn to do X and when you learned to do it.
- Say who taught you to do X.
- Say what their personality was like as a teacher.

Language Steps

1. Use past tenses accurately with times in life words and phrases. ("I *bought* a flute *when I was in University*." / "My parents *gave* me a computer *for my 11th birthday*.")
2. Say who taught you with the preposition "by". ("I was taught *by my grandmother*." / "I was introduced to the guitar *by my friend Stephen*.")
3. Use non-defining relative clauses and adjectives of personality to describe the person who taught you. ("...he was a *patient* and *kind* teacher." / "Miss Clark, *who taught me Maths*, was a *strict* teacher!")

NATIVE SPEAKER WORDS 英语母语词汇

让我们来学习一些英语母语词汇，这些词汇对于回答该类型的问题非常有用，并且能够帮助你理解下面的答案范例。

Native Speaker Word	Part of Speech	Definition	Example Sentence
encouraging 令人鼓舞的	adjective	making you feel more confident or hopeful about something	My friend, Bert, was really encouraging when I was worried about my exams.
strict 严格的	adjective	being quite controlling and making sure someone does what they should do	My teacher, Mr. Hill, was a strict man, but quite fair.
determined 坚决的，确定的	adjective	wanting to do something very much and not letting any difficulties stop you	Mike was determined to climb to the peak of the mountain. He never gave up trying.
supportive 支持的	adjective	helping someone do something by giving them support and advice	I found it hard to learn Japanese at first, but my tutor was remarkably supportive, always encouraging me and praising me whenever I spoke well.
semi-professional 半职业的，半专业的	adjective	describing people who are semi-professional and who are paid for an activity which they take part in but which they do not do all the time	Some of the sports teachers in my school were also semi-professional athletes.
get to grips with 学会，入门		to learn the basics of something	I found the guitar a little hard at first, but with patience and practice I got to grips with it.
learn by trial and error 在反复试验，不断摸索中学习		to learn something by yourself, making mistakes and learning from them	Jimi Hendrix did not have a guitar teacher. He taught himself, and learned by trial and error.

MODEL ANSWERS 答案范例

阅读雅思考生Alice和David的参考答案。

Interviewer Did you ever learn to ride a bike as a child?

Alice Yes, I did! Hmmm...Let me think. It was during the Spring Festival. My parents bought me a really wonderful new bike. I was taught to ride by my uncle, who was incredibly encouraging but quite strict because he was determined to teach me to ride before the end of the holiday.

Interviewer Did you learn to swim when you were in school?

David I did not learn to swim at school because my school did not have any swimming classes, but I learned to swim for a few months one summer when my parents took me to classes at the local swimming pool. I went every other day with a small group of friends. We were taught by a really friendly and supportive man, who was a semi-professional swimmer.

LANGUAGE STEP 1 Past Tenses & Times in Life Phrases
高分语言点 1 过去时态和人生不同时期的表达

我们来看一下雅思考生Alice和David是如何使用过去时态以及如何用英语描述人生的不同时期的。

Alice *Yes, I did!* ...It was *during the Spring Festival*. My parents *bought* me a really wonderful new bike...

David *I did not learn* to swim at school because my school *did not have* any swimming classes, but I learned to swim *for a few months one summer* when *my parents took me to classes* at the local swimming pool. I *went every other day* with a small group of friends...

David and Alice use past tenses accurately. The past simple can be used here in two different ways:

- Using the past simple to talk about something that is finished and in the past:
  "I *learned* to swim..."
  "I *did not learn* to swim, because..."

- Using the past simple to talk about habitual actions in the past:
  "I *went* every other day..."
  "I *practised* playing the guitar three evenings a week..."

It's important to tell the examiner when you did or did not learn to do X using the following times in life phrases:

- when I was + age
  "*When I was 10 years old* my grandfather showed me how to make..."

- on my + birthday
  "*On my* 8th *birthday* I found out how to..."

- during + holiday
  "*During the Spring Festival holiday* my father taught me to..."

- about + number + years ago
  "*About two years ago* I learned how to play..."

- one day
  "*One* cold, wet *day* in December my sister taught me that..."

And for habitual actions remember these adverbs of frequency:

- every day / every other day / every week / every month
  "I went to the swimming pool *every other day* until I could swim."
- about twice a week / month
  "I had classes with my trumpet teacher *about twice a week*."
- occasionally / from time to time / sometimes / quite often / frequently
  "*From time to time* my aunt would teach me a little Spanish."

Exercise 11.1: Sentence Completion & Matching

Complete the sentences 1-5 below by writing the correct forms of the verbs in brackets in the spaces, then match them to the appropriate halves A-E.

1. I first ____________ (start) learning to play the piano when I was 10 years old…
2. I did not learn to drive, but my older brother did. He first ____________ (drive) a car when he was about 16 years old, around my uncle's farm yard…
3. I ____________ (get to grips) with using the Internet quite quickly. Nobody taught me, though…
4. On my 16th birthday my father gave me a water colour painting set and my grandfather, who could paint quite well ____________ (teach) me to paint small birds…
5. When I was a child I ____________ (go) to swimming lessons twice a week during the summer holidays…

A. …Now, I go to the local pool in my city on a regular basis.
B. …I learned by trial and error.
C. …My parents wouldn't let me try because they said I was too young. I've never had an opportunity since, which is a shame!
D. …I played it every day for a couple of hours, through 2nd and 3rd grade.
E. …He had quite a talent for artistic things. He used to practise calligraphy in the local park several times a week.

LANGUAGE STEP 2 Saying Who Taught You
高分语言点 2 描述是谁教你的

我们来看一下雅思考生Alice和David如何描述是谁教他们做某事的。

Alice *…I was taught to ride by my uncle…*
David *…We were taught by…a semi-professional swimmer.*

Notice how Alice and David use the simple structure I was taught (to activity) by + the person who taught them and some information about them. This is a simple language step, but it's important you get it right.

Look at these other examples:

- I was taught (to activity) by + the person

  "*I was taught to knit by my auntie...*"

  "*I was taught to ride a motorbike by my uncle's friend...*"

  "*I was taught to cook by my grandmother...*"

  "*I was taught to write by my father...*"

  "*I was taught to play football by an elder boy* who lived in my street..."

You can also use I learned (how to do) it from + person, to say who taught you:

- I learned (how to do) it from + person

  "*I learned (how) to play the violin from Mr. Chevins*, my teacher."

  "*I learned (how) to sprint from my best friend*, Ben Johnson."

  "I can use spreadsheets well. *I learned (how) to use them from my dad*."

  "I love to make short films with a video camera. *I learned (how) to use it from my friend*, Yorick."

LANGUAGE STEP 3 Non-Defining Relative Clauses and Adjectives of Personality
高分语言点 3 非限制性定语从句和描述人物性格的形容词

首先，我们来看一下雅思考生Alice和David是如何使用非限制性定语从句的。

Alice ...I was taught to ride by my uncle, *who was incredibly encouraging but quite strict...*

David ...We were taught by *a really friendly and supportive man, who was a semi-professional swimmer.*

Notice how after naming the person who taught them, Alice and David go on to say what their personality was like.

Look at the following useful adjectives of personality:

- caring
- supportive
- encouraging
- kind
- understanding
- talented
- firm
- patient / impatient
- strict
- aggressive

These adjectives of personality can also be combined with non-defining relative clause. A non-defining relative clause provides extra information about the person you are talking about, and takes the form who + extra information (for more about relative clauses, see Part Two, Person Monologue Stage 1).

There are two ways to use non-defining relative clauses:

- part of sentence, non-defining relative clause, part of sentence
  "My mother, *who was a fantastic cook*, taught me how to make bread."
- sentence, non-defining relative clause
  "I was taught to make bread by my mother, *who was a fantastic cook*."

Look at these other examples of sentences combining adjectives of personality and non-defining relative clauses:

"I was taught by my brother, *who was very impatient*."

"I was taught by a neighbour, *who was particularly kind and understanding*."

"When I was young, my friend Daniel, *who was firm but fair*, taught me how to play tennis."

"I learned to play cricket from my Mr. Philips, *who was quite an aggressive and quick-tempered teacher*."

Exercise 11.2: Error Correction & Matching

Each of the sentences 1-5 has one mistake. Identify and correct the mistakes, then match the sentences to their counterparts A-E.

1. I learned English by two really good teachers in middle school...
   ____
2. I learned to use spreadsheets from trial and error. I was not taught by anyone...
   ____
3. I was learned how to sing by a friend of my mother,...
   ____
4. I first learn to write characters by my father,...
   ____
5. I taught how to do Web design by using an online tutorial and going through each section every day on my own...
   ____

A. ...who was a friendly, creative woman.

B. ...I got to grips with them pretty fast, because I'm quite good at anything related to mathematics.

C. ...They were both very patient and kind.

D. ...who was an excellent calligrapher and an understanding, encouraging teacher.

E. It took a while to get the hang of, but it was an interesting way to learn.

EXTRA LANGUAGE POINT Phrases to Express Freedom & Constraints
补充语言点 表达自由和限制的短语

我们来看一看下面的句式，学习一下如何用英语表达自由和限制。

It's good to use expressions to say why you did or did not learn to do things in your life. Look at these examples and think how you could use such phrases yourself:

- I was lucky because my parents gave me the chance to + activity.
- I was very fortunate that I had the opportunity to + activity.
- It's a shame I did not have enough time to + activity.
- It's unfortunate I could not do + activity, because my parents couldn't afford it.
- I wish I had had more ambition and patience when I was younger, then I might have learned to do + activity.

For more practice, please go to: www.EQEnglish.com

Formula 12: How has X changed?

AIMS 学习目标

In this lesson you'll master the Formula for "How has X changed?" type questions.

本课的高分公式将教会你如何回答下列同类型的问题，比如：

- How have shops changed in your city in the last five years?
- How has your hometown changed in recent years?
- How have restaurants in your country changed since you were young?

THE FORMULA 高分公式

When the examiner asks you "How has X changed?" type questions, you must:

Answer Order

- Say whether X has changed or not.
- Compare what X was like in past and what X is like now.

Language Steps

1. Use the present perfect tense. ("Since I was young my town *has changed* in a lot of ways...")
2. Control other simple tenses like past and present. ("My town *was* small. Now it *is* quite big." / "The streets *used to be* quiet. Now they *are* very noisy.")
3. Use comparative adjectives. ("The streets are *wider* and the traffic is *heavier* than before.")

NATIVE SPEAKER WORDS 英语母语词汇

让我们来学习一些英语母语词汇，这些词汇对于回答该类型的问题非常有用，并且能够帮助你理解下面的答案范例。

Native Speaker Word	Part of Speech	Definition	Example Sentence
low-rise 不高的，低层的	adjective	describing buildings which are low, usually just one or two stories	My town is fairly small and old. There aren't any skyscrapers or high-rise buildings; all the buildings are low-rise houses and apartments.

续表

Native Speaker Word	Part of Speech	Definition	Example Sentence
narrow 狭窄的	adjective	having a small distance from one side to the other, especially in comparison with the length	The street was so narrow that Arnold could not drive his big lorry down it.
replace 取代，替换	verb	to take the place of something, or to put something or someone in the place of something or someone else	They've taken down the old stone bridge and replaced it with a stronger iron bridge.
facilities 设施	noun	the buildings and equipments provided at a certain place for a particular purpose	There are lots of sports, shopping and medical facilities in my neighbourhood.
eatery 小餐馆，食堂	noun	a small place where one can sit and eat, usually a more simple place than a restaurant	There are a lot of cheap eateries near the drum tower, with excellent local food.
elegant 高雅的，精致的	adjective	attractive and stylish	The restaurant they chose for the wedding was so elegant – the style and decoration was so wonderful!
impersonal 冷淡的，客观的	adjective	lacking in local warmth or individuality	Big expensive hotels are often quite cold impersonal compared to small family-run guest houses.

MODEL ANSWERS 答案范例

阅读雅思考生Alice和David的参考答案。

Interviewer How has your hometown changed in recent years?

Alice I'm from Beijing and it has certainly changed a lot in recent years. Not so long ago there were lots more low-rise buildings and narrow *hutong* streets; now the local government has replaced them with tall apartment buildings with better facilities and modern shopping centres. The streets are now much wider than before. They have also put a lot more parks in the city and have planted thousands of trees in the streets, so the city is more beautiful.

Interviewer How have restaurants changed in your country since you were a child?

David That's a good question. Restaurants and eateries have changed a great deal since I was young. When I was a kid nearly all restaurants in our city were cheap and quite simple. Now, however, a wide range of Chinese and many international restaurants line every street. These are a lot cleaner and more elegant than the small eateries, but sadly are more impersonal and much more expensive!

LANGUAGE STEP 1 The Present Perfect 高分语言点1现在完成时

我们来看一下雅思考生Alice和David是如何使用现在完成时的。

Alice I'm from Beijing and it *has certainly changed* a lot in recent years. Not so long ago there were lots more low-rise buildings and narrow *hutong* streets; now the local government *has replaced* them with tall apartment buildings...They *have also put* a lot more parks in the city and *have planted* thousands of trees...

David ...Restaurants and eateries *have changed* a great deal since I was young...

Notice that Alice and David use the present perfect accurately to talk about changes that have happened.

Remember that the structure of the present perfect is:

- have + past participle

  "She *has invested* lots of money in a KTV bar."

  "The government *has spent* lots of money on public transport recently."

  "The traffic situation has *become* a lot worse in the last few years."

Exercise 12.1: Sentence Completion

Complete the sentences below by writing the present perfect forms of the verbs in brackets.

1. In recent years people ____________ (cut) down a lot of trees in the Brazilian jungle.
2. Cleaner streets, nicer buildings and better transport ____________ (bring) a lot of tourists to this city in the past couple of years.
3. This week the authorities ____________ (fight) to restore law and order to the city, with great success.
4. My university campus ____________ (undergo) a lot of changes in the past few years.
5. My parents ____________ (spend) a considerable amount of money fitting a new kitchen and bathroom in our home.
6. In recent years, fashion ____________ (become) much more interesting and stylish.

LANGUAGE STEP 2 The Past Simple & Present Simple 高分语言点2一般过去时和一般现在时

让我们来看一下雅思考生Alice和David是如何使用现在时和过去时的。

Alice ...Not so long ago there *were* lots more low-rise buildings and narrow *hutong* streets...The streets *are* now much wider than before...the city *is* more beautiful.

David ...Restaurants and eateries have changed a great deal since I *was* young. When I *was* a kid nearly all restaurants in our city *were* cheap...Now, however, a wide range of Chinese and many international restaurants *line* every street. These *are* a lot cleaner and more elegant than the small eateries...

Alice and David use past simple and present simple accurately to talk about changes. This may seem like a very simple language point, but many students get a low score on the test for making basic mistakes with these tenses.

Look at some example sentences that use these tenses to talk about change:

"My town *was* small; now it *is* quite big."

"The streets *used to be* very quiet; now they *are* noisy."

"The shops *sold* poor quality clothes; now they *sell* the latest designer fashions."

"Before, many people *ate* at small eateries or night markets, but now people *choose* more expensive restaurants."

Exercise 12.2: Sentence Completion

Complete the sentences below by writing the correct forms of the verbs (in the present simple or past simple) in brackets.

1. When I was a child everyone in my area of town had to shower in communal bathrooms in the street. Now, however, most people ____________ (be) wealthy enough to have their own, modern bathrooms.
2. Before, many people ____________ (go) to small shops or markets to buy groceries. In recent years, big supermarkets have become very popular.
3. In the past the suburbs ____________ (not look) very attractive. Now, because the government has planted lots of trees and plants, the area ____________ (look) very pleasant.
4. In the past it ____________ (cost) a lot of money to buy aeroplane tickets, but recently prices have gone down and air travel is more accessible to everyone.
5. Many years ago music was very different compared to now. In the past people ____________ (play) traditional instruments and ____________ (enjoy) singing together in parks and gardens.

LANGUAGE STEP 3 Comparative Adjectives
高分语言点 3 形容词的比较级

我们来看一下雅思考生Alice和David是如何使用形容词的比较级的。

Alice ...now the local government has replaced them with tall apartment buildings with *better* facilities...The streets are now much *wider* than before. They have also put a lot more parks in the city and have planted thousands of trees in the streets, so the city is *more beautiful*.

David ...These [the modern restaurants] are a lot *cleaner* and *more elegant* than the small eateries, but sadly *more impersonal* and *much more expensive!*

Notice how Alice and David use a lot of comparatives to explain how their cities have changed and to express whether those changes are good or bad.

This is a very important part of your answer, so now let's review comparatives.

Comparative adjectives

We add an "-er" on the end of the adjective, or we add "more" before the adjective.

To form the comparative of an adjective, you should:

- Add "-er" if the adjective is one syllable long.
- Add "-ier" if the adjective is more than one syllable and ends in -y.
- Add "more" before the adjective if it is two or more syllables long.

Look at the table to refresh your memory.

Short Adjectives		-y Adjectives		Long Adjectives	
Adjective	Comparative Form	Adjective	Comparative Form	Adjective	Comparative Form
cheap	cheaper	easy	easier	expensive	more expensive
large	larger	heavy	heavier	comfortable	more comfortable
fast	faster	pretty	prettier	fashionable	more fashionable
slow	slower	ugly	uglier	useful	more useful

Comparative structure

In comparing the past to the present it is also useful to remember this structure:

- X is + comparative adjective + than + time in the past

  "My city is *prettier* than it was ten years ago."

  "The university library is much *better* stocked now than it was before."

  "The city is a lot *greener* than it was when I was a child."

Exercise 12.3: Gap Fill

Write the correct adjectives in the correct comparative adjective forms to complete the sentences.

fashionable　　fast　　cheap　　expensive　　good　　wide

1. The food is so much ____________ and much ____________ than here in the capital – I really don't like the expensive food here.

2. Since they built the high speed train I can travel home to see my parents on weekends very easily. It's about five times ____________ than the older train.
3. People are, in general, a lot ____________ today than they were years ago. I think it's because they have more money and enjoy buying nice clothes.
4. The downside of all this development is that the gap between the rich and the poor is getting much ____________.
5. As a result of all this rapid, sudden growth, food is considerably ____________ than it was five years ago.

For more practice, please go to: www.EQEnglish.com

Formula 13: How would you improve X?

AIMS 学习目标

In this lesson you'll master the Formula for "How would you improve X?" type questions.
本课的高分公式将教会你如何回答下列同类型的问题，比如：

- How would you improve your apartment?
- How would you change the place where you study to make it better?
- If you could, how would you improve your university / workplace?

THE FORMULA 高分公式

When the examiner asks you "How would you improve X?" type questions, you must:

Answer Order

- Identify problems with X.
- Talk about what you would do to solve them / make them better.
- Say what the positive results of these changes would be.

Language Steps

1. Use changing X phrases to talk about changes you would like to make. ("I *would improve my apartment by buying* new furniture." / "I *suggest that they make it better by employing* more cleaners.")
2. Use the "would have something done" passive to talk about things you'd get professionals / other people to do for you to improve X. ("I *would have the walls painted* a new colour.")
3. Use comparatives of convenience to speculate about how these changes would make X better. ("Having a bigger bed would be *more comfortable*.")

NATIVE SPEAKER WORDS 英语母语词汇

让我们来学习一些英语母语词汇，这些词汇对于回答该类型的问题非常有用，并且能够帮助你理解下面的答案范例。

Native Speaker Word	Part of Speech	Definition	Example Sentence
crowded 拥挤的	adjective	having a lot of people or things	I hate travelling to work by subway in the morning – it's always far too crowded!
stuff 东西	noun	colloquial expression for "things"	There's too much stuff in my house. I need to have a big tidy up soon.
keep track of 了解；记录，留心		to keep an eye on, to keep informed about, to not lose something	I must keep track of my things better. I nearly always lose things because I am not organised enough.
messy 杂乱的	adjective	untidy, badly organised or unpresentable	His bedroom is messy, his hair is messy and his clothes are scruffy. He should care more about his appearance.
cramped 拥挤的，狭窄的	adjective	describing a place where there is too little space, and too many things occupying that space, very crowded	Our dormitory has six people in such a small place. It is so cramped nobody has any personal space.
cosy 温暖舒适的	adjective	comfortable and pleasant, often warm	He has a comfortable sofa and some attractive wall paintings. His flat is very cosy.
get rid of 除掉，扔掉		to throw something out, or give something away that you don't want anymore	I finally got rid of the old, ugly couch. I gave it to Caroline.
scruffy 不整齐的，肮脏的	adjective	untidy, messy, unkempt, unpresentable	I don't like people who wear scruffy clothes and have scruffy hair – people should take care of their appearance and how it affects others.
run down 用坏的，耗尽的		in bad condition because no one has spent money on repairs	The zoo is really run down. It looks like nobody has not looked after the buildings for years and years.
up-keep 维护	verb	to look after, to keep in good condition, to maintain	Recently the authorities have spent quite a lot of money on up-keeping old buildings.
caretaker 看管者，看守员	noun	a person whose job is to care for and maintain a building, usually a school or other large building	The caretaker at my school didn't like me and my friends because we would always make a mess in the classrooms and draw on the walls of the toilet.
modernise 使现代化	verb	to update, to make more modern	They are modernising the entire city centre – building new buildings and improving the roads.

MODEL ANSWERS 答案范例

阅读雅思考生Alice和David的参考答案。

Interviewer How would you improve your apartment?

Alice To start with, the place I'm living in now is quite small and crowded. I have too much stuff, and it makes it hard to keep track of things, and makes everything look messy and very cramped. There's also very little light in my flat. So, firstly, I would make more space by getting rid of some of my things. Then, I would have the windows made bigger and lighter curtains made and fitted. Then my flat would be much cosier.

Interviewer How would you improve your university to make it better?

David My university campus is quite scruffy and run-down. I suggest the authorities improve it by spending more money on up-keeping the grounds and modernising the classrooms. If I were in authority I would have new classrooms built, I would have the sports facilities repaired, and I would hire more caretakers. Having a more modern campus would make life more pleasant for us, and the place more appealing to visitors.

LANGUAGE STEP 1 Changing X Phrases
高分语言点 1 描述对X的改变

我们来看一下雅思考生Alice和David是如何描述对某件事情的改变的。

Alice To start with, the place I'm living in now is quite small and crowded...So, firstly, I *would make more space by getting rid of* some of my things...

David My university campus is quite scruffy and run-down. I *suggest the authorities improve it by spending* more money on up-keeping the grounds and *modernising* the classrooms...

Notice how both Alice and David start by identifying the problem, then go on to use the structure improve X by + verb-ing to talk about changes they would make or they suggest others should make.

For changes you would make

- I would improve X by + verb-ing

  "I *would improve* my bedroom *by putting* posters on the walls."

  "I *would make* my living room cosier *by buying* a new sofa."

  "I *would improve* my flat *by getting* a new wardrobe."

For changes you suggest others make

- suggest someone improve X by + verb-ing

"I *suggest the government improve the air quality by restricting* the amount of cars in the city."

"I *suggest the school authorities improve security by building* a wall around the playground."

"I *suggest they make the city more attractive by planting* more trees and flowerbeds."

Exercise 13.1: Matching

Match the sentence halves.

1. I would improve my area of my office by...
2. I suggest that they make classrooms more comfortable for students by...
3. I would make my flat more cosy by...
4. I suggest they improve the public transport system by...
5. I would make our canteen better by...

A. ...building a few more subway lines.
B. ...suggesting they vary the menu more.
C. ...investing in a more comfortable couch and redecorating it.
D. ...cleaning up some of the mess and being more organised.
E. ...fitting new modern desks and installing new heaters.

LANGUAGE STEP 2 The "Would Have Something Done" Passive
高分语言点 2 请人做某事

我们来看一下雅思考生Alice和David是如何描述请人做某事的。

Alice ...I *would have* the windows *made* bigger and lighter curtains made and fitted...

David ...If I were in authority I *would have* new classroom *built*, I *would have* the sports facilities *repaired*...

Notice how Alice and David use the would have + something + past participle to talk about what they would get others to do.

First look at the difference between the active (what you would do) and the passive (what you would get others to do):

"I *would make* the windows bigger." = "I would do it myself."

"I *would have* the windows *made* bigger." = "I would get someone else to come and do it for me."

Look at these further examples of the passive:

- would have + something + past participle

"I *would have a new kitchen installed*."

"I *would have the walls painted* different colours."

"I *would have my motorbike fixed*."

"I *would have a brand-new bath fitted*."

Exercise 13.2: Error Correction

Some of the sentences below are incorrect, some are correct. Identify the incorrect sentences and write the correct sentences following the rules above.

1. To make my daily routine a bit more interesting, I would do some kind of sporting activity in the evenings.

   ____

2. To make my living room more homely, I put a bookshelf in the corner and some plants.

   ____

3. To make the kitchen better I would get rid of the old units and have a totally new, modern kitchen install.

   ____

4. To make my house look more cheerful I paint the walls of my living room a brighter colour.

   ____

5. To let more light in my house and create more space, I has the balcony extended.

   ____

LANGUAGE STEP 3 Comparatives of Convenience
高分语言点 3 用比较级描述便利性

我们来看一下雅思考生Alice和David是如何运用比较级描述便利性的。

Alice ...Then my flat *would be much cosier*.

David ...Having a more modern campus *would make life more pleasant* for us, and the place *more appealing* to visitors.

To say how the changes you propose would make life better, you should use the following structures:

- ...then X would be + comparative
  "...*then* my university campus *would be warmer*."
  "...*then* my dorm would be *more attractive*."
  "...*then* life would be *more convenient*."
  "...*then* my living room *would be more comfortable*."

- having X / having X done + would make (something / place) + comparative
  "*Having* a carpet fitted *would make* my room *more beautiful and warmer*."
  "*Putting up* a few pictures on the wall *would make* my dorm *more attractive*."
  "*Installing* a new kitchen *would make* life *more convenient* for me."
  "*Buying* a new sofa *would make* my living room much *more comfortable*."

Exercise 13.3: Gap Fill

Write the words below in the correct spaces.

cosier	easier	hanging	having
installing	would make	powerful	warmer

1. ____________ a new heater would make my room considerably ____________.
2. ____________ up some pictures and tidying up a bit would make our flat much ____________.
3. Getting a larger memory for my computer ____________ it more ____________ and faster.
4. We should spend more money on urban planning. Then my city would be much ____________ to get around.
5. ____________ a car would make those picturesque countryside towns in the mountains much more accessible.

For more practice, please go to: www.EQEnglish.com

Formula 14: How important is X?

AIMS 学习目标

In this lesson you'll master the Formula for
"How important is X?" type questions.
本课的高分公式将教会你如何回答下列同类型的问题，比如：

- How important is art in life?
- How important is music for people in your country?
- How important is physical exercise?

THE FORMULA 高分公式

When the examiner asks you "How important is X?" type questions, you must:

Answer Order

- Say whether X is important or not.
- Say HOW important X is.
- Say WHY it is important or unimportant.

Language Steps

1. Use words and expressions to express degree of importance. ("Music is *especially* important in today's society, but I don't think art is very important.")
2. Use positive adjective expressions. ("It is *essential for* all children to learn to draw." / "It is very *beneficial to do* exercise.")
3. Use adjectives of positive and negative feeling to describe feelings about art and culture. ("I find art and music really *inspiring* and *stimulating*.")

NATIVE SPEAKER WORDS 英语母语词汇

让我们来学习一些英语母语词汇，这些词汇对于回答该类型的问题非常有用，并且能够帮助你理解下面的答案范例。

Native Speaker Word	Part of Speech	Definition	Example Sentence
sculpture 雕塑，雕像	noun	a three-dimensional work of art – usually a statue or a figure	I like modern sculptures. Though they are sometimes slightly strange and it is hard to see what they represent, I find looking at three-dimensional shapes interesting.
architecture 建筑	noun	the character or design style of a building	I love 18th century architecture. In fact, I love most old building styles – they look so elegant.
earn 赚得，挣钱	verb	to obtain money, payment for working	John earns a lot of money. He has three jobs and simply doesn't stop working.
inspire 鼓舞，启发	verb	to fill someone with excitement, and be interested in something	I am really inspired by all types of art – art makes me think about life, philosophy and beauty in a passionate way.
reflect on 深思，仔细考虑		to think about deeply or in a deeper way than usual	When I visit museums and see all the ancient collections I start to reflect on the importance of history in life.
contemporary 现代的	adjective	coming from the present day, not the past	Zhang Yimou is a contemporary movie director with a unique style.

MODEL ANSWERS 答案范例

阅读雅思考生Alice和David的参考答案。

Interviewer How important is art in life?

Alice I think art is exceedingly important in life, especially today. People spend most of their lives worrying about working, studying or earning money – and it is easy to forget the value of art – paintings, sculptures and even contemporary architecture. People need to see beauty in their lives...art is really fascinating and can inspire us to think more deeply and reflect on life.

Interviewer How important is music for people in your country?

David Well, it really depends on the types of people you are talking about. In general, music is especially important for young people, in particular, university students from big cities. Personally, I believe that some types of music are good for helping people calm down and relax, and other types are excellent for energising people. Going to live concerts, for example, can be a really stimulating experience.

LANGUAGE STEP 1 Expressing Degree of Importance 高分语言点 1 表达不同程度的重要性

我们来看一下雅思考生Alice和David是如何描述不同程度的重要性的。

Alice I think art is *exceedingly important* in life...

David Well, it really depends on the types of people you are talking about. In general, music is *especially important* for young people...

Rather than saying "art is important", Alice and David use different adverbs of degree to say how important art is. Look at the following ways to express different degrees of importance:

Moderately important

"Art is *fairly important* in life..."

"*To some extent* art is *important*..."

"Art is *important to a point*, but..."

Very important

"Mathematics is *considerably important*..."

"Learning to swim is *incredibly important*..."

"Eating fresh fruit and vegetables is *very important*..."

"I think that art is *very important* in life..."

"I don't think art is *particularly important* for young people..."

"Art is *especially / particularly important* in today's society..."

Note: With "especially important" and "particularly important" we can use "for" or "in" in the following ways:

- for + groups / types of people
  "Art is especially important *for children*."
- in + society / place / country
  "A good education is terribly important *in modern society*."

Unimportant

"Following fashion is *not important at all*."

"Having a camera on mobile phone is *completely unimportant*."

小贴士

我们不可以说 completely important 或者 absolutely important，在英语中 completely 只能用来形容带有否定意义的词语，比如：

"It is *completely* ridiculous!"

"I think art is *completely* unimportant!"

"He is *completely* mad!"

Exercise 14.1: Gap Fill

Write the words below in the correct spaces.

fairly   to some extent   incredibly   completely   especially

1. Physical exercise is important for everyone, but it is ____________ important for older people. If they don't exercise, their bodies will become more and more rigid and unhealthy.
2. I think it depends. Art is important in life ____________, but I think there are many more things that are much more important – like earning money and having a stable life.
3. I don't think art is important at all. Art is quite useless and is a luxury, not a need. All forms of art, in my opinion, are ____________ unimportant in life.
4. Especially for young children, I think art is ____________ important. It can help them learn about the world around them. and help them learn about colours and shapes – these are vital for children's development.
5. I think there are many things in life that are more important than art, but I think art is ____________ important in making the world we live in more beautiful and interesting.

LANGUAGE STEP 2 Positive Adjective Expressions
高分语言点 2 表示积极意义的形容词

让我们来看一下雅思考生Alice和David是如何使用表示积极意义的形容词的。

Alice …art is really fascinating and *can inspire us* to think more deeply and reflect on life.

David …I believe that some types of music are *good for helping people calm down and relax* and other types are *excellent for energising people*…

After stating whether something is important or not, native speakers often say what X is important for, what it is good for or what it is useful for.

Look at these different positive adjective expressions:

- X is important for / excellent for / good for + verb-ing
  "Gardening is *important for helping* people relax."
  "Working out in a gym is *important for keeping fit*."
  "Having massages is *good for helping* people calm down."
  "Drinking hot milk is *excellent for solving* sleep problems."

- X + a good way to + verb
  "Listening to music is *a good way to help* people calm down after a stressful day."
  "Doing physical exercise is *a good way to keep* fit and healthy and happy."
  "Swimming is *an excellent way to release* a lot of energy and maintain a good figure."

- X helps us / helps people / can help us + (to) + verb
  "Spending weekends out in the countryside *helps us (to) wind down*."
  "Taking part in team quizzes *can help people* sharpen their minds."
  "Lifting weights *can help us* develop strong muscles."

Exercise 14.2: Gap Fill

Write the words below in the correct spaces.

can help us	for helping	cycling	excellent way
excellent for	a good way	helps	

1. Running regularly is ____________ to stay slim and strong.
2. Playing team sports is important ____________ children to learn to work together.
3. Doing individual sports like ____________ in the country ____________ us to relax the mind and keep the body in good shape.
4. All forms of physical exercise are ____________ maintaining a healthy heart.
5. Painting is an ____________ to improve our hand-eye co-ordination and creative abilities.
6. I think reading is fairly important in life. Reading ____________ to increase our vocabulary and general knowledge.

LANGUAGE STEP 3 Adjectives of Positive & Negative Feeling
高分语言点 3 表示正面和负面感觉的形容词

我们来看一下雅思考生Alice和David使用了哪些表示正面和负面感觉的形容词。

Alice …art is really *fascinating*…
David …Going to live concerts, for example, can be a really *stimulating* experience.

It's good to complete your answer with just one or two adjectives of positive or negative feeling to explain why you think X is important or not.

Look at the following native speaker adjectives of positive and negative feeling:

- inspiring
- creative
- beneficial
- philosophical
- enriching
- educational
- expressive
- pretentious
- tedious
- frivolous

Here are some examples in context:

- adjectives of positive feeling
  "Art is so *inspiring*."
  "Visiting art galleries is very *enriching*."
  "Learning to play musical instruments is *educational* and *creative*."
  "Painting and drawing can teach children to be more *expressive*."

- adjectives of negative feeling
  "Most art is also very *pretentious*."
  "I think history is a *tedious* subject."
  "Learning about modern art in school is *frivolous* and *unnecessary*."
  "For me, drama is a *pathetic* activity that is incredibly *wasteful* of school time."

Exercise 14.3: Matching

Match the adjectives of positive and negative feeling on the left with their definitions on the right.

1. inspiring
2. creative
3. beneficial
4. philosophical
5. enriching
6. educational
7. expressive
8. pretentious
9. tedious
10. frivolous

A. very boring and repetitive
B. something or somebody which is an unnecessary waste of time or money
C. to be good at imagining new things and thinking about life in a deeper, perhaps more interesting manner
D. to be open about expressing feelings and emotions, passions and ideas in a way that inspires other people
E. relating to philosophy; thinking on a deeper level about life
F. something that teaches you something interesting or useful
G. to be good for someone; to give someone benefits and help someone grow and develop positively
H. to find interesting, fascinating or intriguing in a way which gives you a love for life and creativity
I. when someone is trying to look really intelligent by pretending to be very deep and "more interesting" than other people in a very false way
J. something that gives you a positive and cultural experience, something that enables you to learn and benefit from the learning

Exercise 14.4: Matching

Match the sentence halves.

1. I think it's great to get involved in adventure sports...
2. Going to art galleries and museums with one's partner can be a really...
3. It's good to teach children how to paint and draw...
4. I find watching films from other countries very inspiring...
5. Some people feel that teaching things like art, drama or music in schools is frivolous...

A. ...All kids should learn creative skills from an early age.
B. ...It's a great way to get to know different cultures and their ways of expressing themselves.
C. ...They feel that more serious academic subjects are more important for getting ahead in a future career.
D. ...They are really exciting and stimulating.
E. ...enriching experience, and educational as well as a little romantic!

For more practice, please go to: www.EQEnglish.com

Formula 15: What do you want / hope to do (in the future)?

AIMS 学习目标

In this lesson you'll master the Formula for
"What do you want / hope to do (in the future)?" type questions.
本课的高分公式将教会你如何回答下列同类型的问题，比如：

- Do you hope to do the same job in the future?
- What do you want to do when you finish university?
- What kind of job would you like to do when you finish your studies?

THE FORMULA 高分公式

When the examiner asks you "What do you want / hope to do (in the future)?" type questions, you must:

Answer Order

- Saw WHAT your ambition for the future is.
- Say WHY you want to achieve it.
- Say HOW you hope to achieve it.

Language Steps

1. Use hope to and would like to like a native. ("This is something I really *hope to do*." / "I *would like* to be a really successful businesswoman.")
2. Use future ambition phrases to say why you want to achieve these goals. ("I *would like to achieve this ambition*, because it would be so rewarding!" / "If I succeeded in doing this I *would gain an enormous sense of security*.")
3. Use the first conditional accurately. ("*If I work really* hard and save up enough money *I will go* to Europe and get a master's.")

NATIVE SPEAKER WORDS 英语母语词汇

让我们来学习一些英语母语词汇，这些词汇对于回答该类型的问题非常有用，并且能够帮助你理解接下来的答案范例。

Native Speaker Word	Part of Speech	Definition	Example Sentence
NGO (non-governmental organisation) 非政府组织		an organisation created privately, independent of any government	The WWF, which stands for "the World Wildlife Fund," is a well-known NGO that helps to protect wild animals all over the world.
purpose 目的，目标	noun	an aim, an objective or goal which gives life meaning	I want to achieve something very special in my life. I want my life to have a real purpose.
competitive 竞争激烈的	adjective	involving competition or the desire to do better than other people in the field	Acting is very competitive – you've got to really push yourself if you want to succeed because they're lots of actors but not many acting jobs.
rewarding 值得的，有意义的	adjective	giving you satisfaction, pleasure, or profit	Helping the homeless people was a very rewarding experience for Janet.
challenging 富有挑战的	adjective	used to describing something that is difficult in a way that tests your intelligence, your ability or your determination	Living through those hard times was challenging for us all.
volunteer 志愿 / 志愿者	verb / noun	to do / a person who does something, especially to help other people, willingly and without being forced or paid to do it	I want to volunteer to work in an orphanage during the summer holidays.
stable 稳定的，安定的	adjective	firmly fixed, reliable or not likely to move or change	I don't like these modern relationships when people avoid commitment. I need a traditional stable marriage.
a great sense of + noun 充满……的感觉		experiencing a positive feeling	Working with children gives me a great sense of pleasure and happiness.
strive 争取	verb	to struggle hard for something, to make a real effort to achieve something	If you want to become a top athlete you have to strive incredibly hard to succeed.

MODEL ANSWERS 答案范例

阅读雅思考生Alice和David的参考答案。

Interviewer What do you want to do when you finish university?

Alice What I really hope to do is work for an NGO here in China. I would like to find a purpose in life – I don't want to just worry about success and making money like a lot of people nowadays. I think it would be so rewarding and challenging to work as a volunteer. If I work really hard and save up enough money then I will go to Europe and get a master's.

Interviewer Tell me about your future ambitions.

David What I'd really like to do in the future is pretty simple: I'd like to find a good job, which will hopefully lead to a stable career, get married to a lovely girl and start a family. I hope to be able to afford a nice apartment to bring up our children. I think this would give me a great sense of pleasure and security. If I strive hard I think I can achieve this in less than 10 years.

LANGUAGE STEP 1 Hope To & Would Like To
高分语言点 1 Hope To 和 Would Like To

我们来看一下雅思考生Alice和David是如何使用hope to和would like to这两个短语的。

Alice What I really *hope to do is work* for an NGO here in China. I *would like to find* a purpose in life...

David What I*'d really like to* do in the future is pretty simple: I*'d like to find* a good job...I *hope to be able to afford* a nice apartment...

There are different ways we can use hope to to talk about the future:

- I hope to be able to + verb

  "I *hope to be able to go* abroad after my studies."

  "I *hope to be able to work* in an international hospital."

- I hope I can + verb

  "I *hope I can pass* my driving test."

  "I *hope I can convince* my parents to buy me a car."

- What I really hope to do is + verb

  "What I *really hope to do is travel* around the world."

  "What I *really hope to do is learn* to speak Greek."

You'll notice that Alice and David also use I would like to, which is used in the following way:

- I would like to + verb

  "I *would like to marry* the girl I met in the cake shop."

  "I*'d like to become* the best pool player in Asia."

You can also use these two useful phrases:

"I *would like (to have) the opportunity* to study overseas."

"I *would like (to have) the chance* to fly an aeroplane."

"I *hope (to have) the fortune to* be able to go to Australia."

"I *hope (to have) the chance* to go diving in Thailand."

Exercise 15.1: Error Correction

Some of the sentences below are incorrect, some are correct. Identify the incorrect sentences and write the correct sentences in the spaces provided.

1. In the future I would really like travel in the desert.

____

2. When I finish the university I hope to volunteer for a year for the Red Cross.

____

3. What I really like to do when I am older is live in a wooden house in California.

____

4. I hope have the opportunity to go fishing in lake Tanzania.

____

5. What I'd really like to do learn another foreign language.

____

LANGUAGE STEP 2 Future Ambition Phrases
高分语言点 2 描述未来抱负的短语

我们来看一下雅思考生Alice和David是如何描述自己未来的抱负的。

Alice …I think *it would be so rewarding and challenging to* work as a volunteer…

David …I think *this would give me a great sense of pleasure and security*…

It's always useful to learn a few phrases to talk about future ambitions and why you want to achieve them.

When talking about future ambitions, native speakers will often use common collocations (words that almost always "go together" when native speakers talk) such as the following:

- to achieve an ambition
- to fulfill a dream
- to succeed in doing something
- to manage to do something

Now look at these collocations in the context of the following future ambition phrases:

"I *would like to achieve this ambition* because it would be so rewarding!"

"I*'d love to fulfill this dream* because it would give me a great sense of achievement."

"It's my dream *to succeed in learning* Japanese."

"I *would love to manage to get into art college*."

"Doing this *would* certainly *make me feel that I had really achieved something special* in my life."

You can use these phrases after almost any ambition you mention, to tell the examiner why you want to do it.

Exercise 15.2: Gap Fill

Write the words below in the correct space.

succeed ambition dream manage

1. I would love to ____________ to get into the university basketball team.
2. It would be amazing to fulfill this lifelong ____________.
3. I really want to ____________ in doing this. It would make me so proud.
4. I am pretty confident that I can achieve my ____________ by working hard.

LANGUAGE STEP 3 The First Conditional 高分语言点 3 第一条件句

我们来看一下雅思考生Alice和David是如何使用第一条件句的。

Alice ...*If I work really hard and save up enough money then I will go to Europe and get a master's.*

David ...*If I strive hard I think I can achieve this in less than 10 years.*

We use the first conditional to talk about things that certainly <u>can</u> come true in the future, <u>if</u> we make sure we do certain things.

Remind yourself of the structure of the first conditional:

- if + present simple + will + verb

  "*If* I *work* hard, then I *will be* top of the class."

  "*If* I *train* every day, then I *will become* the best player in the team."

  "*If* I *make sure* I have the discipline to study more, I *will pass* the exam."

  "*If* I *party* too much, then I *will* certainly *anger* my parents."

Don't forget there are two possible orders:

- if + present simple + will + verb

  "*If* I *save* enough money, I *will travel* abroad."

  "*If* I *give* my friend enough help, he *will overcome* this difficulty."

- will + verb + if + present simple

  "I *will travel* abroad *if* I *save* enough money."

  "I *will win* the race *if* I *train* as hard as I can."

Exercise 15.3: Sentence Completion

Think about four things you are sure you will achieve if you fulfill certain conditions. Write full first conditional sentences using the words below to help you.

pass the test | achieve my ambition
have a really happy life | fulfill my dream

1. ____________________

2. ____________________

3. ____________________

4. ____________________

For more practice, please go to: www.EQEnglish.com

Formula 16: Do people do / get enough X?

AIMS 学习目标

In this lesson you'll master the Formula for
"Do people do / get enough X?" type questions.
本课的高分公式将教会你如何回答下列同类型的问题，比如：

- Do people today do enough physical exercise?
- Do children do enough sports in school?
- Do people in your country do enough creative activities in school?

THE FORMULA 高分公式

When the examiner asks you "Do people do / get enough X?" type questions, you must:

Answer Order

- Say whether you believe people get or do enough X.
- Say which types of people get or do not get enough X.
- Say why they should get or do more X.

Language Steps

1. Use opinion phrases. ("*I believe* that many people in my country are very hardworking." / "*In my opinion*, people don't get enough holidays.")
2. Use expressions for quantities and types of people. ("Nowadays *nearly all students* have access to at least one computer." / "*Most bosses* get paid far too much.")
3. Use expressions for suggesting or advising. ("*It's a good idea* to learn more languages in school." / "Everyone *should* get paid more.")

NATIVE SPEAKER WORDS 英语母语词汇

让我们来学习一些英语母语词汇，这些词汇对于回答该类型的问题非常有用，并且能够帮助你理解接下来的答案范例。

Native Speaker Word	Part of Speech	Definition	Example Sentence
the majority 大部分，大多数		the larger number or part of something	The majority of people in my office drink tea.
couch potato 电视迷，终日懒散在家的人		someone who sits on a sofa all day and watches television and is very lazy	John is a real couch potato. He gets no exercise at all. He sits down all day long and never leaves the TV.
cultivate 培养，培育	verb	to try and develop and improve something	It's important that we cultivate good manners so we know how to behave in social situations.
day off 休假，一天的假		a day without work, a day when you don't have to go into work	Everyone was given a day off work to celebrate Women's Day.
vacation 假期	noun	US: a period of one week or more when you travel to another place to have a break and enjoy yourself	I spent my summer vacation in Florida, on the beach. It was wonderful.
break 休息	noun	a time off work, or a short time to relax, sometimes used to describe a small holiday	We had a short break from school when they were making renovations to the west wing – those two free days were marvelous.
holiday 节假日	noun	UK: a public holiday, a day off, or a trip you go on for a week or more US: a public holiday when people don't work	I don't know why, but the UK doesn't have a National Day like the US or China. I think we should, and it'd be nice to have another holiday.
frame of mind 心情，心境		mood, attitude, approach to something	I'm not in the frame of mind to work today. I can't concentrate because I feel a bit sad.

MODEL ANSWERS 答案范例

阅读雅思考生Alice和David的参考答案。

Interviewer Do people do enough physical exercise where you come from?

Alice Well, in my opinion people don't get enough exercise. The majority of people, especially middle class people nowadays, are real couch potatoes. All they do is sit in front of the television all night, and the only exercise they get is going to get more food from the refrigerator. If children are to grow up to be healthy adults, they should learn how to take care of themselves, and they should cultivate an interest in sports like basketball, football or volleyball.

Interviewer Do students get enough holidays in your country?

David I believe that they get too many holidays. Most students have a long summer vacation, a fairly long Spring Festival break, national holidays and all sorts of other days off throughout the year. Because of this a vast amount of students forget a lot of what they've learned during the longer holidays, and take a long time to get back into the frame of mind to study well. It would be good if the holidays were a bit shorter.

LANGUAGE STEP 1 Opinion Phrases 高分语言点 1 表达观点的短语

我们来看一下雅思考生Alice和David用了哪些表达观点的短语。

Alice Well, *in my opinion* people don't get enough exercise…

David *I believe that* they [students] get too many holidays…

It's very easy to learn a variety of different ways to express your opinion when asked a question. Look at these examples:

"*I think that* a large percentage of people over 30 don't exercise enough."

"*I feel that* people should do more to help others in society."

"*I strongly believe that* team sports like basketball teach people to work together."

"*I am quite convinced that* the majority of people would enjoy playing hockey if they just gave it a chance."

"*The way I see it*, sports should be compulsory for elementary school students."

"*In my opinion*, most children naturally enjoy physical exercise."

> 小贴士
> 在表达自己的观点的时候，一定要说出理由并且通过举例来支持自己的观点。

Exercise 16.1: Gap Fill

Write the words below in the correct spaces.

believe   opinion   quite convinced   think that   way

1. I ____________ too many people nowadays don't exercise enough. In my ____________ it would help most people to join a neighbourhood sports team to play football or basketball a couple of times a week.
2. Most people will complain of stress, but I'm ____________ that if they just got out more and played some sports, it would help enormously.

3. The ____________ I see it, it would be beneficial for companies to organise sports teams and outings for their employees. I strongly ____________ that it would increase employee efficiency.

LANGUAGE STEP 2 Quantities & Types of People
高分语言点 2 数量词描述不同类型的人群

让我们来看一下雅思考生Alice和David用了哪些数量词描述不同类型的人群。

Alice ...*The majority of people*, especially *middle class people* nowadays, are real couch potatoes...

David ...*Most students* have a long summer vacation...Because of this *a vast amount of students* forget a lot of what they've learned...

For native speakers it's not very good to make absolute statements like "All Chinese people like..." or "Everyone in Western countries thinks...". This doesn't sound very clever and can sometimes be rude. Even in one country or one culture, many people have different ways of life and different opinions.

You should use quantities of people and types of people to qualify your statements, so that they are not so generalised.

You can use these quantities of people:

- most
- the majority of
- a large percentage of
- nearly all
- a vast amount of
- few
- hardly any
- not many
- a minority of
- only some

You can combine them with types of people to say which people in society usually do something or believe something.

- young people / the younger generation / teenagers / adolescents
- old people / the elderly / the older generation
- office workers / business people / white-collar workers
- the working classes / middle classes / very wealthy people
- unemployed people / the poor / homeless people
- young kids / schoolchildren / university students / graduate students

Look at some examples of how quantities and types of people words can be combined together:

"*Most young people* can play at least one sport."
"*The majority of elderly people* enjoy board games."
"*A large percentage of the population* smokes too much."
"*Nearly all university students* get far too much homework."
"*A vast amount of business people* don't get enough free time."
"*A tremendous amount of young girls* care too much about fashion."

Exercise 16.2: Matching

Match the quantities and types of people on the left with the words and phrases that have the same meanings on the right.

1. a large percentage of	A. young people
2. a minority of	B. white-collar workers
3. children	C. the older generation
4. few	D. only some
5. office workers	E. most
6. teenagers	F. kids
7. the elderly	G. hardly any
8. the majority of	H. a vast amount of

Exercise 16.3: Sentence Completion

Complete the sentences according to your opinions or impressions about different types of people in your society.

1. A tremendous amount of young people don't get enough ____________.
2. In my country, elderly people, in general, like to ____________.
3. A large percentage of famous people don't get ____________.
4. Nearly all students are given far too much ____________.
5. The majority of parents today don't give their sons and daughters enough ____________.

LANGUAGE STEP 3 Suggesting & Advising Expressions
高分语言点 3 意见和建议的表达方法

我们来看一下雅思考生Alice和David是如何表达自己的意见和建议的。

Alice …If children are to grow up to be healthy adults, they *should* learn how to take care of themselves…

David …*It would be good if* the holidays were a bit shorter.

When you've given your opinion and supported it, you should suggest what you'd do to improve the situation. Alice states her disapproval of couch potatoes, then goes on to say how children "should" learn to take care of themselves, so they don't end up like this when they are old. Similarly, David, after saying he believes the holidays to be too long, suggests that "it would be good if" the holidays were shortened.

Here's a summary of ways you can suggest improvements:

- should / shouldn't + verb
  "To get really good at football, you *should practise* every day."
- ought to / ought not to + verb
  "You really *ought to see* a doctor if you feel that ill."
- it would be good if / it wouldn't be good if
  "*It would be good if* everyone learned to play baseball when they were young."
- it's a good idea to / it's not a good idea to + verb
  "*It's not a good idea to run* outside in the winter. You'll catch a cold."
- it would help to + verb
  "*It would help to train* a little bit every day if you want to run a marathon."
- the best thing to do to + improvement phrase + would be to
  "*The best thing to do to improve creativity in schools would be to* introduce art classes in the early years of elementary school."

Exercise 16.4: Gap Fill

Write the words below in the correct spaces.

good idea	ought	it would help if
the best thing	would be	should

1. Everyone ____________ to join a sports team, even if it's just for fun.
2. ____________ to do to make sure people get more holidays is to put pressure on companies to abide by the labour laws.
3. It ____________ good if students learned how to swim competitively at a young age. Kids don't get enough chances to do this nowadays.
4. Many people don't pay enough attention to what the professionals say. You ____________ consider hiring a personal trainer if you want to lift weights.
5. It's not a ____________ to over-exercise. Some people exert themselves too much.
6. ____________ everyone used public transportation instead of driving. Too much traffic clogs the roads and pollutes the air.

For more practice, please go to: www.EQEnglish.com

Formula 17: How can people find out about X?

AIMS 学习目标

In this lesson you'll master the Formula for
"How can people find out about X?" type questions.
本课的高分公式将教会你如何回答下列同类型的问题，比如：

- How can people find out about what's going on in the world?
- How do people obtain information about local events in your city?
- How can you stay up-to-date with the national news where you live?

THE FORMULA 高分公式

When the examiner asks you "How can people find out about X?" type questions, you must:

Answer Order

- Say how people usually obtain information.
- Explain what you do to stay up-to-date.
- Show how reliable these sources are.

Language Steps

1. Use types of media words and phrases. ("You can buy *newspapers* and *magazines* at *newsstands* around my town.")
2. Use finding out information expressions. ("I *surf the Internet* to *stay up-to-date with* what's going on.")
3. Use words to express trust and mistrust of information. ("It is a *well-respected* source of information.")

NATIVE SPEAKER WORDS 英语母语词汇

让我们来学习一些英语母语词汇，这些词汇对于回答该类型的问题非常有用，并且能够帮助你理解下面的答案范例。

Native Speaker Word	Part of Speech	Definition	Example Sentence
current affairs 时事		what is happening in the international or national news at the moment	Daily newspapers are an excellent way to stay up-to-date with current affairs.
mass media 大众媒体		newspapers, television and radio of a nation, designed to reach the entire population	Some people don't fully trust the mass media. Others feel that it is the only reliable source of information.
venue 场所，地点	noun	the place where a concert, play or event is going to take place	I love the Old Theatre in Kemp Town. It's a great venue for a small concert.
events listings 事件列表		lists of events, their dates and venues in local magazines	It's good to check the events listings regularly. There's a lot happening in this city.
gig 演奏会，演唱会	noun	colloquial expression for music concert (usually a pop or rock group)	We saw this great gig in the club D22. It was a fantastic young band from Hubei.
well-respected 受尊敬的	adjective	to describe something that a lot of people respect and appreciate	The hotel is very well-respected. It's got good reviews and all my friends say the service is excellent.
biased / unbiased 有偏见的 / 无偏见的	adjective	showing an unreasonable like or dislike for a person based on personal opinions	The newspapers gave a very biased report on the incident – they obviously wanted to please the president.
viewpoint 观点	noun	perspective; point of view; way of looking at something; opinion	It's usually not a good idea to talk about politics or religion with unfamiliar people – everyone has their own opinion, and people are frequently quite sensitive about such viewpoints.

MODEL ANSWERS 答案范例

阅读雅思考生Alice和David的参考答案。

Interviewer How can you find out about national and international news where you come from?

Alice Nowadays it's easier than ever to stay on top of current events in China. There are many different sources for news. There are newsstands in every major city selling all kinds of magazines and newspapers, which often run interesting features on everything from fashion to international affairs. But generally I surf the Internet to stay up-to-date with what's going on in the blogs. Though some bloggers aren't very objective, their opinions are interesting to read, and usually offer a different viewpoint to what I read in the mass media.

Interviewer How can people find out about local events and entertainment in your city?

David There's quite a lot of ways people can find out about what's going on. There's a local *City Weekend* magazine, which is full of events listings, advertisements and reviews about the latest gigs, classical concerts, art exhibitions and theatre. There's also "dining and drinking" listings – excellent for keeping track of the latest restaurants opening in the city. The magazine is both in physical form and online. It's a great source of information, the reviews are very unbiased and it is very well-respected.

LANGUAGE STEP 1 Types of Media 高分语言点 1 不同类型的媒体

我们来看一下雅思考生Alice和David是如何描述不同类型的媒体的。

Alice ...There are *newsstands* in every major city selling all kinds of *magazines* and *newspapers*, which often run interesting *features* on everything from fashion to international affairs. But generally I surf the *Internet* to stay up-to-date on what's going on in the *blogs*...

David ...There's a local *City Weekend magazine*, which is full of *events listings*, *advertisements* and *reviews* about the latest gigs, classical concerts, art exhibitions and theatre. There's also *"dining and drinking"* listings...The *magazine* is both in *physical form* and *online*...

When we talk about media, we are really talking about "means of communication" in general. This can be anything from mass media – like newspapers, television and radio – to local information, events news and advertisements.

Here's a list of examples:

- newsstands
- newspapers
- advertisements
- features (informative or interesting articles)
- magazines (in physical form / online)
- blogs (online)
- restaurant / bar / events listings
- reviews (of restaurants / bars / events)
- events listings (of current events)
- current affairs

Exercise 17.1: Gap Fill

Write the words below in the correct spaces.

advertisements blogs features magazines newsstands reviews

1. Today, online ____________ are a very popular way in which everyday people put their news, opinions and thoughts out for other people to read.
2. A lot of free magazines fund themselves by charging businesses to display their ____________.
3. The most convenient places to buy newspapers or magazines are ____________ or kiosks on street corners.
4. A lot of "What's On" ____________ have ____________ of new restaurants and bars to help people choose the most suitable places to drink and dine.
5. I enjoy reading the ____________ in magazines for young people. I like the short stories about student life, or the articles about how to deal with certain emotional or social problems young people may face.

LANGUAGE STEP 2 Finding Out Information Expressions
高分语言点 2 描述信息来源

让我们来看一下雅思考生Alice和David是如何描述信息的来源的。

Alice ...generally I *surf the Internet* to *stay up-to-date with* what's going on in the blogs...

David ...There's also "dining and drinking" listings – excellent for *keeping track of* the latest restaurants opening in the city...

Here are some useful native speaker expressions to say <u>how</u> and <u>why</u> you get information:

<u>How</u>

- to surf the Internet
  "I usually *surf the Internet* while drinking my morning coffee."
- to browse through magazines / newspapers / websites
  "I've seen a lot of old people in parks in Kunming, *browsing through newspapers* on warm sunny mornings."
- to watch the news reports
  "My grandfather always *watches* the evening *news reports*."
- to listen to the radio broadcasts
  "Every morning on the bus to school I *listen to the radio broadcasts*."

- to find out by word of mouth
  "I don't read, watch or listen to the news much, but I *find out* a lot from my friends *by word of mouth*."

Why

- to keep track of
  "I believe it's good to *keep track of* what's going on in other countries."
- to keep one's finger on the pulse
  "I don't like to be ignorant about world news. I *keep my finger on the pulse*."
- to stay informed about
  "Online news is a good way to *stay informed about* what's happening in the world."
- to stay abreast of
  "I am too lazy. I don't really care about *staying abreast of* current affairs."
- to stay up-to-date with
  "I am not interested in current affairs. I like to *stay up-to-date with* the sports news though."
- to stay on top of what's going on
  "Taxi drivers often listen to the radio to *stay on top of what's going on*."

Exercise 17.2: Gap Fill & Matching

Write the words below in the correct spaces then match the sentence halves 1-5 (how we get information) with sentence halves A-D (why we get information).

broadcasts	browse through	news reports
blogs	find out about	

1. I listen to radio ____________ on World Service...
2. I occasionally ____________ the local newspapers to keep...
3. I watch ____________ on a small TV in my dorm because I like to keep...
4. I love to surf the Internet, reading sports ____________ by fans and experts. It's a great way to...
5. I am pretty lazy. I don't pay much attention to the news. I ____________ major news stories through...

A. ...abreast of current affairs in my province.
B. ...to keep up-to-date with what's going on in the international news.
C. ...stay informed about which teams are in the lead.
D. ...word of mouth.
E. ...my finger on the pulse. I hate not knowing what's going on around me!

LANGUAGE STEP 3 Words for Trust and Mistrust
高分语言点 3 描述信任和猜疑的词语

让我们来看一下雅思考生Alice和David是如何描述信任或者猜疑的。

Alice ...Though some bloggers aren't very *objective*, their opinions are interesting to read, and *usually offer a different viewpoint to* what I read in the mass media...

David ...It's a great source of information, the reviews are very *unbiased* and it is very *well-respected*...

Usually, when native speakers talk about the ways in which they find information, they will tell each other how much they trust or mistrust that information.

Here's a list of useful words and phrases:

- to express trust
  "It's a very *objective* source of information."
  "It's quite *unbiased*, so I generally believe what I see on that news channel."
  "I believe that the information presented there is *impartial*."
  "I trust that newspaper because it is very *well-respected*."

- to express doubt or slight mistrust
  "I don't like Internet news, I think it can be very *biased*."
  "It's considerably *one-sided* in its approach to discussing international affairs."
  "It's an *untrustworthy* publication."
  "I find the news channel a little *unreliable* to be honest."

Exercise 17.3: Gap Fill

Write the words below in the correct spaces.

objective / impartial   unreliable   well-respected   untrustworthy   biased / one-sided

1. This blog is so ____________; the blogger only likes The Lakers, so he always says good things about the team – even when they do badly!
2. In the Internet age ____________ news is hard to find because everyone has their own opinion and write what they think, not what they can prove.
3. The newspaper my father reads is very ____________. Nearly everyone agrees that it's a good, impartial, trustworthy read.
4. If I think a news channel or radio station has a reputation for being ____________ then I won't pay any attention to it.
5. If we can't really rely on a source of information we usually say it's ____________.

For more practice, please go to: www.EQEnglish.com

Formula 18: Should people be given X?

AIMS 学习目标

In this lesson you'll master the Formula for "Should people be given X?" type questions.

本课的高分公式将教会你如何回答下列同类型的问题，比如：

- Should people be given more holidays?
- Should people be paid more if they work overtime?
- Should children be required to wear a uniform to school?

THE FORMULA 高分公式

When the examiner asks you "Should people be given X?" type questions, you must:

Answer Order

- Show that you are aware the question is asking about PEOPLE IN GENERAL and not about YOU.
- Say whether you think X should or should not be given to people.
- Give reasons to support your opinion.

Language Steps

1. Use common native speaker agreement and disagreement phrases. ("*As I see it*, people in my country often work way too much.")
2. Use common native speaker rights, fairness and permission expressions with the passive. ("All workers deserve to be *provided with* a fair salary.")
3. Express reasons like a native with the zero conditional. ("*If* workers *are treated* fairly they *are* usually more loyal to their company.")

NATIVE SPEAKER WORDS 英语母语词汇

让我们来学习一些英语母语词汇，这些词汇对于回答该类型的问题非常有用，并且能够帮助你理解下面的答案范例。

Native Speaker Word	Part of Speech	Definition	Example Sentence
salary 薪水，工资	noun	an amount of money an employee earns each year, paid to their bank account every month	I hope to get an increase in salary next year. I've worked very hard for this company.
benefits 利益，好处	noun	things you are given by you company for working for them, not including salary, e.g. paid lunches, paid holidays, pension, health insurance etc	My salary is not so high, but I get lots of other benefits from my company – like transport costs and free lunches.
frequently 经常地，频繁地	adverb	often; happening a lot	He is so bad-tempered! He frequently gets angry about such small things.
overtime 超时，加班	noun	working over the normal working hours, doing extra work for the company	I don't do much overtime in my job. I am quite lucky, I get to leave the office at 5 p.m.
loyal 忠诚的	adjective	firm and not changing in friendship or support	Alf is a very loyal dog. He always stays by my side, both in times of danger and times of hope.
long-term 长期的	adjective	taking place a long time in the future	My long-term plan is to get a job in a big multi-national company and get rich!
rebellious 叛逆的，反抗的	adjective	opposing or going against the ideas or rules of authority	This student is so rebellious. He never obeys the school rules! If the teacher tells him to wear his school uniform, he turns up in dirty jeans!

MODEL ANSWERS 答案范例

阅读雅思考生Alice和David的参考答案。

Interviewer Should people be given longer holidays?

Alice Yes, they certainly should! As I see it, people often work very long hours but don't get a high salary or very many benefits in return. In fact, many workers frequently do unpaid overtime for their companies. I strongly believe that workers deserve to be given longer paid holidays so that they can relax more. In my opinion, if people are given more paid holidays they are more loyal to their company in the long term and probably work harder because they are more contented with their job.

Interviewer Do you think that students should be required to wear a school uniform?

David Absolutely not! I strongly believe that students should have the freedom to wear what they like in school. I think it's unfair to make children all look the same. School is a place for hard work and study, but also a place for children to learn to become individuals with their own styles, ideas and opinions. Young people ought to be given more choice in what they wear. If children are controlled too much when they are young, they can become very rebellious in later years.

LANGUAGE STEP 1 Agreement & Disagreement Phrases
高分语言点 1 表示同意和不同意的短语

让我们来看一下雅思考生Alice和David是如何表达同意或是不同意的。

Alice *Yes, they certainly should!* As I see it, people often work very long hours but don't get a high salary or very many benefits in return…

David …*Absolutely not!* I *strongly believe* that students should have the freedom to wear what they like in school…

Look at these ways of expressing agreement and disagreement with a question or proposition.

Agreement

- Yes, they certainly should.
- Absolutely!
- Definitely!
- I couldn't agree more!

Disagreement

- Absolutely not!
- Of course not!
- I don't think so.
- Certainly not!

Introducing your opinion

- I think / believe / feel that...
- The way I see it...
- In my opinion...
- I am convinced that...
- For me...

Exercise 18.1: Gap Fill

Write the words below in the correct spaces.

believe　　course not　　do　　of the opinion　　not　　opinion

John: Do you think that people should be allowed to keep wild animals at home?

Mary: Certainly ____________! I am ____________ that wild animals should be kept in zoos, or in their natural habitat.

John: Do you believe that people get enough holidays?

Mary: Yes, I certainly ____________! This is a developing country and in my ____________ everyone must work hard to make the country better and better.

John: Do you think that parks should be free for everyone to enter?

Mary: Of ____________! I strongly ____________ that parks need to be maintained, plants and flowers need to be watered and the places kept clean. That costs money.

LANGUAGE STEP 2 Rights, Fairness & Permission Expressions
高分语言点 2 权利、公平和许可的表达

首先，让我们来看一下雅思考生Alice和David用了哪些短语表达权利、公平和许可。

Alice ...I strongly believe that workers *deserve to be given* longer paid holidays...

David ...Young people *ought to be given* more choice in what they wear...

When talking about permission and rights, you should use the passive voice. Using the passive voice means that you can say who receives the action without needing to say who does the action.

The passive structure

Remind yourself of the passive structure:

- subject + to be + past participle

  "*The workers are given* three weeks', holiday every year."

  "*The children were allowed to* wear casual clothes last week."

  "*People today are not provided with* enough benefits."

In each case above we know that the people giving the workers three weeks' holiday, allowing the children to wear casual clothes and who ought to be giving people more free time, are bosses, teachers or authorities.

Using the passive to suggest

To make suggestions, native speakers normally combine verbs such as "should" and "ought to" with the passive. Note in the following examples how these are used and that "(to) be" is added before the past participle:

- should (not) be given
- ought to be given
- (don't) deserve to be given
- should (not) be allowed to + verb
- should (not) be permitted to + verb

Look at these in the context of the following examples:

"People who work longer hours *deserve to be paid* more money."

"Workers *ought to be treated* more fairly."

"Women *ought not to be discriminated against* at work."

"Children *should not be allowed to work* until they are 18 years old."

"Employees *should be permitted to wear* causal clothes to work."

"Fathers *should be given* extra holidays to spend time with their family."

"All workers *deserve to be provided with* a safe working environment."

Exercise 18.2: Multiple Choice

Choose the appropriate verb forms from the choices below to complete the sentences.

1. At the moment workers ____________ a bonus if they work hard.
   A. are given　　B. be given　　C. to be given
2. I firmly believe that workers who have to commute a long distance to work ought ____________ with a transport bonus.
   A. provide　　B. be provided　　C. to be provided
3. I think that a person who is lazy at work and makes too many mistakes ____________ given some form of punishment.
   A. should　　B. ought　　C. should be
4. On the last day of every school year I think children ought ____________ to wear casual clothes and have relaxing, fun classes.
   A. to be permitted　　B. to permitted　　C. be permitted
5. The doctor informed me that I ____________ get more exercise and eat more fruits.
   A. should be　　B. should　　C. ought to be
6. For me, workers who are sacked for misbehaviour or poor work don't deserve ____________ money when they leave.
   A. be given　　B. to be given　　C. given

LANGUAGE STEP 3 The Zero Conditional
高分语言点 3 真实条件句

让我们来看一下雅思考生Alice和David是如何使用真实条件句的。

Alice *...if people are given more paid holidays they are more loyal to their company in the* *long term and probably work harder because they are more contented with their job.*

David *...If children are controlled too much when they are young, they can become very rebellious in later years.*

Alice and David use the zero conditional to talk about what generally happens if certain conditions are fulfilled. It's often used for things that are almost always true.

The structure for the zero conditional is as follows:

- if + present verb + present verb

  "*If* we *travel* to work by subway, we usually *get* there quicker."

  "*If* I *go* to music concerts, I always *dance*."

  "*If* workers *are* late, they *get* into trouble."

Look how the zero conditional is used with the passive:

- if + passive + present verb

  "*If* people *are given* more paid holidays, they *are* more loyal to their company."

  "*If* children *are allowed to play* computer games too much, they *get* really lazy."

  "*If* young people *are made to wear* uniforms in school, they *are* generally better behaved."

小贴士

所有的条件句都有两种表达形式。因此，真实条件句的结构可以是 if + present verb + present verb 也可以是 present verb + if + present verb。

当谈论一般性的真实情况时，也可以用 when 来代替 if：

"It's not always true that *when* people *are paid* more money they *work* harder."

"*When* employees *are treated* with respect, they *are* more loyal to the boss."

Exercise 18.3: Gap Fill & Matching

Write the words below in the correct spaces in sentence halves 1-5 then match them to sentence halves A-D.

have punish drive are made are given

1. If children ____________ to wear warm clothes in winter then...
2. If we ____________ students who are rude or behave badly...
3. When people ____________ the chance to learn languages at an early age...
4. If older people ____________ access to computer training programmes...
5. As a general rule, people ____________ more carefully...

A. …they usually understand the younger generation a bit more.
B. …if there is a strong police presence on motorways.
C. …they are more obedient and attentive in class.
D. …they are less likely to catch colds.
E. …they often learn very quickly.

For more practice, please go to: www.EQEnglish.com

Formula 19: Is it difficult to do X?

AIMS 学习目标

In this lesson you'll master the Formula for
"Is it difficult to do X?" type questions.
本课的高分公式将教会你如何回答下列同类型的问题，比如：

- Is it difficult to learn to play a musical instrument?
- Is it difficult to learn another language?
- Is it hard to meet new people when you first go to university?

THE FORMULA 高分公式

When the examiner asks you "Is it difficult to do X?" type questions, you must:

Answer Order

- Say how difficult you think it is to do X.
- Talk a little about the learning process.

Language Steps

1. Use adverbs of degree with adjectives to talk about degree of difficulty. ("Learning to play a musical instrument is *incredibly hard* for some people.")
2. Use a few time marking phrases like a native. ("*In the beginning* speaking English might seem hard, but *after a while* it gets easier.")
3. Use a few native speaker phrasal verbs about learning things. ("Once you *get used to* a new language, you *pick it up* quickly.")

NATIVE SPEAKER WORDS 英语母语词汇

让我们来学习一些英语母语词汇，这些词汇对于回答该类型的问题非常有用，并且能够帮助你理解下面的答案范例。

Native Speaker Word	Part of Speech	Definition	Example Sentence
unfamiliar 不熟悉的	adjective	not familiar; unknown to you	When I got my first job I was unfamiliar with how to use a computer, but I've since learnt how to use one.

续表

Native Speaker Word	Part of Speech	Definition	Example Sentence
a bit 一点，有点儿		a little, a small amount, slightly	In the restaurant, I was a bit embarrassed to admit that I had forgotten my wallet and couldn't pay for dinner.
awkward 不方便的	adjective	uncomfortable; difficult to manage or handle	It was very awkward to carry all my shopping and try to use the subway to get home.
get used to 习惯，适应		to talk about an action that was difficult or unpleasant to do in the beginning, but becomes acceptable or enjoyable	When I lived in France it was difficult to get used to speaking French all the time and getting up so early for my job.
get to grips with 掌握		to master; to succeed in doing something difficult	If you don't get to grips with grammar, you'll never be able to learn that language.
get the hang of 找到窍门		to get used to something; to begin to be able to do something relatively well	I was not good at cooking, but after a few lessons from James, I'm getting the hang of it now.
pick up 学会，获得		to learn, obtain, or develop new skills or abilities	I found learning to play the guitar quite easy – I picked it up quickly.
proficient 熟练的，精通的	adjective	to be very good at something; to have mastered something well	He is very proficient at English. He speaks almost like a native.

MODEL ANSWERS 答案范例

阅读雅思考生Alice和David的参考答案。

Interviewer Is it difficult to learn another language?

Alice I think that learning a language is extremely difficult – probably one of the hardest things someone can do. When you first begin learning, it can be very confusing to remember lots of unfamiliar words and grammar. It often feels a bit awkward and you have to get used to making mistakes. But after a while, everything feels much more comfortable and you can really start getting to grips with the new language.

Interviewer Do you think it's difficult for young people to learn to play musical instruments?

David I believe that learning to play musical instruments is pretty difficult for most people. However, I think that young people usually pick up new things relatively quickly. At first, it's quite hard to get into learning an instrument, but when you get the hang of it, it's not too hard to learn some simple tunes. If you are dedicated in the beginning, I think after a while you become quite proficient.

LANGUAGE STEP 1 Adverbs of Degree 高分语言点 1 程度副词

让我们来看一下雅思考生Alice和David用了哪些程度副词。

Alice I think that learning a language is *extremely difficult* – probably one of the *hardest* things someone can do…

David I believe that learning music instruments is *pretty difficult* for most people…

When asked a question about how difficult / hard something is to do, you must first bear in mind that some things are easier or more difficult to do than others.

Look at this list of adverbs of degree ordered from 1-7 from smallest to largest degree:

1. quite / fairly
2. relatively / comparatively
3. pretty
4. really
5. considerably / very / remarkably
6. extremely
7. incredibly

To talk about how difficult it is to learn things, you can use the above adverbs of degree before a number of different adjectives, including:

- easy / simple / straightforward
- hard
- difficult
- challenging
- awkward
- frustrating

Here are some examples of these adverbs of degree and adjectives combined:

"I think it's *incredibly hard* to learn to play a trumpet."

"I am under the impression that it's *remarkably easy* to play card games."

"I believe it's *exceedingly frustrating* to learn to play the violin."

"A lot of people say that learning Russian is *unbelievably challenging*."

Exercise 19.1: Gap Fill

Write the words and phrases below in the correct spaces.

fairly frustrating	remarkably easy	incredibly
awkward	unbelievably challenging	

1. It's ____________ hard to learn to play the drums well. It took me 10 years!
2. I believe that to master a language to the point when you can speak it fluently is

_____________. It's one of the hardest things in the world.

3. Learning to drive a car is _____________ at first, but pretty easy to pick up if you keep trying.
4. It's _____________ to learn to ride a bike – I learnt in 20 minutes when I was seven years old.
5. Czech pronunciation is very _____________ to learn. I find it hard to be understood clearly when I speak.

LANGUAGE STEP 2 Time Marking Phrases
高分语言点 2 时间标记短语

让我们来看一下雅思考生Alice和David使用了哪些时间标记短语。

Alice …*When you first begin learning*, it can be very confusing…But *after a while*, everything feels much more…

David …*At first*, it's quite hard to get into learning an instrument…If you are dedicated *in the beginning*, I think *after a while* you will become quite proficient.

There are different stages of every learning process. Every activity changes in difficulty according to what stage of the process you are at. For example, learning English is now probably easier for you than it was when you started learning many years ago.

To talk about and compare the difficulty of different stages of learning an activity, you should use the following *time marking phrases*:

- at the outset
- at first
- in the beginning
- When you start doing something...
- When you get into something / doing something...
- for the first few (weeks / months / times)
- after a while
- after a certain point

Examples:

"*At the outset*, learning to drive a car can be quite frightening, but *after a while* it becomes pretty easy."

"*When you start playing* the violin it seems incredibly difficult and doesn't really get any easier until *after the first few months*."

LANGUAGE STEP 3 Phrasal Verbs About Learning Things
高分语言点 3 关于学习某事的短语

让我们来看一下雅思考生Alice和David用了哪些动词短语描述学习某件事情。

Alice ...you have *to get used to* making mistakes. But after a while, everything feels much more comfortable and you can really *start getting to grips with* the new language...

David ...At first, it's quite hard to get into learning an instrument, but when you *get the hang of* it, it's not too hard to learn some simple tunes...

The following native speaker phrasal verbs are extremely useful, especially when answering questions about learning a new skill or language:

- to get used to (somebody / doing something)

  Describes the process where an action that was difficult or unpleasant to do in the beginning becomes acceptable or enjoyable.

  "I don't think Susan is going to *get used to* working in such a small office."

- to get to grips with (something / doing something)

  To try to master, to succeed in doing something difficult.

  "Ask the sales manager to talk to his team please; we really need to *get to grips with* our after-sales service as it isn't good enough."

- to pick up (something) or to pick (something) up

  To learn, obtain or develop (new skills, abilities).

  "While I lived in Barcelona I *picked up* a little Spanish."

- to get the hang of (something / doing something)

  To become skillful, learn how to do something.

  "It doesn't take long to *get the hang of* driving a car; after a few weeks it will be pretty familiar."

Exercise 19.2: Multiple Choice

Choose the appropriate words or phrases from the choices below to complete the sentences.

1. When you start off it's quite difficult, but ____________ you find you start to get better and more confident.

   A. from the outset B. in the beginning C. after a while

2. Computers are relatively easy to ____________ of; you don't need a lot of skill or practise to master the basics.

   A. get to grips B. get the hang C. pick up

3. Learning to bake cakes is not difficult. At first you make a few mistakes, then after a short time, you start ____________ with the basic techniques.

   A. getting the hang B. picking up C. getting to grips

4. Experts say that in the beginning it's incredibly difficult to fly a helicopter, but when you've ____________ it, it's fairly simple.

   A. got used to B. get to grips C. picked it up

5. ___________ to learn to swim, it's really scary and difficult, but after a few weeks of lessons it's not that difficult to get to grips with it.

A. At first   B. When you first begin   C. After a certain point

For more practice, please go to: www.EQEnglish.com

Formula 20: Is X suitable for (types of people)?

AIMS 学习目标

In this lesson you'll master the Formula for
"Is X suitable for (types of people)?" type questions.
本课的高分公式将教会你如何回答下列同类型的问题，比如：

- Is riding a bike suitable for elderly people?
- Are all sports suitable for people of all ages?
- Are computers suitable for young children?

THE FORMULA 高分公式

When the examiner asks you "Is X suitable for (types of people)?" type questions, you must:

Answer Order

- Say whether X is suitable or not.
- Give reasons and examples.

Language Steps

1. Use appropriateness expressions. ("Violent movies are *inappropriate for* children.")
2. Use safety and risk expressions. ("Eating fast food can be *detrimental to* one's health.")
3. Use adjectives and expressions of benefit. ("Vegetables are *excellent for* one's health." / "Yoga is *relaxing* and *therapeutic*.")

NATIVE SPEAKER WORDS 英语母语词汇

让我们来学习一些英语母语词汇，这些词汇对于回答该类型的问题非常有用，并且能够帮助你理解下面的答案范例。

Native Speaker Word	Part of Speech	Definition	Example Sentence
inappropriate 不合适的，不恰当的	adjective	not suitable for a particular purpose or situation	His behaviour at the wedding was rude and his clothes were dirty. How inappropriate he was!

续表

Native Speaker Word	Part of Speech	Definition	Example Sentence
advisable 明智的，可取的	adjective	if something is advisable it means you will avoid problems if you do it, you should do it	It's advisable to book tickets in advance, because the seats for that play will sell out quickly.
detrimental 不利的，有害的	adjective	bad for; damaging; having a negative effect on	So much air pollution is detrimental to our health.
impact 影响	noun	the effect or influence that an event, situation etc has on someone or something	Playing too many contact sports can have a negative impact on a child's physical development.
abseil （用绳索）下降	verb	to go down a very steep cliff / object by holding on to a rope which is tied to the top of the cliff	The special agent abseiled down the tall building to get to the 20th floor secretly.
exhilarating 令人高兴的，使人愉快的	adjective	making you feel extremely happy and excited	Going to the theme park was an exhilarating experience for the kids.
invigorating 精力充沛的	adjective	making you feel full of spirit and energy as well as being excited and thrilled	Going on the speed boat was an invigorating experience – I can't wait to do it again!
lateral thinking 横向思维		logical thinking; clear reasoning; coming to correct conclusions based on clues	Doing puzzles and number games can improve our lateral thinking skills.

MODEL ANSWERS 答案范例

阅读雅思考生Alice和David的参考答案。

Interviewer Do you think that computer games are suitable for young children?

Alice I believe that computer games are inappropriate for very young children. For older children, I think it is reasonable for them to play computer games but it would be advisable for their parents to restrict the amount of time they play games. As most people know, staring at a computer screen for too long can be detrimental to your eyesight; if children play for too long they might harm their eyes. Also, games that are really violent or scary are not suitable as they might have a negative impact upon the child's mental health. In moderation, however, I believe computer games can be ideal for developing children's lateral thinking skills.

Interviewer Are outdoor sports suitable for people of all ages?

David I think that most outdoor sports are suitable for everyone. Though people who do adventurous sports like rock-climbing, abseiling, or white water rafting, should be careful because these sports can be dangerous if you don't know what you are doing. In fact, now I think about it, for kids and elderly people I think these sports are unsuitable. However, for fit and healthy people these sports can be exhilarating and invigorating.

LANGUAGE STEP 1 Appropriateness Expressions
高分语言点 1 如何表达……是恰当的

让我们来看一下雅思考生Alice和David是如何表达……是恰当的。

Alice I believe that computer games are *inappropriate for* very young children...

David I think that most outdoor sports are *suitable for* everyone...for kids and elderly people I think these sports are *unsuitable*...

Native speakers will often use the following adjectives when talking about the appropriateness of an activity:

- suitable for / unsuitable for
- suited to / unsuited to
- appropriate for / inappropriate for
- advisable to / for / inadvisable to / for

You should talk about the appropriateness of the activity in question by combining the above adjectives with the following appropriateness expressions:

- activity is + suitable / unsuitable for + groups of people
  "*Vigorous sports are usually unsuitable for elderly people*."
- it is + suitable / unsuitable for + groups of people + to verb
  "*It is suitable for young people to marry* before the age of 25."
- activity is unsuited / suited to + groups of people
  "*Tai chi is particularly suited to retired and elderly citizens*."
- activity is appropriate / inappropriate for + groups of people
  "*Riding motorbikes is inappropriate for very young children*."
- it is + appropriate / inappropriate for + groups of people + to verb
  "*It is inappropriate for very young children to ride* motorbikes."
- activity is advisable / inadvisable for + groups of people
  "*Doing yoga is advisable for people with back problems*."
- it is + advisable / inadvisable that + groups of people + verb
  "*It's advisable that people with back problems do* yoga."

Exercise 20.1: Multiple Choice

Choose the correct appropriateness expressions from the choices below to complete the sentences.

1. Wearing heavy make-up is ____________ young schoolgirls.
   A. inadvisable that B. unsuitable for C. appropriate for
2. I think ____________ teenagers to go to nightclubs.
   A. it is inadvisable that B. it is unsuited to C. it is inappropriate for
3. Yoga is ____________ people who are stressed.
   A. suited to B. suitable to C. appropriate
4. Working outdoors is especially ____________ for people who like nature.
   A. advisable B. appropriate C. inappropriate
5. I believe ____________ young children to work in factories.
   A. it is totally advisable for B. it is totally appropriate C. it is totally inappropriate for
6. In my opinion, ____________ children to drink alcohol at a young age.
   A. it is inadvisable for B. it is unsuited to C. is unsuitable for

LANGUAGE STEP 2 Safety and Risk Expressions
高分语言点 2 表示安全和危险的短语

让我们来看一下雅思考生Alice和David用了哪些短语表示安全和危险。

Alice ...staring at a computer screen for too long *can be detrimental to* your eyesight; if children play for too long *they might harm* their eyes...they (computer games) *might have a negative impact upon* the child's mental health...

David ...*people...should be careful* because these sports *can be dangerous*...

Using some simple safety and risk expressions you will be able to explain like a native why you think certain activities are suitable or unsuitable.

Examples:

"People *should be very careful* when swimming in the sea."

"Inner city traffic *can be dangerous*."

"Elderly people who are not used to playing sports *may injure themselves*."

"Certain drugs *might be detrimental to* people's mental health."

"Smoking *can cause* cancer."

"Sitting too close to the television *is likely to lead to* eye problems."

"Working too many hours *can have a negative impact on* one's family life."

Note: When using safety and risk expressions, you must try to use different modal verbs to qualify your statement and avoid making absolute statements, as in the examples above. Modal verbs include: "can", "may", "might", "be likely to".

Exercise 20.2: Matching

Match the activities / actions with their potential risks.

1. Being too direct and honest can...
2. Trusting people too much...
3. Doing vigorous sports can...
4. Drinking too much beer might...
5. Increasing traffic on inner city roads is likely to...

A. ...lead to heavy pollution in summer months.
B. ...be detrimental to your health if you do it in excess.
C. ...can lead to being tricked.
D. ...cause you muscle injuries if you are not careful.
E. ...sometimes hurt people's feelings.

LANGUAGE STEP 3 Adjectives & Expressions of Benefit
高分语言点 3 表示益处的形容词和短语

让我们来看一下雅思考生Alice和David是如何表达……是有益的。

Alice ...*In moderation*, however, I believe computer games *can be ideal for* developing children's lateral thinking skills.

David ...However, *for fit and healthy people* these sports *can be exhilarating and invigorating*.

In your answer to this type of question you should express the advantages of doing a particularly activity for certain people, or under certain conditions, as a concluding point.

Look at the following adjectives and expressions of conditions and benefits that you should try to use in your answer:

Conditions

- In moderation
- If not abused
- If not done to excess
- If (type of people) + verb
- If done under supervision
- If we make sure we + verb

Benefits

- can be beneficial
- can be good / excellent / great for
- can be useful (for)
- can be safe
- can be a good / excellent / great / fantastic way to + verb

Now look at the following examples of the above conditions and benefits combined:

Conditions & benefits

"*In moderation*, playing computer games *can be constructive*."

"*If not abused*, alcohol *can be enjoyable* and *good for the health*."

"*If we don't do it in excess* then weight-lifting *can be great for* building strength."

"*If older people get a personal trainer* regular exercise *can be excellent* for their health."

"*If done under supervision* vigorous exercise / adventure sports *can be safe*."

"*If we make sure we do it carefully*, riding motorbikes *can be a fantastic way to travel* in the mountains."

Exercise 20.3: Matching

Match the conditions with their benefits.

1. If done in moderation, drinking alcohol can be...
2. If a person is responsible and careful...
3. If done under supervision contact sports...
4. Skiing can be a fun and safe sport...
5. If we don't do it in excess, then eating lots of cakes and chocolates...

A. ...if we make sure we don't take unnecessary risks in the beginning.

B. ...a good way to lower inhibitions and get to know people in social settings.

C. ...can be good for us and give us boosts of energy during the day.

D. ...then living alone away from home at an early age can be a constructive experience.

E. ...can be very good at building teamwork skills in young people.

For more practice, please go to: www.EQEnglish.com

Part Two 第二部分

第二部分高分公式介绍
INTRODUCTION TO PART TWO FORMULAS

雅思口语考试第二部分介绍

雅思口语考试第一部分结束以后，你将进入口试第二部分。第二部分考试时间为3到4分钟。

考官要求考生就某个话题做一段个人陈述，时间为1到2分钟。考官会给考生准备一张话题提示卡，上面写明考生需要表达的内容，考生有1分钟的时间进行准备。在准备的过程中，考官会向考生提供笔和纸，考生可以做一些笔记。

EQ英语课程第二部分概述

通过对雅思口试第二部分考题的研究和分析，EQ英语发现口试第二部分个人陈述的话题一共可以归纳为4种类型：1）描述一个人；2）描述一个地方；3）描述一件物品；4）描述一件事情。

针对每一类话题的个人陈述，我们提炼出相应的雅思口语高分公式，通过答题思路和高分语言点分别教会考生在回答雅思口语问题时应该说什么和如何说，从而取得雅思口语高分。

如果你掌握了这4种雅思口语高分公式，你就可以轻松应对雅思口试第二部分的所有问题。

Formula 21: Person Monologue

AIMS 学习目标

In this lesson you'll master the Formula for giving a monologue about a person. Typical IELTS part two questions about a person are:

- Talk about a good cook.
- Talk about a famous person you'd like to meet.
- Talk about an animal you find interesting.
- Talk about a person who looked after you as a child.
- Talk about a teacher you know.
- Talk about a neighbour you have or have had.
- Talk about a person you enjoy spending time with.
- Talk about one of your friends.
- Talk about an old person you know who lives near you.

ANSWER ORDER 答题思路

To give a good monologue about a person, you should use the following native speaker answer order.

- Stage 1: Say who they are and how you know them.
- Stage 2: Say what they are like and what they do.
- Stage 3: Say what they have achieved and how they have influenced you.
- Stage 4: Say why they are special and how you feel about them.

MODEL ANSWER 答案范例

阅读雅思考生Sophia的参考答案。

Interviewer Tell me about a person who looked after you as a child.

Stage 1 Say who they are and how you know them.

Sophia I would like to talk about my grandmother. When I was a child my parents were very busy and so my grandmother, who is my father's mother, had to look after me.

Stage 2 Say what they are like and what they do.

Sophia My grandmother is a very gentle and kind woman. Her hair – as far back as I can remember – has always been brilliant white but she is quite self-conscious about this and wears a shoulder-length wig to hide it. Gran is really short, probably about four feet something, but she seems even shorter because she has a permanent stoop. When I think of my grandmother's appearance, the thing which stands out most is her constantly smiling face – she has a very kind face, which is covered in wrinkles.

Stage 3 Say what they have achieved and how they have influenced you.

Sophia Although she was a bit elderly, and had to take care of the house as well as me, she tried to keep me entertained and find interesting things for us to do together. I remember once when we were playing hide-and-seek at home, I ran into the garden and hid so well that she couldn't find me. It was quite a few hours before I decided to come out and my grandmother was so relieved – she had almost called the police!

Stage 4 Say why they are special and how you feel about them.

Sophia My grandmother has always taught me to be more patient and understanding towards other people. She had been a nurse for many years and I think if it hadn't been for her I would never have studied nursing – which I love. Gran was a great role model for me when I was growing up and I still admire her now I'm an adult. I hope that one day I'll have children and grandchildren too, and I hope that I'm as good a grandmother as mine is.

THE FORMULA 高分公式

For STAGE 1 of a person monologue, you must:
Say who they are and how you know them.

Language Steps

1. Use words for relatives, occupations and social positions correctly. ("*My grandfather* was a good man because…" / "A *family friend* once told me…")
2. Use relative clauses with "who" correctly. ("David, *who was my best friend at school*, often played football in the local park.")
3. Use the past continuous and past simple to say how you met someone. ("When I *was studying* at university, my teacher *told* me…")

NATIVE SPEAKER WORDS 英语母语词汇

让我们来学习一些英语母语词汇，这些词汇对于回答该类型的问题非常有用，并且能够帮助你理解下面的答案范例。

Native Speaker Word	Part of Speech	Definition	Example Sentence
look after 照顾		to care for, protect, raise	In China, many children are looked after by their grandparents because their parents have to work during the day.
Roman history 罗马历史		the history of the city of Rome and its ancient empire, usually referring to the period 753 B.C. to 476 A.D.	I don't know why people are interested in Roman history; Chinese history is much more interesting.
college 大学预科（英）， 大学（美）	noun	In the UK, "college" refers to an educational institution that is between school and university. College students are aged 16-18. In the US, "college" means university. College students are aged 17-21.	Sarah didn't enjoy her time at college because it was too much like school; she was much happier when she went to university as it gave her more freedom.
course 课程	noun	a group of classes about a certain topic, often with an exam at the end	I would really like to learn how to paint properly – if I had enough time I would love to take a painting course.
next door （在）隔壁		in the house, room, flat that is immediately next to your own	The postman must be quite stupid; he always gives us letters which should go next door.
(son / daughter / father / mother)-in-law 女婿，儿媳， 岳父，岳母	noun	people who are related to you through marriage, especially your husband's / wife's parents or the husband / wife of your child	I get along really well with my mother-in-law. She's a great woman.
elderly 老年的，上了年纪的	adjective	old, 70 years of age and over	Although my grandmother is now quite elderly, she's still able to look after herself and keep her house clean and tidy.
family home 老家		the house where your family lives, or lived for a long time in the past	I will always remember our family home – it was old, a bit dirty but really comfortable. I haven't got used to living in our new home yet.

MODEL ANSWERS 答案范例

阅读雅思考生Sophia，Mike和Jean的参考答案。

Interviewer Talk about a person who looked after you as a child.

Sophia I would like to talk about my grandmother. When I was a child my parents were very busy and so my grandmother, who is my father's mother, had to look after me...

Interviewer Talk about a teacher you know.

Mike I will always remember Dr. Shotter. He was one of my history teachers at university. I had always loved history at school and college and so I chose history as my major at university. When I was choosing my courses, I decided to try Roman history and so met Dr. Shotter...

Interviewer Talk about a neighbour you once had.

Jean I want to talk about my next-door neighbour Win. We moved to our family home when I was only six months old, so Win is the earliest neighbour that I can remember. Win, who lived with her daughter and son-in-law, was always a very elderly woman...

LANGUAGE STEP 1 Relatives, Occupations and Social Positions
高分语言点 1 描述人物关系、职业以及社会地位

让我们来看一下雅思考生Sophia，Mike和Jean是如何描述人物关系、职业以及社会地位的。

Sophia I would like to talk about my *grandmother*. When I was a child my *parents* were very busy and so my *grandmother*, who is my *father's mother*, had to look after me...

Mike I will always remember Dr. Shotter. He was one of my history *teachers* at university...

Jean I want to talk about my *next-door neighbour* Win. We moved to our family home when I was only six months old, so Win is the earliest *neighbour* that I can remember. Win, who lived with her *daughter* and *son-in-law*, was always a very elderly woman...

When giving a monologue about a person, it's always a great idea to say something about the person's relationship to you, their occupation or social position.

Here are some more examples:

Relatives	Occupations	Relationship
great-grandfather	surgeon	celebrity
grandparents	accountant	star
aunt	architect	politician
uncle	civil servant	TV presenter
cousin	plumber	sports personality
brother-in-law	electrician	friend of the family
mother-in-law	butcher	childhood friend
stepfather	self-employed	(ex-) boy friend / (ex-) girlfriend
nephew	waiter / waitress	distant relation

Examples:

"I would like to talk about my *nephew*, who is a *plumber* like me..."

"I really admire Daniel Craig, who is an excellent *actor* and has recently become a huge *movie star*."

"My grandparents were both *surgeons* during the war..."

Exercise 21.1 Gap Fill

Write the names of the relatives in the appropriate spaces in the family tree below.

Family Tree

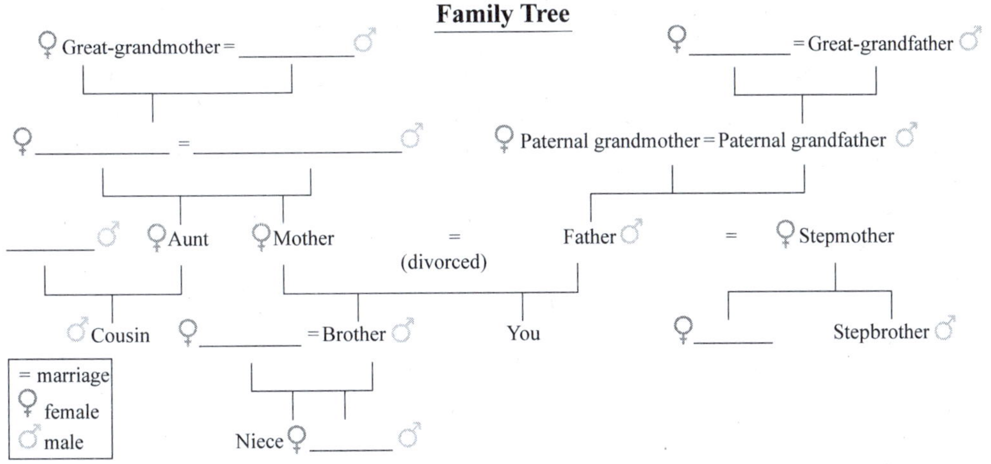

Exercise 21.2 Gap Fill

Write the words below in the correct spaces.

celebrity	childhood friend	ex-boyfriend
friend of the family	sports personality	TV presenter

1. Yao Ming is probably the most popular ____________ in China.
2. I never speak to my ____________, he hurt me too much when our relationship ended.
3. It's great shame that Chris Bailey, who was a ____________ of mine, passed away a few years ago.
4. My family all trust and like Richard Haward. We've known him so long and he always comes to our family events – he's a true ____________.
5. I don't like to watch the show "I Love Movies" because I can't stand the ____________ who hosts the programme.
6. My schoolmate Saskia Clarke has become something of a ____________ after competing in the 2008 Olympics.

LANGUAGE STEP 2 Relative Clauses with Who
高分语言点 2 Who 引导的定语从句

让我们来看一下雅思考生Sophia和Jean是如何使用who引导的定语从句的。

Sophia I would like to talk about my grandmother. When I was a child my parents were very busy and so my grandmother, *who is my father's mother*, had to look after me...

Jean I want to talk about my next-door neighbour Win. We moved to our family home when I was only six months old, so Win is the earliest neighbour that I can remember. Win, *who lived with her daughter and son-in-law*, was always a very elderly woman...

Notice that Sophia and Jean use parts of sentences (clauses) beginning with "who" to provide the examiner with information about the person they are talking about. These are called relative clauses.

There are two main types of relative clause, "defining" and "non-defining". Look at the examples below.

- non-defining relative clause
  "My mother, *who worked as a waitress for many years*, thoroughly dislikes politics."
  "Her good friend Daniel, *who became a very successful businessman*, had suggested to her once that she study computer programming."

In these examples, the relative clause gives "extra" information about the person being spoken about. The information is not "necessary" because if we were to remove the relative clause, the sentence would still make sense: *"My mother thoroughly dislikes politics." / "Her good friend Daniel had suggested to her once that she study computer programming."*

When speaking, you should have a slight pause at the beginning and end of your non-defining relative clauses.

- Defining relative clause
  "The woman *who lived next door to us when I was a child* was extremely ugly."
  "The movie star *who starred in the film* Titanic has become hugely successful."

These relative clauses are necessary to the meaning of the sentence, and are not giving "extra" information. If we removed the relative clause, the sentence would not make good sense as we would not know <u>which</u> woman or <u>which</u> movie star was being talked about: *"The woman was extremely ugly." / "The movie star has become hugely successful."*

When using a defining relative clause, you should not pause but speak continuously.

Note: "whom" is very rarely used in spoken relative clauses – just use "who".

Exercise 21.3 Gap Fill

Write the relative clauses below in the correct spaces.

who lived in Los Angeles
who was a civil servant
who taught us mathematics at school
who lived near our family home
who now studies at Beijing University
who was the President of America

1. Bill Clinton, ______________________, has made a deep impression on me.
2. The teacher ______________________ was particularly strict.
3. A policeman ______________________ once caught me stealing fruit and vegetables.
4. My friend, ______________________, told me once that she hated studying and exams.
5. Her uncle, ______________________, used to come and pick us up in his enormous black car.
6. The relative ______________________ sponsored her visa application to the United States.

LANGUAGE STEP 3 Using the Past Continuous & Past Simple to Say How You Met Someone 高分语言点 3 使用过去进行时和一般过去描述你是如何遇见某人的

让我们来看一下雅思考生Mike是如何描述他是怎样遇到Dr. Shotter的。

Mike I will always remember Dr. Shotter. He was one of my history teachers at university. I had always loved history at school and college and so I chose history as my major at university. *When I was choosing* my courses, *I decided to* try Roman history and *so met* Dr. Shotter...

When introducing somebody, it's often useful to say how, or under what circumstances, you met. Using the past continuous and past simple is a good way to do this.

The past continuous is used together with the past simple for talking about "longer" actions that were happening when a "single" or "shorter" action happened.

The structure of the past continuous is as follows:

- to be + verb-ing
  "I *was walking*..."
  "They *were talking* on the phone..."

"When" or "while" are often used to link the past continuous and past simple, as in the following examples:

"When I *was studying* at university, my teacher *told* me to spend more time researching my subject."

"While my brother *was visiting* Vietnam, he *lost* his passport, wallet, and credit cards."
"We *met* when we *were working* together at the same company."
"I first talked to my girlfriend when I *asked* her the time while we *were waiting* for the bus."

小贴士

感官动词以及描述状态的动词通常没有进行时态。这类动词有 hear, see, smell, have, want, like, love, prefer, know, believe, understand 等。

Exercise 21.4 Multiple Choice

Choose the correct words to complete the sentences.

1. My husband was visiting the city which I lived in ____________ we met.
   A. when   B. while   C. then
2. She gave my brother some help when he ____________ looking for a job.
   A. were   B. was   C. is
3. We were ____________ at university when we joined the same band and started socialising.
   A. study   B. studied   C. studying
4. My roommate was ____________ his friend and so after a few weeks we were introduced to each other.
   A. dating   B. date   C. dated
5. My mother met my father while they were ____________ around the country.
   A. travel   B. travelling   C. travelled

THE FORMULA 高分公式

For STAGE 2 of a person monologue, you must:
Say what they are like and what they do.

Language Steps

1. Use adjectives of personality accurately. ("My mother is a very *conservative* woman." / "Zhang Yimou is quite *humorous* and *open-minded*.")
2. Use adverbs of frequency to talk about past / present behaviour. ("My grandfather was *always* busy when I was young." / "My nephew *often* likes me to read him a story before he goes to bed.")
3. Use the past continuous and past simple and past perfect to tell anecdotes that show people's personality. ("We *were taking* the bus to another city when there *was* a big crash." / "He *had lived* in India for many years so when he *returned* he *looked* very different.")

NATIVE SPEAKER WORDS 英语母语词汇

让我们来学习一些英语母语词汇，这些词汇对于回答该类型的问题非常有用，并且能够帮助你理解下面的答案范例。

Native Speaker Word	Part of Speech	Definition	Example Sentence
brilliant white 亮白的，特别白的		very white, extremely white	I love going to the countryside in winter after it has snowed; everything is so brilliant white – it's beautiful.
self-conscious 自觉的，害羞的	adjective	extremely aware of one's own actions, and feeling very uncomfortable as a result	Jim really dislikes dancing in public because he feels self-conscious; he thinks everybody is watching him and laughing.
wig 假发	noun	artificial (fake) hair that bald people wear on their head to pretend they have hair	Men who go bald really should not wear wigs – they look so obvious and stupid!
stoop 驼背	noun	when someone's back is constantly bent and their head and shoulders are forward	Many extremely tall people have a slight stoop; I think it's because they are very self-conscious of their height.
hide-and-seek 捉迷藏	noun	a children's game often played in the West: everyone hides and one child tries to find them	I remember playing hide-and-seek in the fields near my home; it was such great fun!
beer belly 啤酒肚		a fat stomach caused by drinking a lot of beer for a long time	Most middle-aged men in England have a large beer belly because they drink far too much beer and do too little exercise.
know something (off) by heart 记在心中，背下来		to know something so well that you can recite it, say it from memory	In China most school children are made to learn ancient poems by Li Bai, Du Fu and Wang Wei so well that many years afterwards they still know many of them off by heart.
scowl 皱眉头；怒容	verb / noun	to have a very angry; very annoyed expression	I don't like that waitress; whenever you ask her to do something or you ask her a question she always scowls.
hoarse 沙哑的，嘶哑的	adjective	a rough voice, often caused by a cold, sore throat or smoking	Loads of people love Rod Stewart's songs because of his hoarse voice, but I think he just sounds like he has a cold.
on purpose 故意地，有意		to do something intentionally, not by accident	He said he spilled the drink on her lap by accident, but I know he spilled it on purpose because he was angry at her.

MODEL ANSWERS 答案范例

阅读雅思考生Sophia，Mike和Jean的参考答案。

Sophia ...My grandmother is a very gentle and kind woman. Her hair – as far back as I can remember – has always been a brilliant white but she is quite self-conscious about this and wears a shoulder-length wig to hide it. Gran is really short, probably about four feet something, but she seems even shorter because she has a permanent stoop. When I think of my grandmother's appearance, the thing which stands out most is her constantly smiling face – she has a very kind face, which is covered in wrinkles.

Although she was a bit elderly, and had to take care of the house as well as me, she tried to keep me entertained and find interesting things for us to do together. I remember once when we were playing hide-and-seek at home, I ran into the garden and hid so well that she couldn't find me. It was quite a few hours before I decided to come out and my grandmother was so relieved – she had almost called the police!...

Mike ...Dr. Shotter was about 60 years old and had a huge beer belly. His hair was grey, but quite thick. He always used to have glasses with him but he hardly ever wore them – they usually just dangled around his neck from the glasses strap. I can picture him now, sitting at his desk piled high with manuscripts and reference books, leaning back in his chair and looking out of the window while a cigarette burned between his fingers.

Dr. Shotter was a very experienced history lecturer. I remember that he always brought a lot of teaching notes to class but would then put them down and never look at the notes again the whole time he was teaching – he knew the information off by heart. He was able to bring the history lessons to life, and every student – even the laziest ones – all became interested in the subject when he was speaking. I remember once when he organised a university trip to an historical site. I had brought my girlfriend along, even though my girlfriend always said that history was boring. In the end, Dr. Shotter told my girlfriend about the history of the place and she was amazed...

Jean ...She was a large woman, about 5 feet 8 inches and quite fat. When people saw her, they would be struck immediately by the expression on her face, which often appeared to be a scowl. Actually, she was a very friendly and gentle woman.

Win was originally from London and had a very strong London accent and was never without a cigarette. Because she smoked, whenever she heard something funny she would have this raspy, hoarse laugh. When I visited her she would also be very kind to me, offering to make me a cup of tea, but would usually have some bad words to say about her son-in-law, as he often annoyed her on purpose.

I remember that Win did all the cleaning in the house while her son-in-law, Fred, and her daughter were out at work. To annoy her, Fred would often stub his cigarette out not in the ashtray but on the kitchen floor – making her go crazy!...

LANGUAGE STEP 1 Adjectives of Personality
高分语言点 1 描述人物性格的形容词

让我们来看一下雅思考生Sophia，Mike和Jean用了哪些形容词描述人物的性格。

Sophia ...My grandmother is a very *gentle* and *kind* woman. Her hair – as far back as I can remember – has always been a brilliant white but she is quite *self-conscious* about this and wears a shoulder-length wig to hide it...

Mike ...Dr. Shotter was a very *experienced* history lecturer...

Jean ...When people saw her, they would be struck immediately by the expression on her face, which often appeared to be a scowl. Actually, she was a very *friendly* and *gentle* woman...

When giving a monologue about a person, it's very important to accurately use adjectives of personality to describe what the person is / was like.

Look at some more examples of useful adjectives of personality:

Funny	Shy	Confident	Angry	Happy
humorous	reserved	ambitious	aggressive	charming
witty	introverted	self-confident	bad-tempered	cheerful
funny	quiet	self-assured	moody	vivacious
hilarious	sensitive	extroverted	irritable	lively
amusing	conservative	adventurous	short-fused	
hysterical	timid	arrogant	abrupt	

Helpful	Honest	Kind	Intelligent	Stupid
considerate	straight-forward	gentle	clever	immature
supportive	frank	calm	bright	silly
sympathetic	reliable	generous	mature	dumb
helpful	genuine	loving	talented	dim
	sincere	thoughtful	open-minded	daft
		altruistic	wise	foolish

Examples:

"He is a very *extroverted* person, and really likes to be the centre of attention."

"Gong Li seems like a very *vivacious* and *self-assured* woman, though she's perhaps quite *abrupt* if you make her angry."

"My girlfriend really has two sides to her personality; when she's *happy* she can be *open-minded*, *thoughtful* and really *supportive*, but when she's in a bad mood she can be really *irritable* and *selfish*."

Exercise 21.5: Gap Fill

Write the words below in the correct spaces.

ambitious	moody	bright	charming
supportive	immature	frank	
reserved	humorous	generous	

1. My colleague is really ____________ she is often irritable and angry – sometimes I'm too scared to speak to her!
2. I always have lots of ideas at work but whenever I tell my manager he never listens and nothing changes – I wish my boss was more ____________.
3. My nephew is almost 25 but he still plays computer games and doesn't think about the future. He's far too ____________.
4. Politicians are rarely ____________ with the public; usually they hide the truth or just tell people a part of the truth.
5. Many women really like Brad Pitt not only because he is handsome but because he seems really ____________.
6. Bill Gates is obviously an extremely ____________ man; otherwise he wouldn't have been so successful.
7. One thing I really appreciated about my grandparents was that they were so ____________ – they gave me whatever I needed and didn't really care about money.
8. I think my uncle is still not married because he is extremely ____________. He doesn't like to say much when other people are present and his views are quite traditional.
9. My doctor is fantastic – even though her patients are really nervous about seeing the doctor or going to the hospital, she is so ____________ that she can make them laugh and relax straight away.
10. Although David Beckham is a great football player, he isn't very ____________ – don't ask him any complicated maths questions!

LANGUAGE STEP 2 Adverbs of Frequency for Habits and Behaviour
高分语言点 2 描述习惯和行为的频率副词

让我们来看一下雅思考生Sophia，Mike和Jean用了哪些频率副词描述习惯和行为。

Sophia ...When I think of my grandmother's appearance, the thing which stands out most is her *constantly* smiling face...

Mike ...Dr. Shotter was about 60 years old and had a huge beer belly. His hair was grey, but quite thick. He *always* used to have glasses with him but he *hardly ever* wore them – they *usually* just dangled around his neck from the glasses strap... I remember that he *always* brought a lot of teaching notes to class but would then put them down and *never* look at the notes again the whole time he was teaching – he knew the information off by heart...

Jean ...When people saw her, they would be struck immediately by the expression on her face, which *often* appeared to be a scowl...Win was originally from London and had a very strong London accent and was *never* without a cigarette...When I visited her she would also be very kind to me, offering to make me a cup of tea, but would *usually* have some bad words to say about her son-in-law, as he *often* annoyed her on purpose...

Adverbs of frequency are great for describing people's habits and behaviour.

Refresh your memory of useful adverbs of frequency by looking at the table below.

constantly	frequently	regularly
typically	commonly	often
sometimes	occasionally	rarely
seldom	hardly ever	almost never
always	usually	generally
never	every now and again	from time to time

You can also talk about how often people do or did things by using the structure:

Times + time period

- once a day
- twice a week
- three times a month
- five times a year

Every + time

- every morning
- every evening
- every day at 6 p.m.
- every week
- every month
- every birthday
- every summer vacation

Examples:

"My friend Omar has to wash *five times a day, every day*."

"My grandmother would *regularly* go to the temple to pray and offer gifts."

"*Every summer vacation* my father would think of a special trip for us to go on."

Exercise 21.6: Gap Fill

Write the words below in the correct spaces.

constantly	every now and again	seldom	typically
frequently	twice a year	every night	

1. My sister ____________ did any housework when she was a teenager – she was too lazy and didn't want to help mum.
2. One of my best friends, Adam, is a fantastic cook at a really expensive restaurant. Lots of famous celebrities ____________ go to his restaurant.
3. A teenager that lives near me meets his friends and starts drinking ____________ at 7 p.m.
4. When Tracy was young she went to many different places as her family would ____________ go on vacation ____________.
5. Although my mother loves Chinese food, she only eats at a Chinese restaurant ____________ because they are too expensive.
6. Bob's grandmother had lots of problems with her memory. She couldn't remember new information and ____________ forgot where she lived – she had to have a piece of paper with her address written on it at all times.

LANGUAGE STEP 3 Past Continuous & Past Simple Tenses to Tell Anecdotes 高分语言点 3 用过去进行时和一般过去时讲述小故事

让我们来看一下雅思考生Sophia，Mike和Jean是如何讲述一则小故事的。

Sophia ...I remember once when *we were playing* hide-and-seek at home, I *ran* into the garden and *hid* so well that she *couldn't find* me. It *was* quite a few hours before I *decided* to come out and my grandmother *was so relieved* – she *had almost called* the police!

Mike …I remember once when he *organised* a university trip to an historical site. I *had brought* my girlfriend along, even though my girlfriend always *said* that history was boring. In the end, Dr. Shotter *told* my girlfriend about the history of the place and she *was amazed*…

Jean …I remember that Win *did all the cleaning* in the house while her son-in-law, Fred, and her daughter *were* out at work. To annoy her, Fred *would often stub* his cigarette out not in the ashtray but on the kitchen floor – *making* her go crazy!...

Notice that Sophia, Mike and Jean all tell anecdotes (interesting or amusing short stories) about the people they are describing. This makes their monologue much more interesting and is a great way to show what someone's personality and behaviour is like.

You should remember how to use the past continuous and past simple from the last lesson, where you learnt to talk about how you met somebody. This is very useful for telling anecdotes.

Examples:

"The teacher *was getting* really angry but David *didn't realise*, and *continued* making stupid jokes…"

"I *was travelling* on a bus in Laos when there *was* a loud crash and the bus *started* shaking all over the road…"

You can also use the past perfect and past simple to tell anecdotes.

The structure of the past perfect is as follows:

- had + past participle

  "I *had eaten* a huge dinner…"

  "They *had decided* that they would…"

The past perfect action happened <u>before</u> the past simple action, as in the following examples:

"Last Christmas, I *had eaten* a huge dinner at my mother's house and then my girlfriend's mother *made* me eat another enormous meal."

"They *had decided* that they would visit some historical sites, but on the bus on the way they *were robbed*."

Exercise 21.7: Matching

Match the sentence halves.

1. My mother had had many accidents…
2. Before he became really famous as a kung fu master and a film star,…

A. …but the government protected them and now they are increasing in number every year.

B. …I lied and said a burglar must have done it.

3. My grandparents returned home after I had accidentally knocked over the TV. Instead of telling the truth, ...
4. Forty years ago, American Bald Eagles had almost all died…
5. Our new neighbours tried to steal some of our vegetables from the garden after…

C. …before she finally stopped driving.
D. …my parents had gone away on holiday.
E. …Bruce Lee (李小龙) had been a dancer.

THE FORMULA 高分公式

For STAGE 3 of a person monologue, you must:
Say what they have achieved and how they have influenced you.

Language Steps

1. Use the third conditional accurately to express the importance of somebody to you. ("*If* I *hadn't met* her I *would never have*..." / "I *would have made* a huge mistake if she *hadn't*...")
2. Use the present perfect to talk about changes and achievements. ("He *has taught* me to always put others first." / "My grandfather *has had* a great influence on my life.")
3. Use phrases of achievement to talk about the person's accomplishments. ("She *fought for everything she achieved*." / "He *had a lucky break* at the age of 30, then *rose to fame* quickly.")

NATIVE SPEAKER WORDS 英语母语词汇

让我们来学习一些英语母语词汇，这些词汇对于回答该类型的问题非常有用，并且能够帮助你理解下面的答案范例。

Native Speaker Word	Part of Speech	Definition	Example Sentence
patient 有耐心的	adjective	describing someone who can wait or endure something without getting angry or frustrated	Most successful chefs are not in the least patient – they shout at their staff about the tiniest mistake and always demand that things are done quicker.
understanding 通情达理的	adjective	describing someone who understands what other people are thinking or feeling, and doesn't blame other people for their behaviour or mistakes	At school my Mathematics teacher was not understanding at all; she would get really angry if you made mistakes in your homework and couldn't understand why some things weren't clear to the students.

续表

Native Speaker Word	Part of Speech	Definition	Example Sentence
master's degree 硕士学位		the degree studied at university after the first, or "bachelor's degree"	In China, more and more students are deciding to study for a master's degree in order to improve their chances of finding a good job after leaving university.
over the years 历年，多年以来		over time, as the years pass	I never thought I would learn how to speak Spanish, despite going to Spain every year on holiday. But over the years I have managed to learn quite a lot of the language.
appreciate (somebody or something) 欣赏（某人或某事）		to value, to recognise somebody or understand that something is valuable or important	My mother really appreciated the time she spent in Brazil – during that time she learnt a lot about the country, the people, herself and life in general.
have an influence upon (somebody or something) 对（某人或某事）产生影响		to affect or change someone or something	Nicole Kidman's divorce from Tom Cruise seems to have had a big influence upon her acting career – she's not as big a movie star as she was before.

MODEL ANSWERS 答案范例

在完成下面的练习之前，阅读雅思考生Sophia, Mike和Jean的参考答案。

Sophia ...My grandmother has always taught me to be more patient and understanding towards other people. She had been a nurse for many years and I think if it hadn't been for her I would never have studied nursing – which I love...

Mike ...He had a great influence upon me, and made me want to become a history lecturer myself. I'm sure I wouldn't have studied a Master's degree in Roman History if I hadn't met Dr. Shotter...

Jean ...It was a very sad day when they left, as we had known each other for so long. Although Win was just a normal woman, she had helped our family many times over the years and done small things like looking after our cat which we really appreciated...

LANGUAGE STEP 1 The Third Conditional
高分语言点 1 第三条件句

让我们来看一下雅思考生Sophia和Mike是如何使用第三条件句的。

Sophia ...My grandmother has always taught me to be more patient and understanding towards other people. She had been a nurse for many years and I think *if it hadn't been for her I would never have studied nursing* – which I love...

Mike ...He had a great influence upon me, and made me want to become a history lecturer myself. I'm sure *I wouldn't have studied a Master's degree in Roman History if I hadn't met Dr. Shotter...*

Let's look at how the third conditional is constructed:

- if + had(n't) + past participle + would(n't) have + past participle
  "*If* it *hadn't been* for her I *would* never *have studied* nursing."

- would(n't) have + past participle + if + had(n't) + past participle
  "I *wouldn't have studied* a Master's degree in Roman History *if* I *hadn't met* Dr. Shotter."

Both constructions are possible for each third conditional sentence and mean exactly the same thing.

The third conditional is used to talk about the following things:

- things that did not happen in the past
  "*If* my teacher *hadn't been* so relaxed, I'm sure I *would have studied* harder."
  (My teacher was too relaxed so I didn't study hard enough.)

  "*If* Liu Xiang *had won* the gold medal at the 2008 Olympics, he *would've been* even more famous."
  (Liu Xiang didn't win the gold medal, so he didn't become more famous.)

  "*If* my grandmother *hadn't looked after* me as a child, a babysitter *would have*."
  (My grandmother did look after me, so a babysitter didn't.)

- things that might not have happened – this explains why they happened
  "*If* Bill Gates *hadn't been* so ambitious, he *wouldn't have been* so successful."
  (Bill Gates was very ambitious; and this is why he has been so successful.)

  "*If* my niece *hadn't been* so lazy at school, she *wouldn't have failed* all her exams."
  (My niece was lazy; and this is why she failed all her exams.)

  "Pandas probably *wouldn't have survived if* they *hadn't been* officially protected."
  (Pandas did survive because they were officially protected.)

Exercise 21.8: Matching

Match the sentence halves on the left with those on the right.

1. I would've studied law...	A. ...wolves would've survived for longer in Europe.
2. If we hadn't gone to the same school,...	B. ...I probably wouldn't have met my best friend.
3. I would never have learned to cook...	C. ...if she had had more money.
4. If people hadn't hunted them,...	D. ...I wouldn't have met my boyfriend.
5. My mother would've retired earlier...	E. ...if I had done what my father told me to do.
6. If I hadn't travelled abroad,...	F. ...if my mother hadn't shown me.

LANGUAGE STEP 2 The Present Perfect for Talking About Changes and Achievements 高分语言点 2 用现在完成时态描述变化和成就

让我们来看一下雅思考生Sophia是如何使用现在完成时态的。

Sophia ...My grandmother *has always taught* me to be more patient and understanding towards other people...

When giving a monologue about a person, it's a good idea to talk about the changes or achievements that person has made. For this, you need to use the present perfect.

Remember the structure of the present perfect is:

- have + past participle

  "My grandfather *has had* a great influence on my life."

  "She *has become* one of the most famous actresses in the world."

  "My nephew *has helped* me to see that family is the most important thing."

Exercise 21.9: Multiple Choice

Choose the appropriate verb forms from the choices below to complete the sentences.

1. Jackie Chan (成龙) ____________ over 70 movies in his career.

   A. has made　　B. have made　　C. has been made

2. My parents ___________ me to believe in myself, to do the best that I can.

   A. has always told　　B. have always told　　C. have always tolden

3. Gordon Ramsey, who is a celebrity chef, ____________ for being really rude to his staff and customers.

   A. has become famous　　B. has became famous　　C. has been famous

4. My uncle ____________ always ____________ there to support and comfort me when I couldn't or didn't want to talk to my parents.

   A. has, was　　B. have, was　　C. has, been

5. My grandmother ____________ many experiences in her life; because of her intelligence she has been able to become very wise.

   A. has had　　B. has have　　C. had has

6. Although my cousin ____________ a lot of things that made my family angry and disappointed with her, I still respect her for making her own decisions.

   A. has did　　B. has done　　C. had done

LANGUAGE STEP 3 Phrases of Achievements 高分语言点 3 描述成就的短语

When talking about people that are important to you, or who you admire, you can use phrases of achievements to make you sound more like a native speaker.

Look at the following phrases of achievements:

Working hard

- through sheer hard work
- to struggle for / to do something
- to strive for something
- to fight for something
- to have the determination to do something
- to stand up for something / somebody
- to show perseverance

Examples:

"She *struggled to* get where she is now – she deserves to be so famous!"

"He *fought for* everything he has achieved – I admire him greatly!"

Success

- to have the will to succeed
- to have a desire for success
- to climb the ladder of success
- to have a long and brilliant career
- to earn the respect of somebody
- to get a lucky break

Examples:

"Slowly but surely, she *climbed the ladder of success* and finally reached the top position."

"Mei Lanfang suffered many hardships but nevertheless *had a long and brilliant career*."

Talented

- to have a gift for doing something
- to have an outstanding talent for doing something
- to develop his / her talent for doing something / as a...

For example:

"My brother-in-law has really *developed his talent as* an actor; in recent years he has often appeared in professional plays."

Exercise 21.10: Gap Fill

Write the words below in the correct spaces.

through sheer hard work	earn the respect	has a gift for
to fight for	have the will to succeed	

1. The problem with Ben is that he doesn't ____________ – he just gives up as soon as he meets a problem.

2. I admire Dr. Atkinson, who was my Science professor, because she was from an extremely poor family and it was ____________ that she became an expert in her field.
3. My brother truly ____________ cooking; everything he tries tastes fantastic!
4. Most people are impressed with Nelson Mandela's achievements. He showed the determination ____________ freedom, equality and human rights.
5. In the future I hope to find a well-paid job in an international company so that I can ____________ of my parents.

THE FORMULA 高分公式

For STAGE 4 of a person monologue, you must:

Say why they are special and how you feel about them.

Language Steps

4. Use expressions of admiration correctly. ("I *love her* because..." / "I *will always admire him* because...")
5. Use expressions of imitation accurately. ("I *want to be like him* when I am a grandfather." / "I *hope I am as successful as* he has been.")
6. Use *role model expressions* correctly. ("She has always been *my hero*." / "He was a great *role model* for the younger generation.")

NATIVE SPEAKER WORDS 英语母语词汇

让我们来学习一些英语母语词汇，这些词汇对于回答该类型的问题非常有用，并且能够帮助你理解下面的答案范例。

Native Speaker Word	Part of Speech	Definition	Example Sentence
gran 祖母，外祖母	noun	an informal abbreviation for grandmother	To avoid confusion, when I was young I had to call my maternal grandmother "Gran" and my paternal grandmother "Nan".
role model 榜样		someone who people admire, look up to and try to copy in their behaviour, attitudes, etc	Most hip-hop singers are not good role models for children because they try to make buying guns, shooting people and taking drugs look cool.
academic 学者，大学教师	noun	a person who teaches at university or undertakes scholarly research	I admire most academics because they have had to devote their lives to studying and research in order to become experts in their field.

续表

Native Speaker Word	Part of Speech	Definition	Example Sentence
one day 总有一天		used to talk about an indefinite time in the future	It has been the dream of many different people that one day there will be no war, violence or poverty in the world.
have a positive impact on something 对某事产生积极的影响		to have a beneficial influence on something, to change something for the better	When my father lost his job it actually had a positive impact on his marriage with my mother because they had to work together as a team to get through the tough time.
terrible 糟糕的，可怕的	adjective	very bad, low quality, unpleasant	David is a terrible worker because he's always late, never does his work on time and is a bit rude to his boss.
proud 骄傲的，自豪的	adjective	feeling happy or satisfied because something you have done or someone you are connected to has done something that is good	Lots of people from Hunan are extremely proud that Mao Zedong was from their province.

MODEL ANSWERS 答案范例

阅读雅思考生Sophia，Mike和Jean的参考答案。

Sophia …Gran was a great role model for me when I was growing up and I still admire her now I'm an adult. I hope that one day I'll have children and grandchildren too, and I hope that I'm as good a grandmother as mine was.

Mike …Although I didn't become an academic myself, I feel that Dr. Shotter had a very positive impact on my development. For me, Dr. Shotter was the best teacher I ever had.

Jean …Also, the new neighbours who moved in were terrible so my family really missed Win and her family. We all agree Win was a great neighbour and feel proud to have known her for so many years.

LANGUAGE STEP 1 Expressions of Admiration
高分语言点 1 赞美、钦佩的表达方法

让我们来看一下雅思考生Sophia，Mike和Jean是如何表达对他人的赞美和钦佩的。

Sophia …Gran was a *great role model for me* when I was growing up and I still *admire her* now I'm an adult…

Mike …For me, Dr. Shotter *was the best teacher* I ever had.

Jean …We all agree Win was a great neighbour and *feel proud to have known her* for so many years.

When giving a monologue about a person, you should use expressions of admiration to say why the person is special, or why you admire them.

Here are some more expressions:
"I *love her* because..."
"Everyone *respects* wise and peaceful leaders such as Mahatma Gandhi."
"My niece really *appreciates* what my parents did for her."
"I *look up to* her..."
"I will always *admire* him for..."
"His colleagues all *think highly of* my stepbrother and his work..."
"I *feel proud of* my mother's achievements..."
"She is *special* to me because..."
"I truly *hold in high regard* people such as President Obama who..."
"Many movie enthusiasts *consider him to be the best* actor of his generation."

Exercise 21.11: Gap Fill

Write the words below in the correct spaces.

in high regard	special to me	looked up to
greatly admire	felt proud	hold

1. My brother and I always ____________ our grandfather because he fought during the war and suffered a lot.
2. When I graduated from university with top grades, I felt so happy because I knew both my parents ____________ of me.
3. Because of his practical measures and bravery, I will always ____________ the war hero ____________.
4. Due to the dedication and determination they need to have, I ____________ sports stars such as David Beckham.
5. My kindergarten teacher was really ____________ because she was my first teacher and was so kind and patient.

LANGUAGE STEP 2 Expressions Hoping to Imitate Somebody
高分语言点 2 希望效仿某人的表达方法

让我们来看一下雅思考生Sophia是如何表达希望效仿某人的。

Sophia ...Gran was a great role model for me when I was growing up and I still admire her now I'm an adult. *I hope that one day I'll have children and grandchildren too, and I hope that I'm as good a grandmother as mine was.*

When we talk about people who are special or important to us, we often express the feeling that we want to be the same as them in some way.

Let's look at how to say "I hope...":

- I hope I am as + adjective + as + person
- I hope I will be as +adjective + as + person

Examples:

"*I hope I am as* successful as Bill Gates."

"*I hope I will be as* successful as Bill Gates."

"*I hope I am as happy as* my next-door neighbour when I am old."

"*I hope I will be as* kind a teacher as Mrs. Capp."

Here are some more expressions of imitation:

"*I would love to be like* my mother."

"*I would like to be as* well respected as my grandfather."

"*I want to be like* my neighbour Doris when I'm older."

Exercise 21.12: Multiple Choice

Choose the appropriate words from the choices below to complete the sentences.

1. I would ____________ Zhang Ziyi when I am older; she's beautiful, famous and seems very popular.
   A. like to be as B. like to be like C. love to be like
2. My stepfather is always calm and happy. Now he's stopped working, he has a really relaxed life just fishing, painting and going on trips. I hope my life is ____________ when I retire.
   A. as enjoyable as his is B. as enjoyable as C. enjoyable
3. My babysitter, Margaret, usually had lots and lots of children in her house, so it was really lively and great fun. When I buy a house and have children, I want my house ____________ Margaret's.
   A. to like B. to be like C. to be as
4. My mother is a great cook. Everything she cooks for us is so delicious, the dishes even look mouth-watering too! I hope ____________ well as her.
   A. I will be able to cook as B. I am cook as C. I will be cook as
5. A friend of mine is really confident and out-going; she's always really good at meeting new people so she's popular at parties and things like that and she's successful at work too. I'm quite shy, but I'm trying to believe in myself more – I hope that one day I ________ she is.
   A. will be as confident as B. am as confident as C. as confident as

LANGUAGE STEP 3 Role Model Expressions
高分语言点 3 榜样的表达方法

让我们来看一下雅思考生Sophia是如何描述自己的榜样的。

Sophia ...*Gran was a great role model for me when I was growing up*...

Let's look at some more expressions for describing role models:

- mentor
  "Ringo was his *mentor* for the first year he lived away from home."
- he / she set(s) a fine example for
  "Rita *sets a fine example for* the rest of the team – she works so well."
- hero
  "Paul McCartney was my *hero* for many years. I really admire him."
- pop icon
  "John Lennon became a big *pop icon*. He was all over the media."
- idol
  "George Harrison, who became quite religious for a while, was my *idol* when I was a child – I really looked up to him."
- sex symbol
  "Yoko Ono was a *sex symbol* to some young, alternative people in the 1970s – every young fan wanted to look like her."
- charismatic leader
  "Charles Manson, who was imprisoned for the murder of Sharon Tate, was a crazy *charismatic leader* during the 1960s."
- visionary
  "Some say that the Beatles were not only a talented rock band, but that they were *visionaries* for their generation."

Exercise 21.13: Matching

Match the words on the left with the definitions on the right.

1. he / she sets a fine example for
2. idol
3. hero
4. mentor
5. pop icon

A. somebody who is widely recognised as being beautiful and sexy
B. somebody who is extremely admired / respected
C. somebody who knows how to move the hearts and minds of the people, and can make enormous changes to the world with this power

6. visionary
7. charismatic leader
8. sex symbol

D. somebody who gives another person help or advice for a long time, like a teacher
E. somebody who has the ability to think in a unique and different manner and who can come up with new ideas to promote positive change
F. to say that someone's behaviour / achievements are a very good thing for others to copy or follow
G. somebody who is extremely admired / respected for their achievement(s)
H. somebody who becomes extremely famous and respected for singing or performing music

ANSWER ORDER 答题思路

Remind yourself of the answer order you should use when giving a monologue about a person.

- Stage 1: Say who they are and how you know them.
- Stage 2: Say what they are like and what they do.
- Stage 3: Say what they have achieved and how they have influenced you.
- Stage 4: Say why they are special and how you feel about them.

Exercise 21.14: Ordering

Using the *answer order* above, put the following extracts from a model answer into the correct order.

A. It's probably because of these skills that he has become such a successful actor...
B. As you probably know, he's an incredibly famous Hollywood actor...
C. Brad Pitt has great acting skills – his body language and face expressions are so believable that you immediately accept his new character whatever role he plays...
D. I'd like to talk about Brad Pitt, as I'd love to meet him.
E. I hope that I'll really be able to meet him one day!
F. Interviewer: Tell me about a famous person you'd like to meet.
G. I've really enjoyed watching the movies Brad Pitt has made so far, and I'm sure I'll continue to cry, laugh and be amazed because of his acting in future films...

Formula 22: Place Monologue

AIMS 学习目标

In this lesson you'll master the Formula for giving a monologue about a place. Typical IELTS Part Two questions about a place are:

- Talk about a flat or house you would like to own one day.
- Talk about your ideal home.
- Talk about a shopping centre or mall you have visited.
- Talk about a place where people can do sports.
- Talk about a place you know where people go to listen to music.
- Talk about a friend or family member's house you know and like.
- Talk about museum you have visited.
- Talk about an historic place in your country.
- Talk about a lake or river you know about or have seen.

ANSWER ORDER 答题思路

To give a good monologue about a place, you should use the following native speaker answer order.

- Stage 1: Say what it is and where it is.
- Stage 2: Say what it looks like.
- Stage 3: Say what its purpose is.
- Stage 4: Say why it is special and how you feel about it.

MODEL ANSWER 答案范例

阅读雅思考生Jean的参考答案。

Interviewer A flat or house you would like to own one day.

Stage 1 Say what it is and where it is.

Jean Maybe it's a bit unrealistic, but I would love to own a luxury flat. It's located in the CBD area of Beijing, right in the centre of downtown, close to all the best restaurants and shops.

Stage 2 Say what it looks like.

Jean The flat would be on a high floor – perhaps the top floor – of a brand-new high-rise apartment block with the most modern architectural style. The apartment would have at least two huge bedrooms, one lounge, a massive kitchen and one or two bathrooms – it'd be great if one of the bathrooms was en suite! The style would be modern, with varnished wooden floorboards, leather sofas and colourful rugs on the floor. The flat would be very airy and light, with lots of windows that have great views over the surrounding streets and buildings.

Stage 3 Say what its purpose is.

Jean A flat like this would be perfect for my husband and I to live in and then bring up our child. A new, gleaming kitchen would be great for preparing delicious dishes for our friends when they come to dinner and the guests could be entertained in the comfortable and relaxing sitting room.

Stage 4 Say why it is special and how you feel about it.

Jean I know that this kind of flat will be difficult to buy, especially as my family is not very rich. However, if I am very successful in my career and make loads of money one day, this is the kind of flat I'll buy. I think almost everybody would be happy to live in a flat like this – I just hope that one day I can!

THE FORMULA 高分公式

For STAGE 1 of a place monologue, you must:
Say what it is and where it is.

Language Steps

1. Use words for types of place correctly. ("The *Bird's Nest* is probably the best *stadium* in the world." / "The *Mosque* in Xi'an is an extremely interesting religious *building* because...")
2. Use prepositions of location correctly. ("...it's *above* a Chinese restaurant..." / "...there are many trees *along* the river bank...")

NATIVE SPEAKER WORDS 英语母语词汇

让我们来学习一些英语母语词汇，这些词汇对于回答该类型的问题非常有用，并且能够帮助你理解下面的答案范例。

Native Speaker Word	Part of Speech	Definition	Example Sentence
historic site 名胜古迹		a place where something important in history happened, or where an old building is	The Great Wall is one of the world's most famous historic sites.
suburb 郊区	noun	an area at the edge of a city or large town where most people of that city or town live	A good thing about living in the suburbs is that the houses are much cheaper than in the centre of town, though commuting to work can be a pain.

续表

Native Speaker Word	Part of Speech	Definition	Example Sentence
be located in / near / on / at 坐落在，位于		used to describe where something is	My house is located at the end of the street, whereas hers is located in the middle.
near (to) 离……近	preposition	close, not far away (Note: a common mistake by students of English is to say: "...near from..." This is incorrect.)	When I go on trips, I usually buy my drinks at the shops near the station.
unrealistic 不现实的	adjective	not realistic, not likely to be true or likely to happen	It's unrealistic to expect the world to be peaceful and harmonious in the next few years.
luxury 奢侈品	noun	something which gives comfort, usually very expensive and / or beautiful	Every now and again my mother likes to buy herself luxuries like expensive jewellery and clothes.
downtown 市区 / 市区的	adverb / adjective	towards or in the centre or main business area of a town or city	I would love to live downtown, but I can't afford the rent there.
high-rise / high rise 高层的，多层的 / 高楼	adjective / noun	a tall building with many floors / storeys	Most modern cities have lots and lots of high-rise buildings for business or accommodation.
block of flats / apartment block 公寓楼		a building containing many apartments (Note: British English "block of flats" has the same meaning as American English "apartment block".)	The last block of flats where I lived was really dirty and noisy – my neighbours were so selfish.
flat / apartment 公寓	noun	a place for people to live that consists of a set of rooms that are part of a larger building (Note: British English "flat" has the same meaning as American English "apartment".)	I can't wait to have my own flat one day; I'm sick of living with my parents.

MODEL ANSWERS 答案范例

阅读雅思考生Sophia，Mike和Jean的参考答案。

Interviewer Talk about an historic site you have visited.

Sophia I want to talk about the Summer Palace (颐和园). The Summer Palace is a very famous historic site in the northwest of Beijing, in the suburbs...

Interviewer Tell me about a place where people go to listen to music.

Mike I would like to talk about a bar called D22. D22 is a bar located in Wudaokou, quite near to Beijing University...

Interviewer Talk to me about a house or flat you'd like to own one day.

Jean Maybe it's a bit unrealistic, but I would love to own a luxury flat. It's located in the CBD area of Beijing, right in the centre of downtown, close to all the best restaurants and shops. The flat would be on a high floor – perhaps the top floor – of a brand-new high-rise apartment block…

LANGUAGE STEP 1 Words for Types of Places
高分语言点 1 描述不同地方的词汇

让我们来看一下雅思考生Sophia，Mike和Jean是如何描述各种不同类型的地方的。

Sophia I want to talk about the Summer Palace. The Summer Palace *is a very famous historic site* in the northwest of Beijing, in the suburbs…

Mike I would like to talk about *a bar* called D22…

Jean Maybe it's a bit unrealistic, but I would love to own *a luxury flat*...

The first thing you need to do when giving a monologue about a place is to say what kind of place it is.

Here are some more really useful words for different types of places:

Religious	Tourism	Shopping	Accommodation
mosque	tourist attraction	shopping mall	house
temple	historic site	shopping centre	flat / apartment
church	historic building	plaza	mansion
cathedral	palace	market	campsite
religious building	museum	discount store	youth hostel

Natural	Leisure	Entertainment
scenic spot	gym	bar
park	leisure centre	nightclub
garden	sports ground	theatre
botanical gardens	stadium	cinema
nature reserve	football pitch	concert hall
countryside	sports field	music hall

Examples:

"Let me tell you about *a theatre* I once saw when I was travelling…"

"I would like to talk about the Lavender Fields in Norfolk, which is a very popular *tourist attraction.*"

"I'm going to talk about a lovely little *park* in the *countryside* outside London."

Exercise 22.1: Matching

Match the types of places on the left with the activities people do there on the right.

1. temple
2. market
3. museum
4. nature reserve
5. leisure centre
6. mansion
7. nightclub

A. where people go shopping and try to haggle to get a good price
B. where people can get fit and play sports
C. where people can go to listen to music and dance
D. where people can enjoy trees, mountains and rivers
E. where people go to pray / worship gods
F. where people can see very old and interesting objects
G. a very large house where rich people live

LANGUAGE STEP 2 Prepositions of Location
高分语言点 2 描述地点的介词

让我们来看一下雅思考生Sophia，Mike和Jean用了哪些介词描述地点。

Sophia I want to talk about the Summer Palace. The Summer Palace is a very famous historic site *in the northwest* of Beijing, *in* the suburbs...

Mike I would like to talk about a bar called D22. D22 is a bar *located in* Wudaokou, quite *near to* Beijing University...

Jean Maybe it's a bit unrealistic, but I would love to own a luxury flat. It's *located in* the CBD area of Beijing, *right in the centre of* downtown, *close to* all the best restaurants and shops. The flat would be *on* a high floor – perhaps the top floor – of a brand-new high-rise apartment block...

Notice that Sophia, Mike and Jean all say where their place is located immediately after they have said what the place is – this helps to introduce the place you are describing.

Remind yourself of these essential prepositions of location:

- in + enclosing or larger place
  "...*in* Beijing..."
  "...*in* the countryside..."
  "...*in* the middle of nowhere..."

- at + certain place or location
  "...*at* the top of the mountain..."
  "...*at* the end of the street..."

- on + a surface or roads
  "...*on* the fifth floor..."
  "...*on* a main road..."
  "...*on* the outskirts of the city..."

- over / above + a certain place or location
  "...*above* a Japanese restaurant..."
  "...every day the Chinese flag flies *over* Tian'anmen Square..."

- next to / beside / by + a certain place or location
  "...*by* the seaside..."
  "...*next to* the Bell Tower..."
  "...*beside* Tianchi Lake..."

- opposite / across from + a certain place or location
  "...I work *opposite* my favourite restaurant..."
  "...The Forbidden City is just *across from* Tian'anmen Square..."

- between + two places or locations
  "Suzhou, which is *between* Shanghai and Nanjing..."
  "My house is *between* the mountains and the sea."

- in front of + a certain place or location
  "...the Bund in Shanghai is just *in front of* the main historical buildings..."
  "The Terracotta Warriors (兵马俑) stand *in front of* Emperor Qin Shihuang's tomb."

- outside of (a town / city)
  "Huaqing Pool is just *outside of* Xi'an city."
  "There's a fascinating market *outside of* Urumqi city centre."

- near (to)
  "...Xishuangbanna, which is very *near to* Laos..."
  "...New York City is *near* the sea..."

- far from
  "...it would be *far from* the city centre..."
  "Lhasa is extremely *far from* Shandong Province."

Exercise 22.2: Multiple Choice

Choose the appropriate prepositions of location from the choices below to complete the sentences.

1. My gym is located ____________ my office. When I work, I can see all the people exercising and weight lifting; it makes me feel really guilty if I haven't gone for a while.
   A. outside of　　B. opposite　　C. near

2. The Yangtze River is ____________ northern and southern China.
   A. between B. next to C. in
3. The Great Wall is ____________ where most Chinese people live, so many don't have the chance to visit this fantastic historic site.
   A. outside of B. far from C. beside
4. Many different bands and musicians have played ____________ that concert hall.
   A. of B. on C. at
5. The Bell Tower in Datong is in an awkward position to visit because it's right ____________ a busy road junction.
   A. next to B. on C. opposite
6. I like to go to Double Happy Shopping Centre because it's ____________ my school; I can go shopping there on my way home from class.
   A. on B. between C. near
7. The most amazing house I've ever seen was ____________ a forest; it was made of wood and was built high in the trees.
   A. in B. on C. at
8. The tomb of Liu Bei is a famous tourist site just ____________ Chengdu city centre.
   A. between B. in front of C. outside of
9. I would love to own a small house ____________ the coast so I could fall asleep to the sound of the sea.
   A. in B. at C. on

THE FORMULA 高分公式

For STAGE 2 of a place monologue, you must:
Say what it looks like.

Language Steps

1. Use expressions of size and shape accurately. ("Red Square is a *vast open space* in Moscow..." / "Fogong temple is a *giant, tall, wooden* pagoda.")
2. Use expressions of character and appearance correctly. ("St. Paul's Cathedral in London is a great example of *Gothic* architecture." / "East Oriental Plaza is an *enormous shiny* shopping mall.")
3. Use linking phrases correctly. ("*In addition to* having hosted the Olympic swimming contests, the Water Cube is *also* a fascinating piece of architecture.")

NATIVE SPEAKER WORDS 英语母语词汇

让我们来学习一些英语母语词汇，这些词汇对于回答该类型的问题非常有用，并且能够帮助你理解下面的答案范例。

Native Speaker Word	Part of Speech	Definition	Example Sentence
open area 露天场地		a space that is not enclosed	I'm claustrophobic, which means that I'm scared of small spaces. I always have to be in large rooms or preferably open areas like fields and parks.
represent 代表	verb	to be an example of something, to demonstrate what something is like	The Bird's Nest Stadium represents the way China is changing and becoming more international.
architecture 建筑	noun	the style and / or appearance of a building	I'm not that keen on modern architecture; I think the Bird's Nest and the new CCTV building in Beijing are really ugly.
stage 舞台	noun	a raised platform where actors or musicians perform	I'm singing with a band this weekend and I'm so excited – I can't wait to get on stage!
dingy 昏暗的	adjective	dark, probably dirty (to describe buildings and rooms)	I found the Lu Xun Museum fascinating, although it was a bit hard to see all of the exhibits because the building is so dingy.
permanent / permanently 永久的 / 永久地	adjective / adverb	lasting forever, or for a very long time	People should undertake the development of cities much more cautiously – any old buildings that are destroyed cannot be rebuilt; such changes are permanent.
en suite（浴室和卧室成套的）	adjective	an en suite bathroom is joined onto a bedroom	One sign of an expensive hotel is when the rooms all have en suite bathrooms.
varnished 涂漆的，上漆的	adjective	describing wood that has been painted with a special liquid to protect it and make it shiny	Although varnished furniture is safe to use and more convenient because your furniture doesn't get dirty, I still don't think it looks as nice as simple, natural wood.
airy 通风的	adjective	describing a room with lots of light and space	Studies have shown that employees work better in airy offices with lots of natural light rather than small, dark places.

MODEL ANSWERS 答案范例

阅读雅思考生Sophia，Mike和Jean的参考答案。

Sophia ...For me, the Summer Palace is a beautiful, open area which represents the best of Chinese culture and history. Most of the Summer Palace is actually Kunming Lake, a large open area of water. The lake is surrounded by a large number of hills on which are various examples of traditional Chinese architecture...

Mike ...I would like to talk about a bar called D22...It's really a small place, although it's quite long when you get inside. The bar runs along one side, and at the end of the bar is the stage, where the bands play. To be honest, D22 is not an attractive place: not only does it always seem dark and dingy – no matter how many lights are on – but there is also a permanent smell of cigarette smoke in the air...

Jean ...The flat would be on a high floor – perhaps the top floor – of a brand-new high-rise apartment block with the most modern architectural style. The apartment would have at least two huge bedrooms, one lounge, a massive kitchen and one or two bathrooms – it'd be great if one of the bathrooms was en suite! The style would be modern, with varnished wooden floorboards, leather sofas and colourful rugs on the floor. The flat would be very airy and light, with lots of windows that have great views over the surrounding streets and buildings...

LANGUAGE STEP 1 Expressions of Size and Shape
高分语言点 1 形状和大小的表达方法

让我们来看一下雅思考生Sophia，Mike和Jean是如何描述形状和大小的。

Sophia ...Most of the Summer Palace is actually Kunming Lake, a *large* open area of water. The lake is surrounded by a *large* number of hills on which are various examples of traditional Chinese architecture...

Mike ...I would like to talk about a bar called D22...It's really a *small* place, although it's *quite long* when you get inside...

Jean ...The apartment would have at least two *huge* bedrooms, one lounge, a *massive* kitchen and one or two bathrooms – it'd be great if one of the bathrooms was en suite!...

To describe the place of your monologue well, you should say something about its size.

Have a look at the following really useful size and shape words:

Big	Small	Width	Height	Length
huge / large	little	narrow	towering	long

续表

Big	Small	Width	Height	Length
massive	tiny	wide	high	short
vast	minute	broad	tall	winding
enormous	minuscule	thin	short	endless
gigantic	cramped	thick	low	far-reaching
immense	squat		squat	

However, you should be a little careful about how native speakers use these words to describe different things. It's important to remember these adjective + noun collocations:

- a *vast* mountain range / landscape / lake / desert
- a *massive* / *gigantic* / *huge* / *enormous* / *immense* building / house / shopping complex / room
- a *cramped* room / house / dormitory
- a *broad* avenue / street
- a *squat* house / building
- a *tall* / *high* building / mountain
- a *winding* path / country road / mountain pass
- a *tiny* / *miniscule* / *incredibly small* object / doorway / window

You can also use the following phrases to talk about the dimensions of the place:

- (number) metres / kilometres by (number) metres / kilometres
  "Tian'anmen Square is *880 metres by 500 metres*."
- (number) metres / kilometres squared
  "The size of West Lake at Hangzhou is *5.6 kilometres squared*."

Exercise 22.3: Matching

Match the pictures with the adjectives that describe them best.

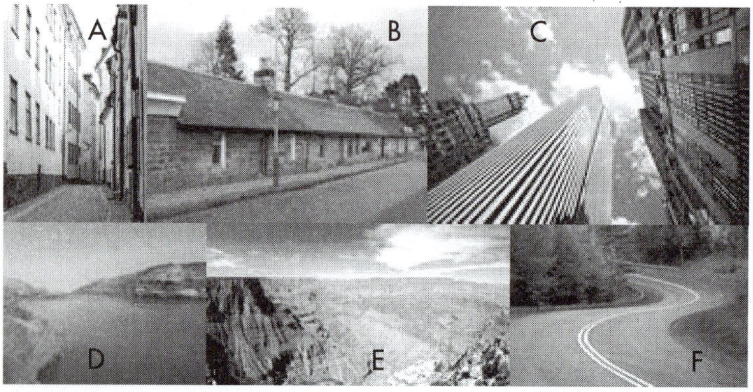

1. vast
2. towering
3. narrow
4. squat
5. broad
6. winding

LANGUAGE STEP 2 Expressions of Character and Appearance
高分语言点 2 特征和外观的表达方法

让我们来看一下雅思考生Sophia，Mike和Jean是如何描述建筑物的特征和外观的。

Sophia ...For me, the Summer Palace is a *beautiful, open area* which represents the best of Chinese culture and history. Most of the Summer Palace is actually Kunming Lake, a large *open area of water*. The lake is surrounded by a large number of hills on which are various examples of *traditional Chinese architecture*...

Mike ...To be honest, D22 is not an attractive place: not only does it always seem *dark* and *dingy* – no matter how many lights are on – but there is also a permanent smell of cigarette smoke in the air...

Jean ...The flat would be on a high floor – perhaps the top floor – of a brand-new high-rise apartment block with the *most modern architectural style*...The style would be *modern*, with varnished *wooden* floorboards, *leather* sofas and *colourful* rugs on the floor. The flat would be very *airy* and *light*, with lots of windows...

As you can see, all of these model answers include words and expressions to accurately describe the appearance and character of a place. You should use such expressions in your monologue to sound much more like a native.

Here are some more great native speaker words:

Light	Dark	Ugly	Beautiful	Impressive
airy	dingy	horrible	appealing	awe-inspiring
bright	gloomy	disgusting	attractive	majestic
well-lit	dim	awful	sovely	thrilling
clear	murky	unappealing	comfortable	significant

Here are a few common adjective + noun collocations:

- an *airy* / *well-lit* / *light* / *dingy* / *horrible* room / house / flat / dormitory
- a *dark* / *gloomy* / *dank* cave / woodland
- a *murky* river / lake / pool / stream
- an *awe-inspiring* work of art / scene / panorama / building
- a *majestic* building / statue
- a *thrilling* scene
- a *significant* area of town / spot / historical site / symbol of our city

Untidy	Age	Luxury
crumbling	old	expensive
tatty	ancient	upmarket
run-down	new	posh
dusty	modern	luxurious
shabby	shining	sumptuous
messy	antiquated	opulent

Here are a few common adjective + noun collocations:

- a *crumbling* old building / wall
- a *tatty* curtain / clothes / fabric / wooden structure
- a *run down* / *shabby* old building
- a *dusty* room / building / yard
- a *luxurious* / *opulent* / *sumptuous* / *up market* palace / mansion / five-star hotel / expensive restaurant

If the place you are giving a monologue about is a building, you can also describe its appearance by saying what materials the building is made of.

- be made of + material
  "The Great Wall *is made of thousands and thousands of bricks*."
  "The 'Gherkin' building in London *is made completely of glass*."

- material + building
  "The Great Wall is an enormous *brick wall*..."
  "The Pantheon in Rome *is* actually a *concrete temple*..."

- be covered in / with + objects / designs
  "A city in southern China *is* completely *covered in graffiti*..."
  "The roofs of the Forbidden City *are covered with yellow tiles*."

- be decorated with + objects / designs
  "The mosque in Xi'an *is decorated with dragons and flowers*."
  "Lots of ancient tombs in Egypt *are decorated with paintings* of ancient Egyptian life."

- be painted + colour
  "...my dream house would *be painted pink*..."
  "...the building *is painted white*, just like the White House in Washington."

Exercise 22.4: Multiple Choice

Choose the appropriate words from the choices below to complete the sentences.

1. At night, lots of people like to go to the Huangpu River in Shanghai to see all the boats that are ____________ in bright lights.
   A. decorated　　B. covered　　C. made of
2. The new CCTV building in Beijing has become a tourist site because of its ____________ architecture.
   A. ancient　　B. modern　　C. sumptuous
3. One place where lots of people go to listen to music is the World of Suzie Wong's in Beijing. It's an extremely ____________ nightclub; all the furniture and decorations are of the highest quality.
   A. lovely　　B. thrilling　　C. sophisticated
4. The Cairo Museum, despite having some of the most important historical artefacts in the world, is an extremely ____________ place. It looks like no one has ever cleaned it. Then again, that actually helps make the museum more ____________ because you can easily imagine the European explorers of the 18th century discovering and researching the objects there.
   A. dirty, significant　　B. dusty, atmospheric　　C. dark, majestic
5. My friend's house is so warm and welcoming because it ____________ bright colours like orange and yellow in every room. It also helps that the house has really big windows so it's extremely ____________ – not ____________ at all!
   A. is painted, well-lit, gloomy　　B. was painted, bright, dark　　C. painted, airy, dingy
6. The gym I usually go to in my hometown is really quite ____________. The showers are dirty, the toilets are awfully filthy and the exercise machines always have lots of sweat all over them.
   A. ugly　　B. messy　　C. disgusting
7. Suzhou is a really an ____________ place; it has tons of history, beautiful gardens and romantic rivers. The gardens are especially famous, and thousands of tourists admire them every year. They are ____________ rock pools, pavilions and carefully planted flowers.
   A. appealing, decorated with　　B. attractive, covered with　　C. awe-inspiring, covered in

LANGUAGE STEP 3 Linking Phrases 高分语言点 3 连接词

让我们来看一下雅思考生Mike是如何使用连接词的。

Mike …To be honest, D22 is not an attractive place: *not only* does it always seem dark and dingy – no matter how many lights are on – *but* there is *also* a permanent smell of cigarette smoke in the air…

When talking about a place, you should say what things can be found there, or talk about the qualities the place has. To do this you should use linking phrases such as the following:

- as well as…also… / as well as verb-ing…also…
  "*As well as* being a place of great natural beauty, it is *also* a place of great historical significance."
- besides…also… / besides + verb-ing…also…
  "*Besides being* one of the most popular music venues in the city, the bar *also* has great food."
- in addition to…(also)… / in addition to verb-ing…(also)…
  "*In addition to having* hosted the Olympic swimming contests, the Water Cube is *also* a fascinating piece of architecture."
- along with…also…
  "*Along with* great shops and designer outlets, Dong Fang Shopping Mall *also* has a number of handy restaurants."
- not only…but also…
  "Tianchi Lake in Xinjiang is *not only* beautiful and tranquil *but* it's *also* a great place to do activities such as fishing and hiking."
- both…and…
  "This gym is *both* conveniently located *and* reasonably priced."

Exercise 22.5: Gap Fill

Write the words below in the correct spaces.

besides	and	in addition to	both
as well as	not only	but also	along with

1. TLA, my secondary school, has a large sports centre that the local community can use ____________ holding evening classes for adults.
2. The kind of flat I dream of owning in the future is one which is ____________ modern ____________ comfortable.
3. ____________ being one of the longest rivers in China, the Yellow River is also a major source of electricity for the country.
4. ____________ being a religious building, the Potala Palace in Lhasa is now also a major tourist site.
5. ____________ having many theatrical performances, Shanghai Grand Theatre also puts on many musical productions, both of which are extremely popular.
6. The British Museum is truly superb; ____________ does it have one of the biggest collections of artefacts in the world, ____________ it's free!

THE FORMULA 高分公式

For STAGE 3 of a place monologue, you must:
Say what its purpose is.

Language Steps

1. Use the passive voice to express purpose / significance of a place accurately. ("Wu Tai Shan *was revered by* the ancestors as a sacred mountain.")
2. Use expressions to talk about past habits correctly. ("I *used to spend* many hours painting by the river." / "*If* I *felt tired* I *would* go to the bar to relax.")
3. Use popularity and fame expressions to say why a place is popular or famous. ("My town *is famous for* the peony flowers that bloom in spring.")

NATIVE SPEAKER WORDS 英语母语词汇

让我们来学习一些英语母语词汇，这些词汇对于回答该类型的问题非常有用，并且能够帮助你理解下面的答案范例。

Native Speaker Word	Part of Speech	Definition	Example Sentence
the public 老百姓，公众		all ordinary people, as individuals – not the government or companies and other organisations	When completed, the museum will be open to the public next year.
take something in 映入眼帘		to enjoy something by watching, to absorb the image you see, suggesting that you want to remember the sight afterwards	After I spent a lot of money travelling to Sichuan and two days climbing Emei Mountain, of course I wanted to sit down and spend some time taking in the surrounding landscape.
hire 出租	verb	to rent, to pay to use something for a relatively short period	Houhai Lake in Beijing has lots of peddle boats which the public can hire for a few hours.
mess around / about 胡闹，瞎混		to act in a carefree, maybe stupid way	Nowadays the shopping mall near my house has arranged people to stop children messing around there – not like when I was a child, when we would always play lots of games there.
pretty 十分，相当	adverb	quite, very	The bands that play at Jiang Jin Jiu Bar in the centre of town are pretty good, but I don't think they'll ever become famous.
used to 过去常常		to say that actions were regularly done in the past or that something was different in the past	I used to go to the MICA Gym to play sports every week, but then they raised their prices and it was too expensive to go.

续表

Native Speaker Word	Part of Speech	Definition	Example Sentence
hang out (with) 与……出去玩		to spend time with somebody or in a certain place	On weekends I generally hang out at the shopping mall with my friends.
bring up 抚养，培养		to raise a child, care for a child from childhood to adulthood	My friend Rachel's house would be a great place to bring up children; there's lots of space, good-sized bedrooms and it's near a good school.

MODEL ANSWERS 答案范例

阅读雅思考生Sophia，Mike和Jean的参考答案。

Sophia …Originally, the Palace was built by the emperor as his private palace and used to be closed to the public. However, now it is open for everybody to enjoy and serves as both a park and a tourist site. I visited the historic halls and grounds of the palace when I was young, but now when I go I like to just walk around the lake and take in the views. Sometimes my friends and I will hire a boat and mess around on the water, which is always great fun!...

Mike …Despite D22 being a bar, it's more of a music venue than a place to go for a drink. In fact, it's pretty famous in Beijing because so many bands play there every week, and on Friday and Saturday nights the atmosphere is fantastic! When I was a student at Qinghua University I would go there all the time and hang out with my friends – it was great!...

Jean …A flat like this would be perfect for my husband and I to live in and then bring up our child. A new, gleaming kitchen would be great for preparing delicious dishes for our friends when they come to dinner and the guests could be entertained in the comfortable and relaxing sitting room...

LANGUAGE STEP 1 The Passive Voice to Express Purpose / Significance of a Place 高分语言点 1 用被动语态描述某地的用途及其重要性

让我们来看一下雅思考生Sophia和Jean是如何描述某个地方的用途及其重要性的。

Sophia …Originally, the Palace *was built by* the emperor as his private palace and used to be closed to the public…

Jean ...A flat like this would be perfect for my husband and I to live in and then bring up our child. A new, gleaming kitchen would be great for preparing delicious dishes for our friends when they come to dinner and the guests could *be entertained* in the comfortable and relaxing sitting room…

Notice that both Sophia and Jean use the passive to talk about the purpose or significance of the place they are describing.

This is a very useful and native speaker way to talk about a place, so let's remind ourselves of the passive structure:

- be + past participle (+ by agent)
  "The Pyramids of Egypt *were constructed* by unpaid workers."
  "Classical music *is performed* there every week."
  "This famous site *is respected and admired* by locals and tourists alike."

Exercise 22.6: Multiple Choice

Choose the appropriate words from the choices below to complete the sentences.

1. Thousands and thousands of fascinating historical relics ___________ in the National Museum.
   A. is kept B. are kept C. are keep
2. The Great Wall ___________ by Chinese emperors to protect the empire.
   A. was build B. was builded C. was built
3. The house I would really love to own ___________ during the reign of Queen Elizabeth – about 400 years ago!
   A. was constructed B. was be constructed C. was be built
4. Unfortunately, Dianchi Lake near my hometown ___________ for many years by the local people so now it's dangerous to swim in the water.
   A. is polluted B. was polluted C. has being polluted
5. The house I lived in as a child ___________ a few years ago, which obviously made me feel very sad.
   A. has been demolished B. is demolished C. was demolished

LANGUAGE STEP 2 Expressions of Talking About Past Habits
高分语言点 2 描述过去的习惯

让我们来看一下雅思考生Sophia和Mike是如何描述过去的习惯的。

Sophia ...Originally, the Palace was built by the emperor as his private palace and *used to* be closed to the public. However, now it is open for everybody to enjoy and serves as both a park and a tourist site. I *visited* the historic halls and grounds of the palace when I *was* young, but now when I go I like to just walk around the lake and take in the views...

Mike ...When I *was* a student at Qinghua University I *would go* there (D22 club) all the time and hang out with my friends – it was great!...

The place that you give a monologue about will often be somewhere you have a personal history with, or somewhere you have been many times. To describe this, the following past simple, "used to" and other habit phrases are extremely useful:

- the past simple

  "I *visited* the river at weekends and *went* swimming."

  "My girlfriend and I *exercised* at Bannatyne's Fitness Gym."

  Note: You can use adverbs of frequency with the past simple.

  "I *always visited* the river at weekends and *went* swimming."

  "My girlfriend and I *regularly exercised* at Bannatyne's Fitness Gym."

- used to

  "I *used to* spend many hours painting by the river."

  "My family *used to* spend every summer camping near Hua Mountain."

- habit phrases

  "If I *felt stressed* I *would go to* the bar to relax."

  "When I *needed* some more designer clothes, my mother *would go to* Jin Hua Shopping Mall."

Exercise 22.7: Gap Fill

Write the words below in the correct spaces.

sometimes	went	had	whenever
took	would	often	always
was	lived	used to	

1. I really don't like the Cutty Sark Museum in London; I've been there too many times. Every year at secondary school we ____________ ____________ go there.
2. My friend's house was beautiful. It was by the seaside, was absolutely enormous and ____________ loads of musical instruments. ____________ I could, I ____________ go and stay there with my friend.
3. A few years ago I played in band. We ____________ ____________ to various bars and clubs around the city. But my favourite bar was The Playhouse because it ____________ so large and lively.
4. When I ____________ in Kent I ____________ went to Lakeside Shopping Centre, but it ____________ quite a while to get there and I found shopping pretty boring to be honest.

LANGUAGE STEP 3 Popularity and Fame Expressions
高分语言点 3 知名度和名气的表达方法

让我们来看一下雅思考生Mike和Jean是如何描述一个地方久负盛名、备受欢迎的。

Mike ...Despite D22 being a bar, it's more of a music venue than a place to go for a drink. In fact, *it's pretty famous in Beijing because* so many bands play there every week, and on Friday and Saturday nights the atmosphere is fantastic!...

Jean ...A new, gleaming kitchen would *be great for* preparing delicious dishes for our friends when they come to dinner and the guests could be entertained in the comfortable and relaxing sitting room...

When giving your monologue, popularity and fame expressions will help you explain why the place you are describing is famous or popular. Let's look at some more great ways of saying this:

- *be famous for* / *be famous for* + noun / verb-ing
- *be famous because* + verb
- *be renowned for* / *be renowned for* + noun / verb-ing
- *be noted for* + noun / verb-ing
- *be popular with* + types of people
- *be great for* / *excellent for* / *particular good for* + noun / verb-ing

Examples:

"Sichuan Province *is famous for* the local cuisine."

"Tiger Leaping Gorge *is famous because* it is so beautiful."

"The Victory Hotel *is renowned for* the live music it has on the weekend."

"The Great Wall *is noted for* its size and historical importance."

"The new shopping mall *is* only really *popular with* wealthy people because the prices are so high."

"The news sports centre *is great for* meeting like-minded sports enthusiasts."

Exercise 22.8: Multiple Choice

Choose the appropriate words from the choices below to complete the sentences.

1. Muslim Street in Xi'an ____________ the delicious snacks that you can buy there.
   A. is famous because　　B. is renowned for　　C. is popular
2. Jiuzhaigou ____________ its beautiful, clear blue water.
   A. is famous because　　B. is famous for having　　C. is noted for
3. The Terracotta Warriors are ____________ people who don't live in Xi'an; most locals have never been there.
   A. popular with　　B. renowned for　　C. noted for being

4. Yan'an is ____________ it was the Communist Party base during the war.
   A. famous for   B. famous because   C. renowned for being
5. Longjing ____________ producing tea which is drunk all over China.
   A. is famous because   B. is noted because   C. is famous for

THE FORMULA 高分公式

For STAGE 4 of a place monologue, you must:
Say why it is special and how you feel about it.

Language Steps

1. Use the zero and first conditional to talk about habits and preferences accurately. ("*If* I *want* to have a good time I just *need* to go to D22 on the weekend." / "I've never been there myself but *if* I *have* the chance I *will* certainly *take* a trip to Malaysia.")
2. Use expressions for how you feel correctly. ("It's important to me because…" / "I always like(d) to…there.")
3. Use adjectives to describe the qualities of a place accurately. ("The waterfall is a *relaxing* yet *energising* place of natural beauty.")

NATIVE SPEAKER WORDS 英语母语词汇

让我们来学习一些英语母语词汇，这些词汇对于回答该类型的问题非常有用，并且能够帮助你理解下面的答案范例。

Native Speaker Word	Part of Speech	Definition	Example Sentence
tranquil 宁静的，安静的	adjective	describing a place that is peaceful and quiet, with nothing to worry about or to disturb you	I get really stressed working in a big city, always rushing around getting stuck in traffic – I'd love to move to a small village where it's really tranquil.
unwind 放松	verb	to relax after doing an activity that has made you tense or worried	After work I like to go to the gym and have a great workout followed by a long, hot shower – it really helps me unwind.
all to myself / yourself / herself etc 我 / 你 / 她专用		for my / your / her etc use only	I especially love my flat when my parents have gone on a trip – that way I get to have the apartment all to myself.
stressful 有压力的	adjective	having a lot of stress, causing a lot of worry and anxiety	Visiting the Taj Mahal in India was incredibly stressful for me – there were so many tourists and people trying to sell me things, it was really hot and I was very tired.

续表

Native Speaker Word	Part of Speech	Definition	Example Sentence
haven 避风港，避难所	noun	a safe and peaceful place, often used to talk about a place where one can escape the noise and stress of one's ordinary environment	I love my house because it's the only place where I can relax and get away from the noise and stress of the city – it's definitely a haven for me.
bring back memories 回忆起		to think of something that happened before because of something that happens now	Every time I see my teddy bear it brings back lots of memories of when I was a child.
nostalgic 感伤的，怀旧的	adjective	to feel happy – or maybe slightly sad – when thinking of things that happened in the past	I met my friends from university last week and had dinner with them. It was great talking about old times and the funny things that happened; I felt nostalgic about my university life the rest of the day.
mosh 狂舞	verb	to dance in a very energetic and possibly violent way (in a mosh pit)	Some people think it's cool to mosh, but I just can't be bothered – I don't understand why people think it's so much fun.
loads 许多，好多	noun	lots, a lot, very many (informal)	I hate going shopping at Wangfujing on a Saturday – there're always loads of people and it feels so cramped.

MODEL ANSWERS 答案范例

阅读雅思考生Sophia，Mike和Jean的参考答案。

Sophia ...The Summer Palace is really important to me because it is so tranquil. If I need a place to relax and unwind, I immediately think of the Summer Palace. Although there are usually lots of tourists walking around, it's still quite easy to find a quiet place all to myself. My work is quite stressful and so it's good to escape the city for a while – the Summer Palace is my haven!

Mike ...I really value D22 because whenever I go there it brings back loads of memories from when I was at university, having fun with my friends. It makes me feel really nostalgic! Besides, D22 is still a cool place to go – if I want to have a good time, I just need to go to D22, drink some beer and get ready to mosh!

Jean ...I know that this kind of flat will be difficult to buy, especially as my family is not very rich. However, if I am very successful in my career and make loads of money one day, this is the kind of flat I'll buy. I think almost everybody would be happy to live in a flat like this – I just hope that one day I can!

LANGUAGE STEP 1 Zero & First Conditional to Talk About Habits & Preferences
高分语言点 1 用真实条件句和第一条件句描述习惯性行为和偏好

让我们来看一下雅思考生Sophia，Mike和Jean是如何描述习惯性行为和偏好的。

Sophia …The Summer Palace is really important to me because it is so tranquil. *If I need a place to relax and unwind, I immediately think of the Summer Palace*...

Mike …Besides, D22 is still a cool place to go – *if I want to have a good time, I just need to go to D22, drink some beer and get ready to mosh*!

Jean …I know that this kind of flat will be difficult to buy, especially as my family is not very rich. However, *if I am very successful in my career and make loads of money one day, this is the kind of flat I'll buy*...

Notice that all of the above model answer extracts use zero and first conditionals to talk about what they like to do at the places they are talking about. You will sound more like a native speaker if you can use these to talk about your habits and preferences.

Zero conditional

This is used to talk about things that are always true.

- if / when + present verb, present verb
  "*If* I *am* hungry, I *go* to a restaurant." / "*When* I *am* hungry I *go* to a restaurant."
- present verb + if / when + present verb
  "I *go* to a restaurant *if* I *am* hungry." / "I *go* to a restaurant *when* I *am* hungry."

First conditional

This is used to talk about things that might happen in the future, if something else happens.

- if + present verb, will + verb
  "*If* I *have* enough time, I *will go* shopping."
- will + verb + if + present verb
  "I *will go* shopping *if* I *have* enough time."

Exercise 22.9: Matching

Match the sentence halves on the left with those on the right.

1. I'll definitely go to England to see Stonehenge...
2. When I go home to Urumqi, ...
3. If I eat too much during my holiday,...
4. I will let my parents live with me...
5. If I go to the Huangpu River,...
6. When I want to see Western operas or classical music,...

A. ...I'll go to the gym and exercise thoroughly.
B. ...if I get the chance – it seems so fascinating!
C. ...I will look at all the ships on the water and think about how fast Shanghai is changing.
D. ...I go to the National Centre for the Performing Arts in Beijing; it never disappoints!
E. ...I always go to the market there because it's so lively.
F. ...if I can afford to buy a house large enough for the whole family.

LANGUAGE STEP 2 Expressions for How You Feel
高分语言点 2 感觉的表达方法

让我们来看一下雅思考生Sophia和Mike是如何描述自己的感觉的。

Sophia ...The Summer Palace *is really important to me* because it is so tranquil...

Mike ...I *really value* D22 because whenever I go there it brings back loads of memories from when I was at university, having fun with my friends. It makes me feel really nostalgic!...

Usually the place you decide to talk about will be one that is special to you. So you should use some expressions to explain how you feel about the place and why it is special to you. Look at the following useful expressions:

- I like / love (the place) because...
- I value (the place) because...
- (The place) is important to me because...
- (The place) makes me feel...
- (The place) reminds me of...
- (The place) provides me with...
- (The place) gives me...
- (The place) lets me...

Examples:

"*I love the Greasy Spoon café* near my house *because* the food is so great and such good value!"

"*The British Museum* always *makes me feel* inspired to learn more about other countries and cultures."

"*The Legion Field provides me* and my friends *with* a pleasant, green space in which to play sports or just hang around."

Exercise 22.10: Gap Fill

Write the words below in the correct spaces.

because	gives me	important to me	I value	lets me
love	makes me feel	provided me with	reminds me	

1. My old family home always ____________ safe and secure; it's a place where I never need to worry about anything.
2. Owning a new, clean, and modern apartment in the future is ____________ because I want to bring up children in a safe and healthy living environment.
3. I really enjoyed going to the Lei Feng Museum in Liaoning Province because it ____________ loads of information about Lei Feng – his life, his achievements and why he is so famous in China.
4. I ____________ going to Far Eastern Shopping Mall ____________ every time I go I always bump into my fellow students and find excellent bargains.
5. ____________ Lush Bar because it has "open mic night" on Sundays when anyone can come and play music. This ____________ a chance to practise my guitar skills and gain confidence playing in front of other people.
6. Shan Hai Guan is special to me because it ____________ that China has a unique and ancient culture that is known and respected all over the world.
7. Going to the People's Park ____________ escape city life for a while – I can get some fresh air, enjoy looking at flowers and trees and, if I want to, get some exercise.

LANGUAGE STEP 3 Adjectives to Describe the Qualities of a Place
高分语言点 3 描述一个地方的特点的形容词

让我们来看一下雅思考生Sophia和Mike用了哪些形容词描述一个地方的特点。

Sophia …The Summer Palace is really important to me because it is so *tranquil*...

Mike …Besides, D22 is still a *cool* place to go – if I want to have a good time, I just need to go to D22, drink some beer and get ready to mosh!

You should try to use a varied range of adjectives to help you describe the place in your monologue; this will make the monologue much more interesting and make you sound more like a native speaker.

Look at the following really useful adjectives to describe a place:

Relaxing	Interesting	Exciting	Beautiful	Busy
cosy	enchanting	exciting	delightful	hectic
comfortable	educational	energising	charming	stressful
quiet	inspiring	breathtaking	magnificent	chaotic
peaceful	fascinating	exhilarating	pretty	bustling
tranquil	engrossing	thrilling	attractive	frantic

Examples:

"I usually love the *bustling* atmosphere of the market, though sometimes I can be a bit too *hectic*."

"Friday Woods is an *enchanting* little forest where you can get a taste of nature."

"I love Helen's Coffee Shop because it provides me with a *cosy* and *comfortable* place to study or relax."

Exercise 22.11: Matching

Match the words on the left with the definitions on the right.

1. enchanting
2. stimulating
3. cosy
4. exhilarating
5. charming
6. hectic

A. very busy and fast, somewhere with lots of activity

B. encourages new thoughts and ideas, makes you feel interested and excited

C. makes you feel very happy and excited

D. extremely pleasant, attractive and enjoyable

E. very comfortable and pleasing, often a place that is small and warm

F. attractive, often a place with a special character

EXTRA LANGUAGE POINT Avoid Saying "China has a long history!"
补充语言点 避免说"China has a long history!"

When taking the IELTS oral test, many students say the following type of sentence:

"China has a very long history…"

"Beijing is a city with a long history…"

While factually and grammatically correct, you need to remember that IELTS examiners become very bored with almost every candidate saying "China has a long history". Also, if you say this kind of thing in an exam it can sound a bit arrogant, because countries like Iran and India also have incredibly long histories of many thousands of years.

It will certainly make you sound more intelligent and original if you do not talk about the long history of China and its cities – try to think of other things that are interesting about your country that will inspire the examiner! Surely there are many more unique things that make your country special.

ANSWER ORDER 答题思路

Remind yourself of the answer order you should use when giving a monologue about a place.

- Stage 1: Say what it is and where it is.

- Stage 2: Say what it looks like.
- Stage 3: Say what its purpose is.
- Stage 4: Say why it is special and how you feel about it.

Exercise 22.12: Ordering

Using the answer order above, put the following extracts from a model answer into the correct order.

A. The Glebe is not an attractive place...

B. Though I am a bit older now, and don't really play sports there anymore, the Glebe is still special to me...

C. I want to talk about "the Glebe", a large public open space in my village.

D. The Glebe is a very useful place for the community because not only does it have tennis and basketball courts but also football and cricket pitches...

E. Interviewer: Tell me about a place where people can do sports.

F. The Glebe is located...

For more practice, please go to: www.EQEnglish.com

Formula 23: Object Monologue

AIMS 学习目标

In this lesson you'll master the Formula for giving a monologue about an object. Typical IELTS part two questions about an object are:

- Talk about something you'd like to buy.
- Talk about something you made yourself.
- Talk about an invention you know and like.
- Talk about a form of transport you use.
- Talk about something you enjoyed wearing.
- Talk about a piece of furniture in your house.
- Talk about a statue or work of art that you've seen.
- Talk about a photograph you have or have seen.
- Talk about a gift you were given.

ANSWER ORDER 答题思路

To give a good monologue about an object, you should use the following native speaker answer order.

- Stage 1: Say what it is and why you have it.
- Stage 2: Say what its purpose is.
- Stage 3: Evaluate it.
- Stage 4: Say why it is important and how you feel about it.

MODEL ANSWER 答案范例

阅读雅思考生Sophia的参考答案。

Interviewer Talk about an invention you know and like.

Stage 1 Say what it is and why you have it.

Sophia I'd like to talk about mobile phones. As you know, mobile phones nowadays are very light, compact and sleek telephones made of plastic which can be carried everywhere very conveniently. My parents bought me my first mobile phone one Spring Festival when I was a teenager and I've had one ever since.

Stage 2 Say what its purpose is.

Sophia I think mobile phones are an extremely practical piece of equipment to have. Not only are mobile phones used for talking to people and sending text messages but also for surfing the Web, keeping a diary and even as an alarm clock! Some of the most expensive mobile phones are bought by people who want to show off and display their wealth – they're often a status symbol.

Stage 3 Evaluate it.

Sophia Today, a mobile phone is an essential piece of technology for everyone, which is used everyday. I last used my mobile phone just before this speaking test – my mum sent me a message to wish me luck!

Stage 4 Say why it is important and how you feel about it.

Sophia Despite being slightly more expensive than a landline, mobile phones are so useful and convenient that many people simply couldn't do without one. If I had to organise trips out with my friends a few days in advance or contact friends who live far way by letter, life just wouldn't be as much fun. I think that everyone has got used to simply picking up their mobile phone and communicating immediately. As for me, I couldn't bear to part with my mobile phone – it gives me so much independence and freedom, and the games are great too!

THE FORMULA 高分公式

For STAGE 1 of an object monologue, you must:
Say what it is and why you have it.

Language Steps

1. Use adjectives of appearance correctly. ("An ipod is a *square*, *compact*, *electronic* device." / "It was a *large*, *colourful*, *light triangular* kite!")
2. Use indirect object to explain possession accurately. ("My parents *bought me* a bike." / "I *made her* a paper airplane.")
3. Use the past simple and past continuous to say how you know the object correctly. ("I *saw one* in a museum *when* I *was* a child.")

NATIVE SPEAKER WORDS 英语母语词汇

让我们来学习一些英语母语词汇，这些词汇对于回答该类型的问题非常有用，并且能够帮助你理解下面的答案范例。

Native Speaker Word	Part of Speech	Definition	Example Sentence
mobile phone 手机		(UK English) a small telephone that can be taken anywhere (American English: cell phone)	I don't even have a phone in my house because using my mobile phone is so convenient and cheap.

续表

Native Speaker Word	Part of Speech	Definition	Example Sentence
compact 紧密的，紧凑的	adjective	describing things that are very close together so that they use very little space	My mother said my new apartment is very small, but I prefer to say it's compact – it's got everything I need, but it doesn't take up much room.
sleek 光滑的，时髦的	adjective	smooth, shiny and (usually) a little sexy	If I win the lottery I'll buy one of those sleek red sports cars.
all by oneself 单独，独自		alone, without anybody else's help	Can you come to my house tomorrow a few hours before the party and help me with the cooking and cleaning? I'll never be able to get everything ready all by myself.
life-size 与实物大小一样的	adjective	a work of art or representation of something that is the same size as what it represents	At Madame Tussauds Museum in London, you can find hundreds of life-size models of famous people made from wax.
statue 雕像，塑像	noun	an object that represents a person or animal, usually made of stone or metal	You must have done something truly special for a city to erect a statue of you in a public place.
depict 刻画，描写	verb	to represent or show something in a story, picture, work of art	Lots of people are concerned about modern movies and television shows because so many of them frequently depict drugs, alcohol and violence.
scene (戏剧的) 一场，(电影、电视的) 一个镜头，(小说的) 一节	noun	a part of a story, play or movie, usually referring to a certain place or a certain situation in which a certain action happens	I love that scene in the movie *Dumb and Dumber* when they go to the evening party wearing stupid suits and fighting.
the real thing 上等货，地道货，原装货		the original, the best	In the theme park "Window of the World" in Shenzhen, there are lots of models of famous buildings such as the Eiffel Tower, the Pyramids and the Tower of London. Although they're not life-size, they're amazing because they look just like the real thing.
figure 画像，肖像	noun	a drawing, painting or model of a person	*The Last Supper* by Leonardo da Vinci has 13 figures in it: Jesus and his 12 followers.

MODEL ANSWERS 答案范例

阅读雅思考生Sophia， Mike和Jean的参考答案。

Interviewer Talk about an invention you know and like.

Sophia I'd like to talk about mobile phones. As you know, mobile phones nowadays are very light, compact and sleek telephones made of plastic which can be carried everywhere very conveniently. My parents bought me my first mobile phone one Spring Festival when I was a teenager and I've had one ever since...

Interviewer Talk about a gift you were given.

Mike I would like to talk about a kite I was given. My father gave me it for my nineth birthday. It was a fairly simple kite: about a metre long, diamond-shaped and it had four colours – red, blue, yellow and orange I think. It was made of plastic and light wood, so it was very light – I remember I was able to carry it to the park all by myself...

Interviewer Talk about a work of art you have seen.

Jean The work of art that I'd like to talk about is *The Laocoon Group*. It is a beautiful, almost life-size marble statue that depicts a scene from the Trojan Wars. The statue includes three figures that are being attacked by snakes. I saw this statue many times in books when I was at school, as my major was art history, but I finally got to see the real thing when I went to Italy for my job about a year ago...

LANGUAGE STEP 1 Adjectives of Appearance
高分语言点1 描述外观的形容词

让我们来看一下雅思考生Sophia，Mike和Jean用了哪些形容词描述物品的外观。

Sophia ...As you know, mobile phones nowadays are *very light*, *compact* and *sleek* telephones *made of plastic* which can be carried everywhere very conveniently...

Mike ...It was a fairly simple kite: *about a metre long, diamond shaped* and it *had four colours* – red, blue, yellow and orange I think. It was *made of plastic and light wood*, so it was *very light*...

Jean ...It is *a beautiful*, *almost life-size marble statue* that depicts a scene from the Trojan Wars...

When giving a monologue about an object, as soon as you have said what the object is you should then describe its appearance.

To describe an object well, it's important that you use the correct adjectival order, as below. (Generally, we don't use more than three adjectives together at the same time.)

Adjective Order:	opinion	size	age	shape	colour	origin	material

Opinion	Size	Age	Shape	Colour	Origin	Material
beautiful	almost life-size					marble
	about a metre long		diamond-shaped			
		old	round	green		
lovely				red	Chinese	

Examples:

"...a *beautiful, almost life-sized marble* statue."

"...the kite was *about a metre long, diamond-shaped*..."

"...an *old round green* ball."

"...a *lovely red Chinese* lantern."

Now look at the following useful native speaker adjectives of appearance:

Opinion	Size	Age	Shape	Colour	Origin	Material
handy	compact	ancient	round	blue	Chinese	cardboard
useful	life-size	old-fashioned	square	multi-coloured	American	cotton
useless	tiny	antique	rectangular	rainbow-coloured	Western	golden
silly	little	worn	diamond-shaped	black and white	European	leather
cute	miniature	aged	oval	grey	African	plastic
terrible	enormous	brand-new	spherical	silver	mass-produced	silk
attractive	huge	modern	curved	gold	factory-produced	stone
ugly	gigantic	state-of-the-art	triangular	white with blue-striped	home-made	wooden
elegant	average-sized	new	cylindrical	black with grey dots	hand-made	woollen

Exercise 23.1: Word Order

Rewrite the words below in the correct order.

1.	statue	golden	life-size	a	
2.	lighter	a	silver	antique	handy
3.	dress	silk	black	an	elegant
4.	a	dictionary	mass-produced	boring	grey
5.	sculpture	spherical	modern	a	glass

EXTRA LANGUAGE POINT "Made of" Expressions
补充语言点 Made of的表达方法

让我们来看一下雅思考生Sophia和Mike是如何使用made of这个短语的。

Sophia ...As you know, mobile phones nowadays are very light, compact and sleek telephones *made of plastic* which can be carried everywhere very conveniently...

Mike ...It was a fairly simple kite: about a metre long, diamond-shaped and it had four colours – red, blue, yellow and orange I think. It was *made of plastic and light wood*, so it was very light – I remember I was able to carry it to the park all by myself...

When talking about an object and its appearance, you might want to talk about what the object is made of. Look at the following expressions:

- made of

  Use "made of" when you can still recognise the material / things used to make the object.

  "The dress *is made of* silk."

  "A light bulb *is made of* glass and metal."

- made from

  Use "made from" when you cannot recognise the material / things used to make the object.

  "My model airplane *was made from* paper and glue."

  "The sculpture *is made from* old tin cans and bicycle parts."

LANGUAGE STEP 2 Indirect Object to Explain Possession
高分语言点 2 使用间接宾语描述物品的所有权

让我们来看一下雅思考生Sophia和Mike是如何使用间接宾语的。

Sophia ...My parents *bought me my first mobile phone* one Spring Festival when I was a teenager and I've had one ever since...

Mike I would like to talk about a kite I was given. My father *gave me it* for my nineth birthday...

If you are talking about an object that you have or had before, you should tell the examiner how you came to possess the object. Using the indirect object sentence structure is a very useful way to do this.

There are two indirect object sentence structures:

- subject + verb + indirect object + direct object
  "She gave me a letter."
  "I bought her a car."
- subject + verb + direct object + to / for + indirect object
  "She gave a letter to me."
  "I bought a car for her."

The indirect object is the receiver of the direct object (e.g. *I* am the receiver of the letter. *She* is the receiver of the car.).

There are quite a few verbs that can be used in these types of sentence, including:

ask	bring	build	buy	get	give
lend	make	offer	paint	read	sell
send	show	take	teach	tell	write

Exercise 23.2: Error Correction

Identify the mistakes in the following sentences.

1. I made he a toy car.
2. I bought a painting to my mother.
3. My friend wrote to I a story.
4. My father bought I a book.
5. It I gave to a classmate.
6. Them I asked to buy for me it.

LANGUAGE STEP 3 Past Simple and Past Continuous to Say How You Know the Object
高分语言点 3 用一般过去时和过去进行时描述你是怎么知道某个物品的

让我们来看一下雅思考生Sophia和Jean是如何描述他们得知某个物品的。

Sophia ...My parents bought me my first mobile phone one Spring Festival *when I was a teenager* and I've had one ever since...

Jean ...I *saw* this statue many times in books *when I was at school*, as my major was art history, but I finally *got to see the real thing when I went to* Italy for my job about a year ago...

When you are giving a monologue about an object you should use the past simple or the past simple with the past continuous to explain why you have the object or how you know about the object.

Look at the following native speaker examples:

Past simple

"I bought myself a laptop many years ago."
"My parents took the photograph when I was very young."
"I saw the work of art when my family went to the art gallery."

Past continuous and past simple

As you may remember, the past continuous is used to talk about "longer" actions that were happening when a past simple "shorter" action happened. So, in the sentence "I was washing the dishes when I broke a plate.", the breaking of the plate was a short action that happened during the longer action of washing the dishes.

The structure is as follows:

- past simple + when / while + to be + verb-ing
  "I *saw* the *Statue of Liberty* *when* I *was studying* in America."
  "My parents *bought* the furniture *while* they *were living* in Shandong."
- when / while + to be + verb-ing + past simple
  "While I *was visiting* my uncle for Christmas, I *got* a great toy."
  "When my sister *was travelling* in Europe, she *took* a fantastic photograph."

Exercise 23.3: Sentence Completion

Complete the sentences below by writing the correct forms of the words in brackets.

1. I ____________ (buy) my first mobile phone when I ____________ (study) at university.
2. I ____________ (see) the painting in an art gallery when I ____________ (to be) a child.
3. My friend ____________ (tell) me about it after he came back from abroad.
4. My grandfather ____________ (make) the desk for me when I ____________ (to be) at high school.
5. Thomas Edison ____________ (invent) the first usable lightbulb in 1879.
6. When I ____________ (date) my ex-boyfriend I enjoyed wearing a baseball cap because he ____________ (buy) it for me.
7. Auntie ____________ (give) me the necklace when I ____________ (stay) at her house for the winter.
8. While I ____________ (work) part time at college, I ____________ (to be able) to save up enough money to buy myself a present.

THE FORMULA 高分公式

For STAGE 2 of an object monologue, you must:
Say what its purpose is.

Language Steps

1. Use the passive voice for application and creation correctly. ("The plane *was invented by* the Wright brothers and it *is used by* people to...")
2. Use expressions of use accurately. ("Radio *provides millions of people with* information, entertainment and advice.")
3. Use phrases for the first / last time correctly. ("*The last time* I *used* my computer *was* yesterday.")

NATIVE SPEAKER WORDS 英语母语词汇

让我们来学习一些英语母语词汇，这些词汇对于回答该类型的问题非常有用，并且能够帮助你理解下面的答案范例。

Native Speaker Word	Part of Speech	Definition	Example Sentence
practical 实用的	adjective	suitable for use in every day life	The clothes models wear in fashion shows may look beautiful, but they're not very practical – they'd be ruined very quickly if you wore them in real life.

续表

Native Speaker Word	Part of Speech	Definition	Example Sentence
text (message) 短信	noun	a message written and sent using a mobile phone (Short message is incorrect.)	Please let me know as soon as you finish this report – but don't phone me as I will be in a meeting; just send me a text.
surf the Internet / Net / Web 上网		to use a computer to visit many Internet sites	When I get home after work I like to surf the Web to find out what's happened in the world.
show off 炫耀，卖弄		to intentionally behave in a way to attract other people's attention	It's embarrassing when Ben drives that really expensive car with such loud music and the roof down; it's so obvious he's trying to show off.
status symbol 地位的象征		something that people want to buy because it shows that they are rich, well educated etc, and others will admire them	The main reason for buying a Ferrari sports car is because it's a status symbol – you have to be incredibly rich to afford one.
essential 必要的，重要的	adjective	necessary, needed, required	To study abroad, a good level of spoken English is essential.
mind 介意，在乎	verb	to care about, be annoyed or worried by something	Do you mind if I open the window? / My manager is really kind; she doesn't mind if I take three weeks' holiday all at the same time.
thrilling 令人兴奋的	adjective	very exciting	I'm currently reading a book by Michael Crichton – it's so thrilling because the story is full of surprises and you never know what's going to happen next!
sculpt 雕刻，造型	verb	(usually by an artist) to create an object out of stone, wood, clay etc	My grandfather was very talented with his hands; once he sculpted a beautifully detailed rose out of a piece of wood he found in the forest.
appreciate 欣赏，重视	verb	to recognise or understand that something is important or valuable	My last girlfriend broke up with me because she said I didn't appreciate her. I guess I should have paid her more attention, said more nice things and sometimes bought things for her.

MODEL ANSWERS 答案范例

在完成下面的练习之前，阅读雅思考生Sophia，Mike和Jean的参考答案。

Sophia …I think mobile phones are an extremely practical piece of equipment to have. Not only are mobile phones used for talking to people and sending text messages but also for surfing the Web, keeping a diary and even as an alarm clock! Some of the most expensive mobile phones are bought by people who want to show off and display their wealth – they're often a status symbol. Today, a mobile phone is an essential piece of technology for everyone, which is used everyday. I last used my mobile phone just before this speaking test – my mum sent me a message to wish me luck!...

Mike ...The kite was made by my father, probably because he couldn't afford to buy one from a shop. Although it wasn't such a valuable gift, I didn't mind because I was just pleased to receive such a cool present! I remember feeling really excited when my father gave me the present and we went to the park to try flying it. It seemed so thrilling to have a brand-new kite to fly, and my dad to help me fly it. That first day we flew the kite for hours and hours, my dad showing me how to get the kite into the air, then how to fly it...

Jean ...Nobody really knows who *The Laocoon Group* was sculpted by, but it was probably made in the first century B.C. As a work of art, it is obviously appreciated for its beauty – despite the unpleasant nature of the subject – and many tourists see it every day when they visit the Vatican in Rome...

LANGUAGE STEP 1 Passive Voice for Creation & Application
高分语言点 1 用被动语态描述物品的制造及功能

让我们来看一下雅思考生Sophia，Mike和Jean是如何描述物品的制造及功能的。

Sophia ...Not only *are* mobile phones *used for* talking to people and sending text messages but also for surfing the Web, keeping a diary and even as an alarm clock! Some of the most expensive mobile phones *are bought* by people who want to show off and display their wealth – they're often a status symbol. Today, a mobile phone is an essential piece of technology for everyone, which *is used* everyday...

Mike ...The kite *was made* by my father, probably because he couldn't afford to buy one from a shop. Although it wasn't such a valuable gift, I didn't mind because I was just pleased to receive such a cool present!...

Jean ...Nobody really knows who *The Laocoon Group* *was sculpted* by, but it *was probably made* in the first century B.C. As a work of art, it *is obviously appreciated* for its beauty...

Notice that all of the above model answers use the passive voice to explain who the objects were made by and what they are made or used for.

You probably remember the structure of the passive voice from previous lessons, but here's a quick reminder:

- to be + past participle (+by + agent)

"The plane *was invented by* the Wright brothers."

"The wheel is an invention that *has been used* for hundreds of years in millions of different tools and machines all over the world."

"The photograph *was taken* before I was born."

Exercise 23.4: Multiple Choice

Choose the appropriate forms of the passive from the choices below to complete the sentences.

1. *The Mona Lisa* ____________ by Leonardo da Vinci.
   A. is painted　　B. was painted　　C. has been painted
2. Online language lessons ____________ more and more frequently in the future.
   A. are going to be used　　B. is going to be use　　C. are going to use
3. Apparently email ____________ first ____________ by the army for military purposes.
   A. was, invent　　B. had been, invented　　C. was, developed
4. That gold ring ____________ by my great-grandmother all her life, so it's very important to my family.
   A. were weared　　B. was weared　　C. was worn
5. My first radio-controlled car ____________ for me by my parents one Christmas.
   A. was bought　　B. was brought　　C. is brought
6. An electric blender can ____________ to make soups, drinks, milkshakes and sauces.
   A. is used　　B. be used　　C. to be used

LANGUAGE STEP 2 Expressions for Uses
高分语言点 2 用途的表达方法

让我们来看一下雅思考生Sophia和Jean是如何描述物品的用途的。

Sophia ...Not only are mobile phones *used for talking to people and sending text messages but also for surfing the Web, keeping a diary and even as an alarm clock*!...

Jean ...As a work of art, *it is obviously appreciated for its beauty* – despite the unpleasant nature of the subject...

As in the above model answers, you should use expressions for uses in your monologue to explain how your object is used and / or why it is useful.

Look at the following useful expressions:

- can help (people) to + verb
  "The Internet *can help people to communicate* across the world cheaply and quickly."
- (it) is used to do / for verb-ing...
  "Microwave ovens *are used for cooking, heating and defrosting* food and drinks."

- (it) is useful for verb-ing...
  "The Internet blog I write *is useful for developing* my research and writing skills."

- (it) is great for verb-ing...
  A pocket digital camera *is great for taking* quick photos while on holiday."

- (it) provides...
  "Online English classes *provide* an environment for students to speak to real, live native English speakers."

- (it) provides (people) with...
  "Cars *provide ordinary people with* the freedom to travel independently anywhere, at any time."

- (it) is valued for...
  "Egyptian mummies *are valued for* their historical significance."

- (it) is appreciated because / for...
  "The movie *Lilies of the Field* *is appreciated because* one of the actors, Sidney Poitier, was the first black actor to win an Oscar."

- (it) is important for...
  "When I become a father, I want to buy a baby carry bag as *it's important for* carrying the baby around outside safely."

Exercise 23.5: Gap Fill

Write the words below in the correct spaces.

provides people with	are great for	can help	is important for
are used for	useful for	are valued for	
it's appreciated because	provide		

1. My favourite pair of shoes is my Reebok running shoes; they ____________ running, exercising or just as causal shoes when I'm relaxing.
2. Internet chat rooms ____________ discussing all kinds of things, ranging from personal matters, hobbies and interests, relationship problems and even politics.
3. The electric light bulb ____________ safe, reliable and cheap lighting.
4. Mobile phones ____________ a way for people to communicate and stay in touch with business partners, family and friends wherever they are.
5. The Internet has become such a part of everyday life that now it ____________ every company to be on the Internet and to have email access.
6. There is an old, yellowing photograph that hangs on the wall in my house. Though it's really old, in my family ____________ it's the only photo we have of our great-grandfather.
7. A cheongsam ____________ quite ordinary looking women look more sexy and elegant.

8. My watch has so many functions – it's amazing. Not only is it ____________ telling the time and date, but it can also tell me where I am in the world, how deep under water I am and even surf the Internet.
9. Solar panels ____________ their potential to help save the environment and reverse global warming.

LANGUAGE STEP 3 Phrases for the First / Last Time
高分语言点 3 关于第一次和最后一次的短语

让我们来看一下雅思考生Sophia和 Mike是如何描述自己第一次或者最后一次做某事的。

Sophia ...*I last used my mobile phone just before this speaking test* – my mum sent me a message to wish me luck!...

Mike ...I remember feeling really excited when my father *gave* me the present and we *went* to the park to try flying it. It *seemed* so thrilling to have a brand-new kite to fly, and my dad to help me fly it. That first day we *flew* the kite for hours and hours, my dad *showing* me how to get the kite into the air, then how to fly it...

If you are talking about an object that you used or still use, you should talk about the first or last time that you used it, just like Sophia and Mike do in their model answers.

To do this, you can use phrases for the first / last time:

Phrases for the first / last time

- the first / last time + past verb + was + time period (ago)
  "*The first time* I *used* a computer *was* about *10 years ago*."
  "*The last time* I *saw* the painting *was* in *1997*."

- I + first / last + past verb + time period (ago)
  "*I first used* a computer about *10 years ago*."
  "*I last saw* the painting in *1997*."

Of course, you can also use some of the grammar that you studied in the last lesson – the past simple or the past simple with past continuous.

Past simple and past continuous

- past simple
  "My aunt *gave me* the karaoke machine for my birthday and we all – my family and I – immediately *started* singing and dancing."
  "My elder sister *took* me to the cinema and we *watched* the movie together."

- past simple with past continuous
  "I *saw* the pyramids of Egypt for the first time when I *was travelling* in the Middle East."

Exercise 23.6: Word Order

Rewrite the words below in the correct order.

1. ago years two watch the wore last I

____

2. took time the The was in I 1989 first subway

____

3. The yesterday the watched time last I was film

____

4. very first long a I dictionary time used a ago

____

5. painting looked month at I the was last The time last

____

6. I 2003 a cell bought in first phone

____

THE FORMULA 高分公式

For STAGE 3 of an object monologue, you must:
Evaluate it.

Language Steps

1. Use adjectives for evaluation correctly. ("Electronic dictionaries are so *convenient* because they are *compact*, *cheap* and highly *practical*.")
2. Use linking phrases for uses and evaluation accurately. ("*Although* Van Gogh's painting *Sunflowers* is much more famous, I *still* prefer *Crows over Cornfields* because…")
3. Use comparatives and comparative structures accurately. ("…a cell phone is certainly *much more convenient than* a conventional phone…")

NATIVE SPEAKER WORDS 英语母语词汇

让我们来学习一些英语母语词汇，这些词汇对于回答该类型的问题非常有用，并且能够帮助你理解下面的答案范例。

Native Speaker Word	Part of Speech	Definition	Example Sentence
slightly 轻微地	adverb	a little, a very small amount	You would never know my sister is pregnant; apart from being slightly bigger than before, she looks exactly the same.

续表

Native Speaker Word	Part of Speech	Definition	Example Sentence
landline 座机，固定电话	noun	the traditional kind of telephone that is fixed and not mobile	Sorry. I can't hear you on my cell phone, can you phone my landline instead?
do without 没有……也行		to manage without something, often in the negative "can't do without"	If you want to start your own company, you must remember that successful businesses can't do without good staff, a strong market and a great location.
cool 极好的，绝妙的	adjective	good, fashionable or attractive	For some reason, lots of people think that Hip Hop singers who sing about having lots of girlfriends, money and guns are cool – I don't. I think they're stupid.
portray 描绘，描述	verb	to represent or describe something / somebody in a film, play, or piece of art etc	The movie *Titanic* portrays how the ship sank and how all the passengers reacted.
vivid 生动的，栩栩如生的	adjective	describing descriptions, pictures etc that make it very easy to clearly and in detail imagine what happened	Although Van Gogh's painting *Wheatfield with Crows* is not exactly "realistic", it is very vivid – you can imagine being in the field yourself, feeling the wind blow and hearing the birds crowing.
sympathise (with) 同情	verb	to understand and care about someone else's problems	Though I can sympathise with Clare and the way she feels after breaking up with Richard, there's nothing we can do about it because Richard loves someone else.
suffering 痛苦，苦难	noun	physical or mental pain and difficulty, or an experience of this	Whenever you watch news on TV and see people all over the earth dying, starving and fighting, you're reminded how much suffering there is in the world.

MODEL ANSWERS 答案范例

阅读雅思考生Sophia，Mike和Jean的参考答案。

Sophia ...I think mobile phones are an extremely practical piece of equipment to have. Not only are mobile phones used for talking to people and sending text messages but also for surfing the Web, keeping a diary and even as an alarm clock!...Today, a mobile phone is an essential piece of technology for everyone, which is used everyday...Despite being slightly more expensive than a landline, mobile phones are so useful and convenient that many people simply couldn't do without one...

Mike ...Although it wasn't such a valuable gift, I didn't mind because I was just pleased to receive such a cool present!...

Jean ...I think the statue is such a fantastic work of art because although it portrays men suffering, it's a wonderfully vivid sculpture. Whenever I see it, I immediately sympathise with the pain and suffering of the figures whilst at the same time I can appreciate the extremely high quality of the work...

LANGUAGE STEP 1 Adjectives for Evaluation
高分语言点 1 评价某物的形容词

让我们来看一下雅思考生Sophia，Mike和Jean是如何评价某物的。

Sophia ...I think mobile phones are an *extremely practical* piece of equipment to have...Today, a mobile phone is an *essential* piece of technology for everyone, which is used everyday...Despite being *slightly more expensive* than a landline, mobile phones are *so useful and convenient* that many people simply couldn't do without one...

Mike ...Although it wasn't *such a valuable* gift, I didn't mind because I was just pleased to receive *such a cool* present!...

Jean ...I think the statue is *such a fantastic* work of art because although it portrays men suffering, it's a *wonderfully vivid* sculpture. Whenever I see it, I immediately sympathise with the pain and suffering of the figures whilst at the same time I can appreciate the *extremely high quality* of the work...

Notice that Sophia, Mike and Jean all use adjectives for evaluation in their monologues to describe the object in more detail. This makes the monologue more interesting, more accurate and more like a native speaker's.

Let's look at some more really useful adjectives for evaluation:

Age	Appearance	Value	Quality
state-of-the-art	vivid	over-priced	high quality
innovative	striking	expensive	reliable
fashionable	colourful	costly	well made
advanced	eye-catching	dear	dependable
brand-new	attractive	reasonable	poorly made
cutting-edge	lifelike	good value for money	unreliable
modern	realistic	economical	low quality
outdated	charming	reasonably-priced	poor quality

续表

Age	Appearance	Value	Quality
old-fashioned	ugly	low-cost	
dated	unattractive	cheap	
unfashionable	unappealing	a waste of money	
antique	unrealistic		

Use	Importance	Size / Weight	Fun	Speed
practical	essential	compact	enjoyable	sluggish
convenient	vital	bulky	fantastic	slow
useful	indispensable	heavy	beneficial	fast
useless	crucial	light	delightful	speedy
impractical	needless	thick	pleasant	quick
informative	dispensable	thin		
enlightening	superfluous	soft		
educative	unnecessary	hard		
helpful				

Examples:

"My laptop is quite old now, so although it seemed an absolutely *cutting-edge* piece of technology when I bought it, it's now relatively *sluggish* compared to other computers now."

"My mother's necklace is an *antique*, *high quality* and *charming* which is an item of jewelry."

"Despite being extremely *costly*, aeroplanes provide passengers with a *convenient*, *safe* and *economical* way to travel."

Exercise 23.7: Matching

Match the adjectives for evaluation on the left with their synonyms / meanings on the right.

1. outdated
2. economical
3. unreliable
4. state-of-the-art / innovative / cutting-edge
5. vital / indispensable
6. striking
7. reasonably priced
8. well made
9. practical
10. informative
11. superfluous
12. sluggish
13. dear

A. new; using new ideas and / or technology
B. old, old-fashioned
C. attractive, easily noticed
D. bad quality, easily breaks
E. good quality
F. cheap
G. good value
H. expensive
I. useful, helping solve problems
J. not needed, unnecessary
K. essential, extremely important
L. providing a lot of information
M. slow

LANGUAGE STEP 2 Linking Phrases for Uses & Evaluation
高分语言点 2 用连接词描述用途及评价

让我们来看一下雅思考生 Sophia，Mike 和 Jean 用了哪些连接词描述物品的用途及评价。

Sophia ...*Not only* are mobile phones used for talking to people and sending text messages *but also* for surfing the Web, keeping a diary and even as an alarm clock!...*Despite* being slightly more expensive than a landline, mobile phones are so useful and convenient that many people simply couldn't do without one…

Mike …*Although* it wasn't such a valuable gift, I didn't mind because I was just pleased to receive such a cool present!...

Jean ...I think the statue is such a fantastic work of art because *although* it portrays men suffering, it's a wonderfully vivid sculpture...

Notice that in the above model answers, the candidates use linking phrases to talk about the uses of an object or to evaluate an object. This is a very native speaker way to talk about an object. Look at the following linking phrases:

Linking phrases for uses

- in addition to…also…
  "*In addition to* being a worker's tool, a computer *also* provides people with the ability to communicate worldwide."

- besides…also…
  "The subway is a great means of transport because *besides* being more environmentally friendly, it *also* helps reduce traffic."
- as well as…also…
  "I really valued the scarf my mother knitted me because *as well as* keeping me warm, it *also* reminded me of her love for me."
- not only…but also…
  "The electronic dictionary I have *not only* has millions and millions of definitions, *but also* has recordings of native speakers saying the words."

Linking phrases for evaluation

- although…(still)…
  "*Although* Van Gogh's painting *Sunflowers* is much more famous, I still prefer *Crows over Cornfields* because…"
  "I prefer Van Gogh's *Crows over Cornfields* *although* *Sunflowers* is much more famous."
- despite…(still)…
  "*Despite* buses in Beijing always being crowded, they're *still* the cheapest and most convenient way to travel."
- even though…
  "*Even though* it has caused many problems, the invention of gunpowder is extremely important historically."
- apart from…
  "*Apart from* the very low battery power, my new mobile phone is excellent."

小贴士

in addition to, besides 和 as well as 这三个短语只能与动词的 -ing 形式连用。

与中文不同的是，在英语中 although 和 but 不能出现在同一个句子中。因此，"Although the phone is good, but it is too expensive." 这个句子是错误的。

Exercise 23.8: Multiple Choice

Choose the appropriate linking phrases to complete the sentences.

1. My family's photographs of me as a child are really embarrassing. ____________ do I have a weird hairstyle in many of them, ____________ I'm often naked!
   A. As well as, also B. Not only, but also C. Apart from, also

2. ____________ *Titanic* was a big movie in Hollywood, I thought it was pretty terrible.
   A. Despite　　B. Apart from　　C. Even though
3. I really think nuclear power plants are a bad invention – ____________ being extremely dangerous, they ____________ pollute the environment.
   A. besides, also　　B. despite, still　　C. although, still
4. ____________ the prints of *Marilyn Monroe* are some of the most famous pictures in the world, a lot of people don't know the artist who created them – Andy Warhol.
   A. Despite　　B. Apart from　　C. Although
5. ____________ a few small scratches and marks, our dining table still looks brand-new.
   A. In addition to　　B. Apart from　　C. Although
6. ____________ having lots of useful vocabulary and grammar, a good English textbook should also have interesting exercises and fun games.
   A. As well as　　B. Not only　　C. Even though
7. ____________ their high cost, the last pair of shoes I bought were not good quality; they broke within the first two months.
   A. Although　　B. Even though　　C. Despite
8. Netball is a fantastic sport. ____________ being a great way to exercise, it's ____________ a good way to learn how to be part of a team.
   A. Not only, also　　B. In addition to, also　　C. Despite, also

LANGUAGE STEP 3 Comparatives & Comparative Structures
高分语言点 3 比较级和比较结构

让我们来看一下雅思考生Sophia是如何使用比较级和比较结构的。

Sophia ...Despite being slightly *more expensive than* a landline, mobile phones are so useful and convenient that many people simply couldn't do without one...

When evaluating an object, you should use comparatives and comparative structures to compare the object to others.

Comparatives

As you may remember from previous lessons, when we want to make a comparative we add an "-er" or "-ier" to the end of the adjective, or we add "more" before the adjective.

- We add "-er" to adjectives that are one syllable long.
- With adjectives that finish in "-y" and are two or more syllables long, we add "-ier".
- We put the word "more" before adjectives that are two or more syllables long.

Look at the table to refresh your memory:

Short Adjectives		-y Adjectives		Long Adjectives	
cheap	cheaper	easy	easier	expensive	more expensive
large	larger	heavy	heavier	comfortable	more comfortable
fast	faster	pretty	prettier	fashionable	more fashionable
slow	slower	ugly	uglier	environmentally friendly	more environmentally friendly

小贴士

下列形容词的比较级形式是不规则的。

Adjective	Comparative
good	better
bad	worse
fun	more fun

Comparative structures

- X is COMPARATIVE than Y
  "Buses are slower than taxis."
- X is COMPARATIVE than + time in the past
  "Mobile phones are smaller and more advanced than 10 years ago."

小贴士

如果你想让上述句子的语气更强烈一点，你只需要在比较级前加 much 或 far 即可，比如：

"Buses are *much* slower than taxis."
"Buses are *far* slower than taxis."
"Mobile phones are *much* smaller and more advanced than 10 years ago."
"Mobile phones are *far* smaller and more advanced than 10 years ago."

- X + to be + as adjective as + Y
  "*Watching TV is as enjoyable as going to a party.*"
- X + to be + not as adjective as + Y
  "*My hometown's traffic is not as crowded as Beijing's.*"
- X + to be + not as adjective as + time in the past
  "*Movies are not as interesting to watch as they were when I was a child.*"

Exercise 23.9: Sentence Completion

Complete the sentences below by writing the correct comparative forms of the words in brackets.

1. The toy my father gave me was ____________ (important) to me than the other presents I received because he chose it himself.
2. Though Chinese goods are ____________ (not reliable) as Japanese goods, I think it's important for Chinese people to buy Chinese goods.
3. I like my old cell phone, although it's ____________ (not advanced) more modern phones.
4. I think Chinese art is much ____________ striking and innovative than 10 years ago.
5. Although Jackie Chan's movies are ____________ (not enlightening) many other movies, I think they are much more enjoyable.
6. Buying my own apartment one day is ____________ (equally important) to me ____________ having my own child.
7. For me, going to look at Turner's paintings is ____________ (pleasant) than spending time with family and friends.
8. My last coat was ____________ (warm) and ____________ (colourful) ____________ the one I wear now.

THE FORMULA 高分公式

For STAGE 4 of an object monologue, you must:
Say why it is important and how you feel about it.

Language Steps

1. Use words and phrases for attachment to objects accurately. ("The kite *makes me feel nostalgic about* the fun I had with grandpa.")
2. Use the second and third conditionals for expressing the importance of objects correctly. ("*If* I *didn't* have my laptop, I *wouldn't* be able to do all of my writing so easily.")
3. Use the present perfect for expressing the importance of objects accurately. ("Computers *have become* essential to every business everywhere in the world.")

NATIVE SPEAKER WORDS 英语母语词

让我们来学习一些英语母语词汇，这些词汇对于回答该类型的问题非常有用，并且能够帮助你理解下面的答案范例。

Native Speaker Word	Part of Speech	Definition	Example Sentence
trip 旅行，旅程	noun	a short journey, where you travel for a short time and then return (Note: avoid the common mistake "to trip" – you should say "to have / take a trip".)	When I was at school we had a trip to France for the day. But it wasn't that exciting because we spent much more time on the motorways and ferry travelling there than we did in France.
in advance 提前		before a certain time, before you do something else	On Friday nights you have to book in advance otherwise there's no way you can get a table – there's just too many people.
contact 联系	verb	to communicate with somebody using something, e.g. a phone, letter etc (Note: avoid the common mistake "to connect with somebody", "to contact with somebody".)	When I went to America to study, my parents got worried if I didn't contact them once a week to let them know how I was.
bear 忍受，承担	verb	to accept, endure or tolerate something unpleasant	David and I broke up because I found out he was seeing another girl when he was supposed to be my boyfriend. After I found out, I couldn't bear to see him anymore.
part with something 放弃，丢掉		to give something to somebody else or to lose something, especially when you don't want to	My mother still has all my old baby clothes because she says it will make her too upset to part with them.
breeze 微风	noun	a light and pleasant wind	I love walking in the park when the weather's sunny and there's a gentle breeze.
nostalgic 怀旧的	adjective	feeling pleasure and maybe slightly sad when thinking about something that happened in the past	I went back to my old kindergarten a few days ago. I felt so nostalgic looking at our old classrooms, thinking about all the fun we had together and wondering what has happened to all my classmates.
combination 混合物	noun	a mixture of two or more things	Though you might not expect it, the combination of orange and duck in one dish is really delicious.
inspire 鼓舞，激励	verb	to make somebody want to do something and believe that they can succeed at doing it	My school trip to France inspired me to start learning French.

MODEL ANSWERS 答案范例

阅读雅思考生Sophia，Mike和Jean的参考答案。

Sophia ...If I had to organise trips out with my friends a few days in advance or contact friends who live far way by letter, life just wouldn't be as much fun. I think that everyone has got used to simply picking up their mobile phone and communicating immediately. As for me, I couldn't bear to part with my mobile phone – it gives me so much independence and freedom, and the games are great too!

Mike ...After that birthday, I used to go to the park with my dad every chance I got – when there was even a gentle breeze I would start asking him to take me there. Some years later the kite got broken, I don't remember how. But I remember seeing the broken kite and feeling really upset, like I'd lost a part of my childhood. Now, whenever I see children flying kites at my local park, I always start feeling nostalgic, and think about when I was young.

Jean ...For me, the combination of making viewers feel emotions with excellent workmanship is sign of a truly great work of art. In fact, this statue has been famous throughout history and has inspired many other artists and their works of art.

LANGUAGE STEP 1 Words and Phrases for Attachment to Objects
高分语言点 1 描述对某物的喜爱

让我们来看一下雅思考生Sophia和 Mike是如何描述自己对某物的喜爱的。

Sophia ...As for me, *I couldn't bear to part with* my mobile phone – it gives me so much independence and freedom, and the games are great too!

Mike ...Some years later the kite got broken, I don't remember how. But *I remember seeing the broken kite and feeling* really upset, like I'd lost a part of my childhood. Now, *whenever I see children flying kites at my local park*, *I always start feeling nostalgic*, *and think about* when I was young.

Notice that both Sophia and Mike use the above phrases to indicate why the object they are describing is special or important to them. Let's look at some more useful words and phrases for attachment to objects:

Adjectives for how an object makes you feel

- nostalgic
- sentimental (about)
- homesick
- inspired
- intrigued
- fascinated

- enthusiastic (about)
- delighted
- thrilled
- exhilarated
- relieved
- relaxed

Phrases for how an object makes you feel

- (it) makes me feel…
- (it) makes me think of / about…
- Whenever I (do something) I feel…
- (it) reminds me of…
- I couldn't bear to part with…
- (it)'s important to me because…
- (it)'s indispensable to me because…

Look at the following examples of some of the above words and phrases for attachment to objects:

"My new mobile phone, with all its gadgets, *makes me feel delighted* that my life is getting better and better."

"My car *is important to me because* without it I wouldn't be able to do my job."

"I'm quite *sentimental* about my teddy bear because it *reminds me of* my happy childhood in England."

"*Whenever I read* a novel by Stephen King, *I feel enthusiastic* about writing something myself."

Exercise 23.10: Gap Fill

Write the words below in the correct spaces.

inspired   intrigued by   nostalgic   relaxed   sentimental   thrilled

1. I like to sit in front of my TV and watch my favourite programmes while eating my dinner or drinking tea; it makes me ____________.
2. I'm quite ____________ about my father's bike, which is why I've kept for so many years even though it's really old and actually not very nice to ride.
3. I am ____________ Cai Guoqiang's works of art using stuffed wolves. Although they are a bit strange, and I'm not sure if I understand them, these sculptures make me think about many different things when I look at them.
4. Going home makes me feel ____________ because I always think of all the things that my brother and I did together when we were growing up.
5. They say Christmas is all about giving, not receiving, and I couldn't agree more. When I

gave my daughter a doll last Christmas it was great to see how ____________ she was to have her own little "person" to play with.

6. After I watched the movie *Schindler's List* I was ____________ to try and make the world a better place.

LANGUAGE STEP 2 The Second & Third Conditionals for Expressing the Importance of Objects
高分语言点 2 用第二条件句和第三条件句描述物品的重要性

让我们来看一下雅思考生Sophia是如何描述物品的重要性的。

Sophia *...If I had to organise trips out with my friends a few days in advance or contact friends who live far way by letter, life just wouldn't be as much fun.*

Notice that Sophia uses the second conditional to emphasise the importance of the object she is describing.

Second conditional

The structure of the second conditional is as follows:

- If + past verb, would(n't) + verb

  "*If* I *didn't have* my laptop, I *wouldn't be able to study* English online."

  "*If* my parents *had* a dishwasher, we *wouldn't need* to spend so much time washing up."

  "*If* I *won* the lottery, I *would buy* an enormous truck."

- would(n't) + verb + if + past verb

  "I *wouldn't be able to study* English online *if* I *didn't have* my laptop."

  "My family *wouldn't need* to spend so much time washing up if my parents *had* a dishwasher."

  "I *would buy* an enormous truck *if* I *won* the lottery."

As you can see from these examples, the second conditional is used to talk about present or future situations that are very unlikely or impossible to happen. So, you can use the second conditional to talk about what your life would be like if you had or didn't have the object you are talking about.

> 小贴士
>
> 当第二条件句中的谓语动词是 be 动词的时候，根据正式的文体规则，我们需要将 be 动词改成 were。比如，"If I *were* richer, I would buy a boat." 然而，在口语中，大多数英语母语者同时使用 was 和 were。

Third conditional

You can also use the third conditional to explain why a certain object is important. Let's look at how the third conditional is constructed:

- If + had(n't) + past participle, would(n't) have + past participle
  "*If* computers *hadn't been invented*, the world economy *wouldn't have developed* so quickly in the last 30 years."
  "*If* I *had seen* the movie on my own, I *would've been* really *scared*."
- would(n't) have + past participle + if + had(n't) + past participle
  "The world economy *wouldn't have developed* so quickly in the last 30 years *if* computers *hadn't been invented*."
  "I *would've been* really *scared if* I *had seen* the movie on my own."

Notice from the above examples that the third conditional is used to talk about:

1. Things that did not happen in the past
2. Things that might not have happened – this explains why they happened

Notice also in the examples that to make Type 2 sentences (about situations that did not happen in the past), you must have "not" (or a negative) in both halves (clauses) of the third conditional.

Exercise 23.11: Sentence Completion

Second conditional

Complete the sentences below by writing the correct second conditional forms of the words in brackets.

1. If the movie *Dirty Harry* ____________ (make) now, it ____________ (not be) as good as the original with Clint Eastwood.
2. I ____________ (play) basketball every single day of the week if I ____________ (have) enough time.
3. I ____________ (to be) extremely upset if all my old family photographs ____________ (to be lost).

Third conditional

Complete the sentences below by writing the correct third conditional forms of the words in brackets.

4. If my parents ____________ (not buy) me that penknife for Christmas, I ____________ (to be) really disappointed.
5. Damien Hurst ____________ (not become) a famous artist if he ____________ (not make) a controversial work of art using a dead cow.
6. If the Harry Potter movies ____________ (to be made) using American actors, they ____________ (not to be) so enjoyable to watch.

LANGUAGE STEP 3 The Present Perfect for Expressing the Importance of Objects 高分语言点 3 用现在完成时描述物品的重要性

让我们来看一下雅思考生Sophia和Jean是如何使用现在完成时描述物品的重要性的。

Sophia ...I think that everyone *has got used to* simply picking up their mobile phone and communicating immediately...

Jean ...In fact, this statue *has been* famous throughout history and *has inspired* many other artists and their works of art.

As you can see from the above extracts, Sophia and Jean use the present perfect to explain why their objects are important or special.

As you will probably remember from previous lessons, the present perfect is constructed like this:

- have / has + past participle

  We use the present perfect to talk about recent changes ("Computers *have become* essential to business..."), for things that happened in the past that are connected with the present ("The government *has greatly developed* the subway system...") or for experiences ("I *have watched* every movie by Zhang Yimou...").

> 小贴士
>
> 现在完成时不可以与 finished-time words 连用，比如 yesterday, last week, two years ago, in 2008 等等。它只能和 unfinished-time words 连用，比如 today, this week, this year, recently 等等。

Exercise 23.12: Multiple Choice

Choose the appropriate forms of the present perfect from the choices below to complete the sentences.

1. My cell phone is such good quality that I ____________ the same phone for about 10 years now.
   A. have have　　B. have had　　C. had had
2. The old vase my family has had for years ____________ quite valuable – though we wouldn't want to sell it.
   A. has become　　B. has became　　C. has becomed
3. Nuclear power ____________ make the environment much cleaner.
   A. have helped　　B. had helped　　C. has helped
4. I ____________ the first suit I bought for many years and it still looks brand-new!
   A. have weared　　B. have wore　　C. have worn

5. I ____________ many times by people for the wooden truck I made when I was a teenager.

   A. have been complimented B. have be complimented C. have be compliment

6. I ____________ thousands of words using a computer that would have taken me much longer if I had had to write them by hand.

   A. have write B. have written C. have wrote

ANSWER ORDER 答题思路

Remind yourself of the answer order you should use when giving a monologue about an object.

- Stage 1: Say what it is and why you have it.
- Stage 2: Say what its purpose is.
- Stage 3: Evaluate it.
- Stage 4: Say why it is important and how you feel about it.

Exercise 23.13: Ordering

Using the answer order above, put the following extracts from a model answer into the correct order.

A. Cable cars are used very rarely in cities, but…
B. I think it'd be great if every city had cable cars, just like Chongqing.
C. Not only are cable cars environmentally friendly, but they are extremely cheap…
D. Interviewer: Talk about a form of transport you use.
E. When I was living in Chongqing, I used a cable car every day…
F. If Chongqing didn't have cable cars…
G. I'm going to talk about cable cars…

For more practice, please go to: www.EQEnglish.com

Formula 24: Past Event Monologue

AIMS 学习目标

In this lesson you'll master the Formula for giving a monologue about a past event. Typical IELTS Part Two questions about a past event are:

- Talk about a party you attended.
- Talk about a stage in your life that you enjoyed most.
- Talk about a sports event you attended.
- Talk about a journey you have been on.
- Talk about a story you heard as a child.
- Talk about a time when you were late for something.
- Talk about something you did that helped you learn a language.

ANSWER ORDER 答题思路

To give a good monologue about a past event, you should use the following native speaker answer order.

- Stage 1: Say what it was and when it happened.
- Stage 2: Say why it happened, where it happened and who was there.
- Stage 3: Say what happened.
- Stage 4: Say why the event was special and how you feel / felt about it.

MODEL ANSWER 答案范例

阅读雅思考生Sophia的参考答案。

Interviewer Talk about a story you heard as a child.

Stage 1 Say what it was and when it happened.

Sophia I want to talk about a story called "The Boy Who Cried Wolf". When I was a child, my mother always used to read me bedtime stories to help me get to sleep. My mother would lie next to me on the bed and read a different story every night. When she was reading, I would often lay my head on her chest and listen to the voices she made for the different characters in the stories. The story I remember best is "The Boy Who Cried Wolf".

Stage 2 Say why it happened, where it happened and who was there.

Sophia In the story there was a boy who was a shepherd. His job was to look after his father's sheep in the fields outside his village, but he found it very boring to be by himself all day.

Stage 3 Say what happened.

Sophia Once, he decided to play a trick on his fellow villagers. He ran into the village shouting "Wolf! Wolf! There's a wolf killing my sheep!" Immediately, all the villagers stopped working and ran to the field to help protect the sheep. When they found there was no wolf, the boy laughed at them. Another day, the boy played the same trick on the villagers and again laughed at them when they came running into the field looking for a wolf. One day, a real wolf did get into his field and start attacking his sheep. Again, the boy ran into village shouting "Wolf! Wolf! There's a wolf killing my sheep!" But to his surprise nobody believed him and all his sheep got killed.

Stage 4 Say why the event was special and how you feel / felt about it.

Sophia The moral of this story is that you shouldn't lie otherwise people won't believe you – even when you are speaking the truth. I liked this story as a child and I think it has a good message. I will definitely read this story to my children in the future.

THE FORMULA 高分公式

For STAGE 1 of a past event monologue, you must:
Say what it was and when it happened.

Language Steps

1. Use words & phrases for events accurately. ("It was a great *family holiday* in the German countryside.")
2. Use prepositions of time and time phrases correctly. ("*In* 1989..." / "*Quite a while ago* I went to a great party...")
3. Use the past continuous & past simple and past perfect & past simple for setting the scene correctly. ("I *had been* at university for a couple of years, so I *decided* to have a huge party...")

NATIVE SPEAKER WORDS 英语母语词汇

让我们来学习一些英语母语词汇，这些词汇对于回答该类型的问题非常有用，并且能够帮助你理解下面的答案范例。

Native Speaker Word	Part of Speech	Definition	Example Sentence
used to 过去常常		to say that something always happened or was true in the past (especially if this is not true now)	I used to go running every few days to keep fit, but nowadays I hardly do anything; I'm getting fatter and fatter.
get to sleep 入睡		to fall asleep, to go to sleep (especially if it is a little difficult to fall asleep)	I couldn't get to sleep for a long time last night; I was too worried about today's exam.
bedtime 就寝时间，睡觉时间	noun	the time when you usually go to sleep (especially for children)	Now listen to your mother: bedtime was an hour ago and you've got school tomorrow. It's time to go to sleep.
character 人物，角色	noun	a person in a film, story or play	I'm bored of watching Ben Stiller films; he always plays the same type of character – a nice, ordinary guy who is really unlucky or who experiences strange things.
5-a-side 5人制的	adjective	to describe the size of a sports team, where usually the team has more members; also 7-a-side, 3-a-side etc	I'm really tired after playing 5-a-side football all day – you need so much energy to run all over the pitch for so long.
secondary school 中学	noun	UK: secondary school vs. US: high school, the type of school for students aged 11-16 or 11-18	Lots of people love their time at secondary school. God knows why; I hated every minute of it and couldn't wait to go to university.
affect 影响	verb	to influence, alter, change	Lucy hasn't been doing very well at university since she broke up with her boyfriend. It's really affected her grades.

MODEL ANSWERS 答案范例

阅读雅思考生Sophia，Mike和Jean的参考答案。

Interviewer Talk about a story you heard as a child.

Sophia I want to talk about a story called "The Boy Who Cried Wolf". When I was a child, my mother always used to read me bedtime stories to help me get to sleep. My mother would lie next to me on the bed and read a different story every night. When she was reading, I would often lay my head on her chest and listen to the voices she made for the different characters in the stories.

The story I remember best is "The Boy Who Cried Wolf"...

Interviewer Talk about a sports event you attended.

Mike I'd like to tell you about a football competition I participated in. It was a 5-a-side football competition held when I was working for my last company, about four years ago...

Interviewer Talk about a time when you were late.

Jean I'd like to talk about the time that I was late for an exam. It was in my last year at secondary school, when I was taking my final exams. Obviously, these exams were very important, as they affected what university I would be able to go to after school...

LANGUAGE STEP 1 Words & Phrases for Events
高分语言点 1 描述事件的词和短语

让我们来看一下雅思考生Sophia，Mike和Jean用了哪些词语来描述一件事情。

Sophia I want to talk about a *story* called "The Boy Who Cried Wolf". When I was a child, my mother always used to read me *bedtime stories* to help me get to sleep...

Mike I'd like to tell you about a *football competition* I participated in. It was a *5-a-side football competition* held when I was working for my last company, about four years ago...

Jean I'd like to talk about *the time that I was late for an exam...*

Obviously, the first thing you should do when beginning your monologue about a past event is to say what type of event it was. Look at the following words and phrases:

Stories	Competitions / Sports	Learning a Language	Journeys
children's story	sports match	class	school trip
bedtime story	boxing match	activity	educational trip
novel	sports competition	exercise	road trip
poem	athletics competition	role-play	day trip
play	chess competition	summer camp	holiday / vacation
film	speech contest	English corner	family holiday
opera	the Olympic Games	a friendly game	tour
fable	the Asian Games	class discussion	romantic weekend away
fairy tale		debate	
legend			

续表

Party	TV
birthday party	TV programme
housewarming party	TV drama
hen party	TV show
stag party	soap opera
wedding reception	documentary
ball	comedy

As well as the above, you can also use the following phrases to say what the event was:

- the time (that / when) + did something

  "...*the time when* I *saw* an interesting story on TV..."

  "...*the time that* my friends and I *went on* a day trip..."

  "...*the time* I *went to* the Houston Rockets..."

- the first time + did something

  "...*the first time* I *learned to* ride a bike..."

  "...*the first time* I *played* chess..."

  "...*the first time* I *flew* in a plane..."

Exercise 24.1: Gap Fill

Write the words below in the correct spaces.

fairy tale	legend	poems	road trip	role play
speech contest	romantic weekend away	the first time	the time when	

1. I would like to talk about ____________ I went abroad. My boyfriend and I went to Rome for a ____________ and he proposed to me. Since then, we've had many such short trips.
2. I want to tell you about the ____________ of King Arthur. It's a very old story, though it's probably not true.
3. I'd like to speak about ____________ I ride my motorcycle for hundreds of kilometres around Inner Mongolia. It was a fantastic ____________.
4. One thing that really helped me to learn Spanish was the time that I competed in a Spanish ____________. As well as giving a long talk, we also had to recite famous ____________ and act in a ____________ with the other contestants.
5. The story I really like is the ____________ "Cinderella", which is about the girl with two ugly sisters who marries a prince.

LANGUAGE STEP 2 Prepositions of Time & Time Phrases
高分语言点 2 与时间和时间短语搭配的介词

让我们来看一下雅思考生Sophia，Mike和Jean是如何描述时间的。

Sophia I want to talk about a story called "The Boy Who Cried Wolf". *When I was a child...*

Mike ...It was a 5-a-side football competition held when I was working for my last company, *about four years ago*...

Jean I'd like to talk about *the time that I was late for an exam*. It was *in my last year at secondary school*, when I was taking my final exams...

As you can see from the above model answer extracts, it's important to use prepositions of time or time phrases in your monologue to explain when the past event happened like a native speaker. First, remind yourself of the following essential prepositions of time for <u>specific</u> times:

- last (weeks, weekends, months, years, festivals)
  "...*last* weekend..."
  "...*last* month..."

- in (months, seasons, years, long periods of time)
  "...*in* December..."
  "...*in* 1979..."

- on (days, special days)
  "...*on* the 5th of November 2005..."
  "...*on* my parents' 25th wedding anniversary..."

- at (specific times, noons, midnights, festivals)
  "...*at* noon on my birthday..."
  "...*at* Christmas..."

- during (months, seasons, long festivals, long periods of time)
  "...*during* the Spring Festival..."
  "...*during* the spring..."

You can also use the following phrases for <u>unspecific</u> times:

- around / about (times, months, occasions, festivals, special days)
  "...*around* Christmas..."
  "*About* my 10th birthday..."

- once
  "*Once* I went on a school trip."
  "I attended a strange party *once*."

- one day
  "*One day* I watched a football match with my cousin."
  "*One day* I took a bus into the countryside."
- a few years ago
  "*A few years ago*, I was late for work."
  "I was late for work *a few years ago*."
- quite a while ago / some time ago
  "I started going to English corners *quite a while ago*."
  "*Some time ago* a friend gave me this piece of advice…"
- when
  "*When* I was a child…"
  "I went on a trip *when* I was at university."

小贴士

你不可以把 before 单独和时间短语连用来描述过去发生了某件事情，它只能用来描述某件事情发生在过去的其他事情之前。因此"It happened a few years *before*."的说法是不正确的。你应该说"It happened a few years ago."或者"It happened a few years *before* I went to university."

Exercise 24.2: Multiple Choice

Choose the appropriate prepositions of time or time phrases to complete the sentences.

1. ____________ I was studying at school…
   A. During B. In C. When
2. I think it was ____________ my 8th birthday that my family…
   A. at B. on C. when
3. ____________ August 2008 I bought tickets for the Olympics…
   A. In B. At C. On
4. I travelled by myself ____________ years ago.
   A. some time B. a few C. about
5. My friends and I saw the TV show ____________ the summer vacation.
   A. during B. about C. on
6. I remember the match very clearly; it only happened ____________ week!
   A. in B. during C. last
7. ____________ I was late for my dentist appointment…
   A. Some time B. During C. Once
8. The appointment was ____________ 3:35 p.m.
   A. on B. at C. about

9. I graduated from university ____________, so I haven't had classes or exams recently.
   A. quite a while ago　　B. some time　　C. one day
10. I was at work ____________ when my boss came and told me...
   A. one day　　B. some time　　C. quite a while
11. I caught the plane home ____________ Easter, so all the family were together.
   A. on　　B. in　　C. around

LANGUAGE STEP 3 Past Continuous & Past Simple and Past Perfect & Past Simple for Setting a Scene
高分语言点 3 用过去进行时和一般过去时以及过去完成时和一般过去时设定场景

让我们来看一下雅思考生Sophia，Mike和Jean是如何设定场景的。

Sophia ...My mother would lie next to me on the bed and read a different story every night. *When* she *was reading*, I *would often lay* my head on her chest and listen to the voices she made for the different characters in the stories...

Mike ...It *was* a 5-a-side football competition held when I *was working* for my last company, about four years ago...

Jean I'd like to talk about the time that I was late for an exam. It *was* in my last year at secondary school, *when* I *was taking* my final exams...

Notice that in the above model answers, the candidates all "set a scene" of their monologues by using the past continuous and past simple to help them say when the event occurred.

Past continuous & past simple

When using the past continuous and past simple, the "shorter" past simple event happened during the "longer" past continuous (was / were + verb-ing) action.

Let's look at the two structures of the past continuous and past simple again:

- (while / when) + was / were + verb-ing (when) past verb
  "*While* / *when* I *was studying* at university, I *heard* an interesting story."
  "I *was studying* at university *when* I *heard* an interesting story."

- past verb (while / when) + was / were + verb-ing
  "I *heard* an interesting story *while* / *when* I *was studying* at university."
  "I *wrote* this letter while I *was travelling* back to my university."

Past perfect & past simple

You can also use the past perfect and past simple to "set a scene" of your monologue.

The past perfect (had + past participle) action happened before the past simple action. The two structures for the past perfect and past simple are:

- had (already) + past participle + past verb
  "I *had studied* at university for a few months before my teacher *told* me..."
  "Because I *had already performed* really well on the school sports day, the headmaster *made* me attend another competition."

- past verb + had + past participle
  "My teacher *told* me something really important after I *had studied* at university for a few months."
  "The headmaster *made* me attend another competition because I *had already performed* really well on school sports day."

Exercise 24.3: Multiple Choice

Choose the appropriate forms of the past continuous & past simple or past perfect & past simple to complete the sentences.

1. My friends and I ____________ football in the street when a car ____________ up and squashed the ball.
   A. were playing, driving B. were playing, drove C. played, drove
2. I ____________ to listen to BBC programmes when I ____________ for my university entrance exams.
   A. started, was studying B. was starting, studied C. had started, was studying
3. While I ____________ in Japan, I ____________ to take a trip to Tokyo.
   A. had travelled, was deciding B. was travelling, decided C. travelled, was deciding
4. I ____________ quite a few parties in my house so I ____________ it was only fair that someone else have a party.
   A. have had, thought B. was having, think C. had had, thought
5. I only ____________ I didn't have my wallet after we ____________ for about 30 miles.
   A. realised, had travelled B. had realised, travelled C. realised, were travelling

THE FORMULA 高分公式

For STAGE 2 of a past event monologue, you must:
Say why it happened, where it happened and who was there.

Language Steps

1. Use the passive voice for location or cause of event accurately. ("The party *was held* in a restaurant.")
2. Use prepositions of location correctly. ("She lived *above* a Chinese restaurant." / "There were many trees *along* the river bank.")
3. Use relationship, occupation and group words accurately. ("My *uncle*, *who lived in Tianjin*, was an *engineer*.")

NATIVE SPEAKER WORDS 英语母语词汇

让我们来学习一些英语母语词汇，这些词汇对于回答该类型的问题非常有用，并且能够帮助你理解下面的答案范例。

Native Speaker Word	Part of Speech	Definition	Example Sentence
shepherd 牧羊人	noun	a person responsible for taking care of sheep	I think it must be quite nice to be a shepherd as you have no stress or anything to worry about, just sit in fields all day with your sheep.
find 觉得	verb	to think, feel a certain way about something or somebody	I find Ben really boring; all he does is talk about himself and his car.
all over somewhere 到处都是，遍地都是		everywhere in a particular place	My husband Lee is so messy; whenever I come home I always find his dirty clothes, plates and cups all over the living room, kitchen and bedroom.
senior 高级的	adjective	high-level, high-ranking	We are only low level staff, the decision about who will be the next CEO of the company will be made by senior management.
out of shape 走形的，变形的		saying that somebody is unfit, not in a good physical condition	Although it was really hot on the beach I didn't feel comfortable taking my T-shirt off like the other guys because I'm so out of shape.
goalkeeper 守门员	noun	the player in certain sports who protects the goal for their team	Stephanie never agreed to be the goalkeeper in hockey because she was too scared of getting hit by the ball or other players.

续表

Native Speaker Word	Part of Speech	Definition	Example Sentence
loads 许多，很多	noun	(informal) a lot, very many, very much	I love you loads. / I can't come to the party; I've got loads of work to do.
revise 复习	verb	to study something again in preparation for an exam	It's not surprising that Bob didn't do well in the history exam; he didn't revise at all.
all-nighter （在大学）通宵学习	noun	(informal) spending the whole night studying, either writing homework or preparing for an exam	I must go to sleep early tonight; I'm exhausted after doing an all-nighter last night.
cram 死记硬背，临时抱佛脚	verb	to study very hard and learn many things in a very short period of time, usually before an exam	Most students in China have a habit of trying to cram before their exams, though this isn't a very effective way to study.

MODEL ANSWERS 答案范例

阅读雅思考生Sophia，Mike和Jean的参考答案。

Sophia ...In the story there was a boy who was a shepherd. His job was to look after his father's sheep in the fields outside his village, but he found it very boring to be by himself all day...

Mike ...The competition was organised by a national football association, and teams from all over the country came to my hometown to compete. The other members of our team were all my colleagues, who either worked in different departments to me or were more senior managers than I was. Most of us were quite out of shape, and a few players were getting a little bit too old to play competitive football. Our main concern though was our goalkeeper, Mark, who was absolutely awful!...

Jean ...There were loads of exams and I had been revising really hard in preparation for them, especially my English exam. I had studied so hard that I got more and more tired as time went by. Then, the night before my English exam, I did an all-nighter to try and cram as much as I could...

LANGUAGE STEP 1 Passive Voice for Location or Cause of Events
高分语言点 1 用被动语态描述事件发生的地点或者原因

让我们来看一下如何用被动语态描述事件发生的地点及原因。

In his model answer, Mike says: "...The competition *was organised by* a national football association..."

When talking about a past event, native speakers will often use the passive voice to say why or where an event occurred in the past.

You may remember the passive voice from previous lessons, but remind yourself of its structure:

- subject + to be + past participle (by + agent)
  "*I was given* a present for my 8th birthday."
  "*The party was held* in an office."
  "*I was told* the story *by my teacher*."
  "*The competition was organised by my school*."
  "*I was taken* to the swimming pool *by my father*."

Exercise 24.4: Sentence Completion

Complete the sentences below by writing the correct passive forms of the words in brackets.

1. Our basketball matches ____________ (play) at the local park.
2. I ____________ (invite) to the party ____________ my sister-in-law.
3. Lots of stories ____________ (read) to me ____________ my grandparents.
4. I ____________ (promote) ____________ my boss, and as a result I became the manager of my colleagues.
5. The English corners at university ____________ (teach) in a corner of the library.
6. We ____________ (take) to the cinema ____________ my aunt before she took us to lunch in a really expensive restaurant.
7. The Christmas tree ____________ (carry) into the living room and then my sister and I spent ages decorating it.
8. Thankfully, my plane ticket to Japan ____________ (buy) for me ____________ my parents.

LANGUAGE STEP 2 Prepositions of Location 高分语言点 2 地点介词

让我们来看一下雅思考生Sophia和Mike是如何使用地点介词的。

Sophia ...His job was to look after his father's sheep *in* the fields *outside* his village, but he found it very boring to be by himself all day...

Mike ...The other members of our team were all my colleagues, who either worked *in* different departments to me or were more senior managers than I was...

Obviously, when you are talking about a past event, you need to say where it happened. To do this well, you need to use prepositions of location correctly.

Remind yourself of these prepositions of location:

- in + enclosing or larger place
  "...*in* the countryside..."

"...*in* the middle of nowhere..."

- at + specific place or location
  "...*at* the top of the mountain..."
  "...*at* the end of the street..."

- on + a surface or roads
  "...*on* the fifth floor..."
  "...*on* a main road..."

- over / above + a certain place or location
  "...*above* a Japanese restaurant..."
  "Every day the Chinese flag flies *over* Tian'anmen Square."

- next to / beside / by + a certain place or location
  "...*by* the seaside..."
  "...*next* to the Bell Tower..."
  "...*beside* Tianchi Lake..."

- opposite / across from + a certain place or location
  "I work *opposite* my favourite restaurant."
  "The Forbidden City is just *across from* Tian'anmen Square."

- between + two places or locations
  "Suzhou, which is *between* Shanghai and Nanjing..."
  "My house is *between* the mountains and the sea."

- in front of + a certain place or location
  "The Bund in Shanghai is just *in front of* the main historical buildings."
  "The Terracotta Warriors stand *in front of* Qin Shihuang's tomb."

- outside of (a town / city)
  "The rowing events of the Olympics were held on the *outside of* Beijing."

- near (to)
  "Xishuangbanna, which is very *near* to Laos..."
  "New York City is *near* the sea."

- far from
  "I live *far from* the city centre."
  "Lhasa is extremely *far from* Zhejiang Province."

Exercise 24.5: Multiple Choice

Choose the appropriate prepositions of location from the choices below to complete the sentences.

1. I was sitting ____________ the living room when my mother told me a great documentary was going to be ____________ TV.
   A. at, on　　B. in, at　　C. in, on
2. An interesting story I heard as a child was about Yu Gong (愚公), who lived ____________ a mountain.
   A. outside　　B. beside　　C. inside
3. I was later for the meeting than anyone else because I lived so ____________ the office. Ben's house, on the other hand, is just ____________ where we work.
   A. far from, opposite　　B. outside of, near to　　C. above, in front of
4. I once went to a fantastic party ____________ the beach.
   A. on　　B. in　　C. over
5. The basketball tickets my brother bought were fantastic; there was only a few metres ____________ our seats and the basketball players.
   A. outside of　　B. in front of　　C. between
6. A great journey I had a few years ago was when my wife and I flew in a helicopter ____________ the Grand Canyon in the USA.
   A. over　　B. under　　C. in front of
7. I remember having my photograph taken ____________ the Great Wall when a bird landed on my head.
   A. outside　　B. far from　　C. in front of
8. Last year I went to Yunnan and visited the Stone Forest just ____________ Kunming.
   A. next to　　B. outside of　　C. between

LANGUAGE STEP 3 Relationship, Occupation and Group Words
高分语言点 3 描述关系、职业和人群的用语

让我们来看一下雅思考生Sophia和Mike是如何描述关系、职业以及人群的。

Sophia …In the story there was a boy who was a *shepherd*. His job was to look after his *father*'s sheep in the fields outside his village, but he found it very boring to be by himself all day…

Mike …The other members of our team were all my *colleagues*, who either worked in different departments to me or were more senior *managers* than I was…Our main concern though was our *goalkeeper*, Mark, who was absolutely awful!...

Most past events native speakers talk about involve other people, as in the above model answers. You should similarly use relationship, occupation and group words to describe the people involved.

We've already looked at some words of relatives, occupations and social positions (Person Monologue Stage 1, Language Step 1). The following table contains a few of these words to remind you, as well as words to describe groups of people.

Relatives	Occupations	Relationship	Groups
grandparents	accountant	friend of a friend	a crowd of people
aunt	waiter / waitress	next-door neighbour	loads of people
uncle	musician	colleague	a big group of people
			(sport) supporters
			party-goers
			a tour group
			audience
			guests
			passengers
			players

You can also use the following structure to introduce and describe the people in your past event monologue (for more information about relative clauses, see Person Monologue Stage 1, Language Step 2).

- person + relative clause
  "Susan, *who was an accountant with HSBC*, was waiting for me outside."
  "My grandfather, *who was a very kind and gentle man*, got so angry that he..."
  "All of the party-goers *who had been dancing all night* decided to go to another bar."

Exercise 24.6: Table Completion

Write the following words in the correct places in the table above.

friend of the family	acquaintance	spouse	mother-in-law
nephew	childhood friend	distant relation	

Now, think about who you are likely to talk about when you give a monologue about a person. Write the appropriate relationship and occupation words for these people in the table above until it is complete.

Exercise 24.7: Rephrasing

Combine the following sentences. For each, write one sentence that combines both items of information using a relative clause.

For example:

Many students had been studying hard. They all decided to have a party after their exams.

All of the students who had been studying hard decided to have a party after their exams.

1. Simon gets carsick very easily. He felt very ill on the school bus one day.

____

2. Susan is very forgetful. She forgot her handbag.

____

3. Many tennis fans didn't manage to buy tickets. They all watched the match on TV screens outside.

____

4. Ralph was a friendly old man. He used to talk to me every day on my way home from school.

____

5. Lots of passengers hadn't bought a ticket. They were thrown off the bus.

____

6. Some members of the tour group were American. They didn't understand what I said.

____

THE FORMULA 高分公式

For STAGE 3 of a past event monologue, you must:
Say what happened.

Language Steps

1. Use direct and indirect speech accurately. ("*He said I would never go to university.*" / "*She said 'You are my best friend'.*")
2. Use the past simple with sequence markers correctly. ("My cousin went next door to get the ball. *Shortly afterwards* he came running back…")
3. Use the past continuous & past simple and the past perfect & past simple with adverbs of surprise. ("While *we were cycling* along the road, *suddenly* a man *jumped* out of the trees!")

NATIVE SPEAKER WORDS 英语母语词汇

让我们来学习一些英语母语词汇，这些词汇对于回答该类型的问题非常有用，并且能够帮助你理解下面的答案范例。

Native Speaker Word	Part of Speech	Definition	Example Sentence
play a trick on somebody 捉弄某人，搞恶作剧		to confuse somebody or cause somebody a problem for one's own amusement	Every year, April 1st is a great day in our office because everybody tries to play a trick on each other.
intimidated 胆小的，害怕的	adjective	feeling frightened or nervous because you are not confident in a situation	Students of a new language often feel intimidated speaking in front of their classmates.
draw 平局 / 打成平局	noun / verb	where two teams / players have an equal score and so both sides neither lose nor win	If there is a draw in the World Cup final, the teams have to take part in a penalty shoot-out to decide who wins the cup.
manage 完成，达成，设法做到	verb	to succeed in doing something	Unfortunately Shirley didn't manage to get enough points in her exams to enter Beijing University.
get sent off 被罚下场		to be ordered to leave a game / match because you have behaved badly or broken the rules	David Beckham is a very popular player now, but after he got sent off in the 1998 World Cup lots of English football fans were extremely angry with him.
referee 裁判	noun	the person in charge of a game who makes sure the rules are followed	Most football fans and players shout at referees, but they're an essential part of every match.
whistle 口哨	noun	a small plastic or metal object that you put in your mouth to make a loud, high sound	In tennis, the umpires don't use whistles when a problem happens, but just shout or use their loud microphone.
stream in / out / through 涌入 / 涌出 / 流过		to move continuously in one direction	When school finishes, you can see hundreds of students streaming out of their classrooms.
why / how / what / when / who / where on earth 到底为什么 / 究竟怎么样 / 到底有什么/ 到底什么时候 / 究竟是谁 / 究竟在哪里		used when you are very surprised, angry or confused about something	When I was young, I played with my friends near the sea and got covered in mud. I looked really strange so when I got home my mother asked me where on earth I'd been to.
give somebody a look / get a look 给某人脸色看		to show somebody / receive a disapproving or angry expression	At university there was a rugby party where all the players dressed in women's clothes. They got lots of looks from the teachers and staff.

MODEL ANSWERS 答案范例

阅读雅思考生Sophia，Mike和Jean的参考答案。

Sophia ...In the story there was a boy who was a shepherd...Once, he decided to play a trick on his fellow villagers. He ran into the village shouting "Wolf! Wolf! There's a wolf killing my sheep!" Immediately, all the villagers stopped working and ran to the field to help protect the sheep. When they found there was no wolf, the boy laughed at them. Another day, the boy played the same trick on the villagers and again laughed at them when they came running into the field looking for a wolf. One day, a real wolf did get into his field and start attacking his sheep. Again, the boy ran into village shouting "Wolf! Wolf! There's a wolf killing my sheep!" But to his surprise nobody believed him and all his sheep got killed...

Mike ...Two weeks before the competition we all started playing football and training together, though not very seriously. On the day, we arrived at the football arena quite early, and we all waited nervously for the matches to begin. Looking at the other teams, we felt quite intimated because many of them looked much younger and fitter than our team. Anyway we played our group matches, and did surprisingly well; we managed to draw most matches and even won a couple. I was also pleased because I had managed to score the most goals for our team – usually I don't score at all because I play in defence. We got through to the next round where we played a team that was very aggressive. The match was very close but right at the end one of their players got sent off for fouling me. One of my teammates passed me the ball then I ran to the other end and smashed it into their goal – just before the referee blew the whistle!...

Jean ...I remember studying by myself in my bedroom and feeling exhausted. I'm not really sure what happened next, but I must have fallen asleep when I was studying because the next thing I knew it was the next day and the sunlight was streaming through the window. Straight away, I started panicking as it felt very late. Looking at my watch, I found that I was already 20 minutes late for my exam! So without showering or changing my clothes I ran out of the house and caught the bus to school. I think I was about 40 minutes late by the time I entered the examination hall. As soon as my teacher saw me he asked what on earth I thought I was doing. But he didn't wait for an answer and just helped me to find my seat. I got a few looks from my classmates, but of course nobody said anything. I remember hurriedly opening my exam paper, taking a deep breath and then writing as fast as I could...

LANGUAGE STEP 1 Direct & Indirect Speech
高分语言点 1 直接引语和间接引语

让我们来看一下雅思考生Sophia是如何使用直接引语和间接引语的。

In her model answer, Sophia says: "...In the story there was a boy who was a shepherd...He ran into the village *shouting 'Wolf! Wolf! There's a wolf killing my sheep!'*..."

There are two ways to report what somebody has said: direct speech and indirect speech.

Direct speech

The above example is direct speech, as Sophia uses quotation marks to say what another person said. (Obviously quotation marks can't be heard by the examiner during the IELTS test, but you can still use this way to report speech.)

Other examples are:
"She always says: 'Wear more clothes; don't catch a cold.'"
"He said: 'I really don't like this party.'"
"I said: 'I will not go home now.'"

This is probably the easiest way to report what someone has said, because you do not need to change the language used.

Indirect speech

When you do not use quotation marks and instead use what the person has said as part of your own sentence, this is indirect speech. When using indirect speech, you usually have to change the pronouns, time markers and the tense of all verbs in the sentence.

The tense should "go back" one tense further into the past, so that present simple becomes past simple, past simple becomes past perfect etc.

Examples:
"She said: 'I love you.'" becomes "She said that she *loved him*."
"I said: 'I have never loved you.'" becomes "I said that I *had never loved her*."

When reporting questions, "yes / no" questions should be changed using "if", while questions that use question words such as "how", "who", "why" etc should be included in the indirect speech.

Examples:
"I asked her: 'Will you go?'" becomes "I asked her *if* she *would* go."
"She asked him: 'Why don't you love me?'" becomes "She asked him *why he didn't* love her."

Look at the following examples:

Direct Speech	Indirect Speech
My mother said: "I won't have time to read you a story."	My mother said that she wouldn't have time to read me a story.
Our teacher said: "Stay together so you won't get lost."	Our teacher told us to stay together so that we wouldn't get lost.
She said: "John was hungry yesterday."	She said that John had been hungry the day before.
He said: "Mary will go to New York tomorrow."	He said that Mary would go to New York the next day.
She asked him: "Do you like ice cream?"	She asked him if he liked ice cream.
The teacher asked: "Why didn't you come to class today?"	The teacher asked me why I hadn't gone to class that day.

小贴士

在间接引语中，动词 could, should, would, might, must, needn't, ought to, used to 不需要变换形式。

Exercise 24.8: Rephrasing

Rewrite the following sentences, changing them from direct to indirect speech.

1. He said: "I'm Chinese."

____

2. She said: "I'm not going to study next year."

____

3. He asked me: "Can you come to my house tonight?"

____

4. She told him: "I don't love you anymore."

____

5. I said: "I won't be able to leave the party now."

____

6. My dad said: "I went to Beijing many years ago."

____

7. I asked Jack: "Where is Jill?"

____

8. I said to my parents: "I can't tell you, it's a secret."

____

9. He said: "I have never been to Tian'anmen Square."

____

LANGUAGE STEP 2 Past Simple with Sequence Markers
高分语言点 2 有先后次序的一般过去时

让我们来看一下雅思考生Sophia和Jean是如何使用序号标志词和一般过去时的。

Sophia ...In the story there *was* a boy who *was* a shepherd...He *ran* into the village shouting "Wolf! Wolf! There's a wolf killing my sheep!" *Immediately*, all the villagers *stopped* working and *ran* to the field to help protect the sheep. *When* they *found* there was no wolf, the boy *laughed* at them...

Jean ...I remember studying by myself in my bedroom and feeling exhausted. I'm not really sure what *happened next*, but I must have fallen asleep when I *was* studying because the next thing I *knew* it *was* the next day and the sunlight *was* streaming through the window. *Straight away*, I *started* panicking as it *felt* very late. Looking at my watch, I *found* that I *was* already 20 minutes late for my exam! *So* without showering or changing my clothes I *ran* out of the house and *caught* the bus to school...

When describing a past event, you need to use the past simple accurately. You should also use sequence markers to structure your monologue – this makes it clear what order things happened in and also makes you sound much more like a native speaker.

Look at the following useful sequence markers:

- to start with
- at the beginning
- at first
- as soon as
- immediately
- straight away
- by the time that
- then
- so
- afterwards
- following that
- following on from that
- after (that)
- next

- soon after / afterwards
- shortly after / afterwards
- in the end
- finally

Examples:

"*To start with* I felt very nervous but *after* a few dances I relaxed and *in the end* had a really great time."

"*As soon as* we entered the stadium we realised we were very early."

"I watched a documentary about wild animals a few years ago. *Following that*, I decided not to eat meat anymore because I think it's cruel."

Exercise 24.9: Multiple Choice

Choose the appropriate sequence markers from the choices below to complete the sentences.

1. I remember when I started learning Italian by using a CD. __________, I found it very useful and I learnt a lot quickly. But __________, when I went to Italy and tried to speak Italian, I had lots of problems and realised it wasn't a good way to learn a language.
   A. To start with, as soon as B. At first, next C. At the beginning, finally
2. The party started at 7 p.m., but I was really late. __________ I got there, most of the guests had already left.
   A. By the time that B. As soon as C. Immediately
3. I got in a bus in Tokyo to go to Kyoto but __________ leaving the bus station we crashed into a car.
   A. following that B. shortly after C. afterwards
4. At school there was an organised trip to Tian'anmen Square. __________, we ate ice cream and sang songs on the way home.
   A. So B. Next C. Afterwards
5. I really loved the end of my high school, although there were lots of exams. __________, it was really hard work, __________ I was tired all the time. __________ I got used to the excitement of the exams and rushing to write so much, and found that I actually enjoyed the exams!
   A. At the beginning, then, Following that
   B. To start with, so, Then
   C. At first, following that, In the end
6. In the story, Goldilocks eats the bears' porridge. __________, she feels really tired and sleeps in one of their beds. __________, the three bears come home and find her.
   A. Soon afterwards, In the end
   B. As soon as, Next
   C. Following that, So

LANGUAGE STEP 3 Past Continuous & Past Simple and Past Perfect & Past Simple with Adverbs of Surprise
高分语言点 3 表示意外或突然的副词用于过去进行时和一般过去时以及过去完成时和一般过去时

让我们来看一下雅思考生Sophia和Jean是如何使用表示意外的副词的。

Sophia …Again, the boy ran into village shouting "Wolf! Wolf! There's a wolf killing my sheep!" But *to his surprise* nobody believed him and all his sheep got killed…

Jean …I'm not really sure what happened next, but I must have falien asleep when I was studying because *the next thing I knew* it was the next day and the sunlight was streaming through the window…

Notice that both Sophia and Jean use adverbs of surprise in their monologues. These are very frequently used by native speakers when they talk about past events or stories as they add interest and drama.

Look at the following highly useful adverbs of surprise:

- suddenly
- all of a sudden
- to (one's) surprise
- out of the blue
- surprisingly
- unexpectedly
- unbelievably
- incredibly
- the next thing I knew

> 小贴士 如果 when 或者 and then 出现在句子中间的时候，它们必须放在 suddenly, all of a sudden, to (one's) surprise 和 out of the blue 这些词语的前面。

These phrases are commonly used in combination with the past continuous and past simple or past perfect and past simple, as in the example below:

- with past continuous & past simple
  "We *were quietly walking* along the road *when suddenly* a car *crashed* right in front of us."
  "I *was sleeping* in my parents' car on the way to the airport *and then the next thing I knew* we *were flying* in an aeroplane!"
  "We *were watching* the basketball match on TV *when* the electricity *unexpectedly stopped*."

"When we *were learning* the first conditional, the activity our English teacher *made* us do *was surprisingly* enjoyable and useful."

- with past perfect & past simple

"I *had* just *sat down* in the restaurant *when all of a sudden* a woman *came* to my table and *threw* a glass of wine over me!"

"My girlfriend *had told* me that there *was* a problem with our flat, and *asked* me to come home quickly. *Incredibly*, when I *got* home I *found* all my friends and family *were* there, to give me a surprise birthday party!"

"I *had prepared* for the presentation for a very long time and although I *was* nervous, it *went unbelievably* well."

"My classmates and I *hadn't prepared* well for the exam and so *were* really worried. *Out of the blue*, our teacher *told* us it was cancelled – it *was* such a relief!"

"We *had asked* our parents for a pet dog many, many times and they always *said* no. Then one day, *to our surprise* they *said* yes!"

Exercise 24.10: Matching

Match sentence halves 1-9 with sentence halves A-I.

1. I had left my house just wearing shorts and a T-shirt when…
2. My class was visiting an old castle together when…
3. I had volunteered to join a classroom activity and then…
4. I was trying to paint a picture – and not doing very well – when…
5. We had been told that it would take a long time to get through customs at the border…
6. I was delivering newspapers for my paper round when…
7. We were watching the football match in the stadium when…
8. We hadn't seen my mother's family for many years before that Spring Festival...
9. I didn't want to watch this particular programme although my mother had told me to.

A. …but when we got there it was incredibly easy and straightforward.
B. …However, when I watched it I found it was unexpectedly fascinating.
C. …unbelievably our teacher started buying us all ice creams!
D. …out of the blue a footballer jumped off the pitch and into where we were standing!
E. …suddenly an enormous dog started chasing me!
F. …to my surprise my cat ran across the painting.
G. …But her family was surprisingly friendly and generous with us.
H. …all of a sudden it started to rain really heavily.
I. …the next thing I knew I was doing a role-play in front of everybody.

THE FORMULA 高分公式

For STAGE 4 of a past event monologue, you must:
Say why the event was special and how you feel / felt about it.

Language Steps

1. Use adjectives for describing events & adjectives of feeling well. ("This event was important to me because it was such a *crazy time*!" / ("I feel very *nostalgic* whenever I think of those times.")
2. Use the third conditional & present perfect to express the importance of an event accurately. ("*If* I *hadn't had* this experience I *would never have had* the confidence to learn the language.")
3. Use concluding phrases correctly. ("*I wish I hadn't* done it; I still feel stupid whenever I think about it!")

NATIVE SPEAKER WORDS 英语母语词汇

让我们来学习一些英语母语词汇，这些词汇对于回答该类型的问题非常有用，并且能够帮助你理解下面的答案范例。

Native Speaker Word	Part of Speech	Definition	Example Sentence
the moral of something 某事的寓意，启示		the moral of an experience or story refers to what one learns from it about how to behave	Last week I shouted at my boyfriend for not phoning me or sending me a text message for ages. Eventually I realised that my phone had no money on it. The moral of that story is that I should check the facts first before I blame somebody.
take part in something 参加，参与		to join others in doing an activity	When I was young I was too shy and nervous to take part in school plays.
horrible 可怕的，恐怖的	adjective	very unpleasant, very bad	I don't know why so many women ask men what they look like before they go out; even if they look horrible the men will always say they look good.
pretty 十分，相当	adverb	quite, extremely	I have to say that last night's party was pretty boring. There were only a few interesting people there.
anxious 焦急的，紧张的	adjective	worried and nervous	Before meeting a boy on a date I always feel really anxious; I worry about my clothes, my hair and whether he will like me.

续表

Native Speaker Word	Part of Speech	Definition	Example Sentence
worried sick 非常担心的		extremely worried	A few years ago I went out with my friends but didn't take my mobile phone. When I got home really late, I remember my mum being really angry with me and saying that she had been worried sick – she had even phoned all the local hospitals to make sure I hadn't been in an accident.
wonder 想知道	verb	to think, to ask yourself questions about something	Whenever I spend the night on my uncle's fishing boat, I always look at the stars and wonder how big the universe is and whether there are different people on different planets.
punctual 准时的	adjective	arriving or doing something at the right time, not late	To make a good first impression, you should never be late for a job interview; always be punctual.

MODEL ANSWERS 答案范例

阅读雅思考生Sophia，Mike和Jean的参考答案。

Sophia …The moral of this story is that you shouldn't lie otherwise people won't believe you – even when you are speaking the truth. I liked this story as a child and I think it has a good message. I will definitely read this story to my children in the future.

Mike …Although we lost the next match and so didn't win any cups or anything, I was really pleased with my performance. Besides, it was a really fun day for all of us. I've always liked playing football, but that was probably the most enjoyable football competition I've ever taken part in.

Jean …Needless to say, this was a pretty horrible experience for me to go through. Apart from feeling so anxious on the day of the exam, I was also worried sick about what my result was going to be for weeks afterwards. In the end, my exam result was much better than I had expected, although not great. I got into a good university, but I always wonder what my life would have been like if I had done better in the exam and gone to a better university. This event taught me the importance of not being late – I've always been punctual ever since!

LANGUAGE STEP 1 Adjectives for Describing Events & Adjectives of Feeling
高分语言点 1 描述事件和感觉的形容词

让我们看一下雅思考生Mike和Jean用了哪些形容词描述事件和感觉。

Mike ...I was really pleased with my performance. Besides, it was a really fun day for all of us. I've always liked playing football, but that was probably the most enjoyable football competition I've ever taken part in.

Jean ...Needless to say, this was a pretty horrible experience for me to go through. Apart from feeling so anxious on the day of the exam, I was also worried sick about what my result was going to be for weeks afterwards...

As you can see in Mike's and Jean's model answers, you should use adjectives for describing events in your monologue.

Here are some more adjectives for you to use:

Interesting	Strange	Surprising	Good	Bad
funny	unusual	amazing*	inspiring*	horrible
amusing*	bizarre	astounding*	life-changing	terrible
interesting*	weird	astonishing*	enjoyable	awful
fascinating*	mysterious	awe-inspiring*	wonderful	depressing*
curious	peculiar	incredible	fun	unpleasant
stimulating*	random	breathtaking	refreshing*	frustrating*
thought-provoking	crazy		encouraging*	disappointing*
enlightening*	wild		moving*	embarrassing*

In addition to describing what the past event was like, you should also talk about how you felt. This makes your monologue more interesting to the examiner and explains why this event was important to you.

Let's look at some useful native speaker adjectives of feeling:

- embarrassed
- irate
- incredulous
- moved
- pleased
- delighted

- thrilled
- over the moon
- enthusiastic
- reassured
- satisfied

Here are some examples using both kinds of adjectives:

"I felt extremely *satisfied* to see my paper be published in the school newspaper."

"Although it was *embarrassing* at the time, when I think about it now I guess it's pretty *amusing*."

"I was really *moved* to visit a place with such an *awe-inspiring* history."

Exercise 24.11: Table Completion

The above adjectives for describing events that are marked with * can all be changed into adjectives of feeling. Complete the following table by changing the adjectives for describing events into adjectives of feeling.

Adjectives for Describing Events	Adjectives of Feeling
amazing	
amusing	
astonishing	
astounding	
awe-inspiring	
depressing	
disappointing	
embarrassing	
encouraging	
enlightening	
fascinating	
frustrating	
inspiring	
interesting	
moving	
refreshing	
stimulating	

Have you noticed the pattern for changing adjectives for describing events into adjectives of feeling? Think of some more adjectives that can describe events and feelings and write them in the above table.

LANGUAGE STEP 2 The Third Conditional & Present Perfect to Express the Importance of an Event
高分语言点 2 用第三条件句和现在完成时描述事件的重要性

让我们来看一下雅思考生Mike和Jean是如何描述事件的重要性的。

Mike ...I've always liked playing football, but *that was probably the most enjoyable football competition I've ever taken part in*...

Jean ...This event taught me the importance of not being late – *I've always been punctual ever since!*

In your monologue about a past event you should also tell the examiner what you learned from it or how it has affected your life. This is a great way of saying why the event was important.

To do this, you can use either the third conditional or the present perfect.

The third conditional

We've already looked at the third conditional in previous lessons, but just remind yourself of its structure before looking at some examples bellow.

- If + had(n't) + past participle, would(n't) have + past participle
  "*If* I *hadn't participated* in the speaking competition, I *wouldn't have had* the confidence to continue studying Italian."

- would(n't) have + past participle + if + had(n't) + past participle
  "I probably *wouldn't have chosen* architecture for my major *if* our school *hadn't taken* us to St. Paul's Cathedral in London."

The present perfect to express the importance of an event

To talk about the importance of a past event, you can use the present perfect in the following ways:

- (event) was the superlative (type of event) I have ever past participle
  "*That match* was *the best* match I *have ever played* in."
  "*This story* was *the most memorable* tale I *have ever heard*."

- since (event) I have (adverb of frequency) past participle
  "*Since* I saw that TV programme, I *have often thought* about all the animals that become extinct every year."
  "*Since* that party I *have been* much more interested in foreign cultures and customs."

Exercise 24.12: Sentence Completion

Complete the sentences below by writing the correct third conditional, superlative or passive forms of the words in brackets.

1. If I ___________ (not be) late to work that day I possibly ___________ (to be) promoted.
2. I ___________ (not take) up photography as a hobby if I ___________ (not travel) through the Vietnamese countryside.
3. If I ___________ (go) to a different university, I'm sure I ___________ (not make) such good friends or ___________ (enjoy) myself so much.
4. I ___________ (keep) in contact with those old workmates if I ___________ (not lose) that cell phone.
5. That class was ___________ (good) I ___________ (ever have).
6. Since my mother gave me this advice, I ___________ (always try) to pay more attention to other people's feelings.
7. That family day out was ___________ (exciting) day trip I ___________ (ever be) on.
8. Since that interview I ___________ (never arrive) late for anything – honestly!

LANGUAGE STEP 3 Concluding Phrases 高分语言点 3 结束语

让我们来看一下雅思考生Sophia和Jean是如何结束自己的个人陈述的。

Sophia *...I liked this story as a child and I think it has a good message. I will definitely read this story to my children in the future.*

Jean *...This event taught me the importance of not being late – I've always been punctual ever since!*

When talking about a past event, native speakers will often use a concluding phrase to sum up or conclude their monologue – you should too!

Here are our "top ten" concluding phrases:

- The (event) taught me that...
  "*Writing this letter and the effect it had on my friend taught me that* making just small signs that you care about someone can have a big impact on their life."
- The (event) was important to / for me because...
  "*This trip was important to me because* I learnt a lot about travelling alone and staying safe."
- Through this experience I learnt the importance of...
  "*Through this experience I learnt the importance of* studying as well as I could, and not being lazy."

- I will always remember...
  "*I will always remember* that sunny afternoon in the park with my boyfriend."
- I will never forget...
  "*I will never forget* watching that crazy basketball match with my father."
- Overall, it was a rewarding experience and I learned a lot.
- I'm glad I did it – it was a very (adjective) experience.
  "*I'm glad I did it – it was a very inspiring experience.*"
- I would love to do it again if I had the chance.
- Although I enjoyed it at the time, I wouldn't want to do it again because...
  "*Although I enjoyed it at the time, I wouldn't want to do it again because* I don't think it would be as much fun now that I'm older."
- In the future I will...
  "*In the future I will* try and share the same piece of advice with others."

Exercise 24.13: Gap Fill

Write the concluding phrases below in the correct spaces.

this event taught me
I will never forget
a very stimulating experience
I wouldn't want to do it again
important for me
in the future I will
I would love to do it again
rewarding experience and I learned a lot
I learnt the importance of

1. I'm glad I did it – it was ____________.
2. Through this experience ____________ not believing everything I am told.
3. ____________ make sure my children have the opportunity to do the same kind of things.
4. ____________ that everyone, even people younger than yourself, can give good advice – you just have to listen.
5. ____________ my 10th birthday party.
6. Although I enjoyed it at the time, ____________ because looking back I guess it was quite dangerous.
7. Overall, it was a ____________.
8. It was ____________ because it made me realise that people everywhere are basically the same.
9. ____________ if I had the chance.

ANSWER ORDER 答题思路

Remind yourself of the answer order you should use when giving a monologue about a past event.

- Stage 1: Say what it was and when it happened.
- Stage 2: Say why it happened, where it happened and who was there.
- Stage 3: Say what happened.
- Stage 4: Say why the event was special and how you feel / felt about it.

Exercise 24.14: Ordering

Using the answer order above, put the following extracts from a model answer into the correct order.

A. I was out partying with my friends when....

B. On the whole, it was an enlightening experience, though I certainly wouldn't want to do it again!

C. Then suddenly, I realised...

D. Interviewer: Tell me about a time you lost you something.

E. I got in a taxi and we started travelling on the way home...

F. I want to tell you about the time I lost my mobile phone.

For more practice, please go to: www.EQEnglish.com

Part Three 第三部分

第三部分高分公式介绍
INTRODUCTION TO PART THREE FORMULAS

雅思口语考试第三部分介绍

雅思口语考试第三部分考试时间为4到5分钟。考官将就一些比较广泛的社会问题与考生进行双向讨论。

考生需要清晰地表达并支持自己的观点，同时向考官展示出自己能够运用英语母语者讨论问题的技巧，并就一些不太熟悉的话题进行广泛而深入的讨论。

EQ英语课程第三部分概述

通过对雅思口试第三部分考题的研究和分析，EQ英语总结了英语为母语者讨论问题的技巧，在此基础上提炼出7种非常实用的雅思口语高分公式。本书第三部分把这7种高分公式分成7课来讲解。每一课都提供了讨论范例，这些范例向考生展示了如何把这些高分公式运用到雅思口试中。每一种雅思口语高分公式均包含答题思路以及高分语言点解析。掌握了这7种雅思口语高分公式，考生就能够轻松自如地就任何话题进行讨论了。

Formula 25: Giving and Supporting Opinions

AIMS 学习目标

In the following lessons you'll learn how to give good discussion answers to IELTS Part Three questions.

In this lesson you'll master the Formula for Giving and Supporting Opinions. This is a skill that you will need to use in all Part Three lessons. It is a basic native speaker discussion skill.

你将学会如何回答雅思口试第三部分的常见问题，比如：

- Do you think children should be made to wear a uniform to school?
- Do you believe it is acceptable that animals are used for cosmetics testing?
- Do you feel that city life is suitable for elderly people?
- What do you think about there being a single international language?

THE FORMULA 高分公式

To give and support opinions, you should:

Answer Order

- Introduce and state your opinions clearly.
- Support your opinions with reasons or examples.

Language Steps

1. Use native speaker opinion phrases. (*"I believe that..." / "I feel that..." / "I hold the opinion that..."*)
2. Use native speaker phrases for talking about why you believe something. (*"It is good for..." / "It is essential for..." / "It has a positive effect on..."*)

NATIVE SPEAKER WORDS 1 英语母语词汇 1

让我们来学习一些英语母语词汇，这些词汇对于回答该类型的问题非常有用，并且能够帮助你理解下面的答案范例。

Native Speaker Word	Part of Speech	Definition	Example Sentence
identity 身份	noun	who somebody is, what makes them different to other people	She reacted very angrily when I said she should stop wearing a leather jacket and changing the colour of her hair to pink and green – she said these were part of her identity.
unity 统一，一致	noun	the concept / idea of being one, being a united group, being together, being the same as others in the same group	There has been a great sense of unity in the whole community after the terrible disaster.
snobbish 势利的	adjective	being arrogant, believing and acting like you are better or superior to others	He is incredibly snobbish. He thinks he's better than his classmates just because he has really expensive shoes and fashionable jackets.
ridicule 嘲笑，愚弄	verb	to make fun of, to mock, to pick on, to criticise and make jokes about somebody	Sometimes kids can be quite cruel and ridicule their classmates and friends.
pick on 找茬，捉弄		to make fun of, to mock, to be nasty to someone unfairly	The boys always picked on Mike because he was smaller than any of the other boys in the class.
designer clothes 名牌服装		clothes made by famous, "high-end" fashion designers; clothes and shoes with famous "names"	He's a really rich man. He is always wearing the latest designer clothes and likes to show off about it.
discriminate (against) 歧视	verb	to treat somebody or a group of people differently (usually in a worse way) for a superficial reason such as the colour of their skin, sex, or age	In recent years, there have been a lot of new laws to stop black and Asian people being discriminated against by employers.
inappropriate 不适当的，不相称的	adjective	to be unsuitable or not correct for a particular person or situation	Most people would agree that it's inappropriate to laugh, chat and smoke at a funeral.
patronising 盛气凌人的	adjective	having an attitude or behaviour of looking down on others, believing others to be inferior or less worthy or less able to think intelligently or make decisions of their own	I can't stand Ben, he's such a patronising idiot; he talks to me as if I am about ten years old and don't know anything!!

MODEL ANSWER 1 答案范例 1

阅读雅思考生Sophia的参考答案。

Interviewer Do you think that children should wear a uniform to school?

Sophia Yes, I think that children in middle school and high school should wear a uniform to school. I strongly believe that it is essential for giving children a sense of identity and unity. Young children can be very snobbish about fashion and often ridicule and pick on children who don't wear expensive or designer clothes. If all school children have to wear a uniform, they will all look the same and so poorer children won't be discriminated against by the richer children.

Interviewer What about in university? Should university students all wear a uniform?

Sophia Certainly not! We are all adults by the time we get to university, so I believe that we should have the freedom to choose what we want to wear and when we want to wear it. It would certainly be inappropriate to make university students wear a uniform, and incredibly patronising too!

NATIVE SPEAKER WORDS 2 英语母语词汇 2

让我们来学习一些英语母语词汇，这些词汇对于回答该类型的问题非常有用，并且能够帮助你理解下面的答案范例。

Native Speaker Word	Part of Speech	Definition	Example Sentence
convinced 确信的，深信的	adjective	to be certain, sure	Many people say that society is getting better and better, but I'm not convinced.
emphasis 强调，重点	noun	special stress laid upon, or importance attached to something	When I was in school there was a strong emphasis on academic success rather than on doing well in sports.
academic 学术的	adjective	relating to schools, universities, studying in general rather than practical things	Universities in the UK are investing millions of pounds in their science departments. But this is mainly so that they can make scientific discoveries which they can sell, not just for purely academic reasons.
facilities 设施，设备	noun	the various buildings and equipment available for use at a certain place	The medical facilities at my local hospital are fantastic; all of the beds are brand-new, the buildings are well-designed and the hospital has the latest machines for examining and testing for cancer, heart disease and other problems.
co-operate 合作，协作	verb	to work together with other people in a group towards the same goal	The team did especially well in the competition because each member co-operated really well with the other members.
build (up) 建立	verb	to develop; to make stronger (skills, abilities)	He's been building up his leadership skills since becoming manager of the team.
mature 成熟的	adjective	to be responsible, mentally and emotionally developed, to behave well	Some people think that people under the age of 18 should be given the right to vote, but I don't agree; at that age nobody is mature enough to make such big decisions.
competitive 竞争的	adjective	having or causing people to have a strong desire to compete with others	The banking industry is highly competitive – everyone is constantly striving and competing to do better than their co-workers so they can get better promotions and raises.

MODEL ANSWER 2 答案范例 2

阅读雅思考生Mike的参考答案。

Interviewer Do you think that young people should do more sport in schools today?

Mike I certainly do. I think that young people today are getting quite lazy and this is bad for their health. I'm convinced that schools put too much emphasis on academic subjects, so I firmly believe that good sports classes and sports facilities are very important.

Interviewer Do you believe that children can learn a lot from team sports?

Mike Yes, I do. Children need to learn to work in groups and co-operate as well as build leadership skills. Sport is also good for children to learn to be competitive in a mature manner. It's also very important that children keep fit and healthy. For example, it's been proven that children who learn to play team sports grow up to be more understanding and co-operative adults.

LANGUAGE STEP 1 Giving and Supporting Opinions
高分语言点 1 表达并支持你的观点

To express your opinions like a native you must:

1. Introduce your opinions and give your opinions clearly.
2. Support your opinions with reasons or examples.

首先，让我们来看一下雅思考生Sophia和Mike的参考答案。

Interviewer Do you think that children should wear a uniform to school?

Sophia Yes, I think that children in middle school and high school should wear a uniform to school. *I strongly believe that it is essential for giving children a sense of identity and unity. Young children can be very snobbish about fashion and often ridicule and pick on children who don't wear expensive or designer clothes…*

Interviewer Do you believe that children can learn a lot from team sports?

Mike Yes, I do. *Children need to learn to work in groups and co-operate as well as build leadership skills. Sport is also good for children to learn to be competitive in a mature manner. It's also very important that children keep fit and healthy. For example, it's been proven that children who learn to play team sports grow up to be more understanding and co-operative adults.*

Giving and Supporting Opinions is a basic skill you'll need for any type of IELTS Part Three answer. You should use this skill in every one of your EQ Part Three lessons and consider it as a basic requirement for all native speaker discussions.

Notice how Sophia and Mike both follow their introduction of opinion with reasons and examples. Sophia says that she believes that children in middle school and high school should wear a school uniform because:

"...it is essential for giving children a sense of identity and unity."

"...children can be very snobbish about fashion and often ridicule and pick on children who don't wear expensive or designer clothes."

When asked whether university students should wear a uniform Sophia says that she thinks they certainly should not and gives her reason:

"We are all adults...we should have the freedom to choose what we want to wear..."

Remember to state your opinion and then give a reason or example to back it up.

It's a simple formula:

- opinion
- reasons / examples

Exercise 25.1: Matching

Match sentence halves 1-6 (opinions) with sentence halves A-F (reasons / examples).

1. The law that people can't steal is a good law...
2. Charities are really important in a society...
3. No, it's not necessary to give expensive gifts to people...
4. It is very important that the government protect the environment more...
5. The Internet is a great educational tool because...
6. It is important all children learn to read from a young age...

A. ...because we should help people who are less fortunate than ourselves.
B. ...it gives us instant access to a wealth of information.
C. ...because clean food and water are essential for the health and happiness of a nation.
D. ...for it is the thought and intention which carries more meaning than the price of a present.
E. ...because in a competitive society a good education is vital if you want to get a good job.
F. ...because a society would not function properly if people stole other people's possessions.

LANGUAGE STEP 2 Introducing Opinions 高分语言点 2 表达观点

让我们来看一下雅思考生Sophia和Mike是如何表达自己的观点的。

Interviewer Do you think that children should wear a uniform to school?

Sophia *Yes, I think that* children in middle school and high school should wear a uniform to school. *I strongly believe that* it is essential for giving children a sense of identity and unity…

Interviewer What about in university? Should university students all wear a uniform?

Sophia *Certainly not!* We are all adults by the time we get to university, *so I believe that* we should have the freedom to choose what we want to wear and when we want to wear it…

Interviewer Do you think that young people should do more sport in schools today?

Mike *I certainly do. I think that* young people today are getting quite lazy and this is bad for their health. *I'm convinced that* schools put too much emphasis on academic subjects, *so I firmly believe* that good sports classes and sports facilities are very important.

Interviewer Do you believe that children can learn a lot from team sports?

Mike *Yes, I do.* Children need to learn to work in groups and co-operate as well as build leadership skills…

Notice how Sophia and Mike both use native speaker phrases to introduce their opinions.

Expressing agreement or disagreement with the question

- Yes, I do.
- Sure.
- Certainly.
- Certainly not!
- Absolutely not!
- Not really.
- I'm not sure I agree.

Introducing opinion phrases

- I believe that… / I think that…
- I don't believe that… / I don't think that…
- I really think that…
- I strongly believe that…
- I am of the opinion that…
- For me…
- The way I see it…

- I am convinced that…

Examples:

"A: Do you think that vegetables are an important part of a diet?

B: *Sure. I think that* they give people a lot of vitamins."

"A: Do you believe people should pay to enter public parks?

B: *No, absolutely not! The way I see it*, all public parks should be free for everyone."

Exercise 25.2: Gap Fill

Write the words below in the correct spaces.

believe that	certainly do	convinced that	don't think
of the opinion	not really	strongly believe	

1. I really ____________ people are happier if they live in a big house rather than a small apartment. People need space to live in and space to think.
2. I ____________ that people should buy products from their own countries as much as possible, and not from outside.
3. I am ____________ it's very important to have good, friendly relationships with one's neighbours. It helps build community spirit and good feeling.
4. Yes, I ____________! I am firmly ____________ that older people should be taken care of by their sons and daughters.
5. I ____________ young people should be made to do chores in the household, because they need to spend their free time working towards their exams.
6. ____________. I think that animals have their rights too and shouldn't be used in scientific experiments.

LANGUAGE STEP 3 Supporting Your Opinions
高分语言点 3 论述你的观点

让我们来看一下雅思考生Sophia是如何解释为什么学生应该穿校服的。

Sophia ...I strongly believe that it *is essential for* giving children a sense of identity and unity...

Supporting a positive opinion

Look at these other positive phrases to say why something is a good thing:

- It's good for + verb-ing
- It's essential for + verb-ing
- It's vital for + verb-ing
- It's very important for / that + verb-ing
- People should all + verb

- It gives us the opportunity / freedom to + verb
- People should make an effort to + verb

Examples:

"I really think that *people should all* try and eat healthily."

"A solid education *is essential for finding* a good job."

"Better public transport *gives us the opportunity to stop* using private vehicles which hurt the environment."

Supporting a negative opinion

Look at how Sophia expresses why making students in university wear a uniform would be bad:

Sophia It would certainly be inappropriate to make university students wear a uniform, and incredibly patronising too!

Look at these other negative phrases to say why something is a bad thing:

- It would be inappropriate to + verb / for + noun
- It could have a bad effect on...
- It's not good for society if people...
- It's unfair to + verb / somebody...
- It's not necessary to + verb
- It's unethical to + verb
- It's unreasonable to + verb

Examples:

"I'm convinced that *it would be inappropriate to make* children under the age of 12 work for a living."

"I feel that *it's unfair to* deny people healthcare just because they are poor."

"For me, *it's not necessary to* make education free because it's already extremely cheap."

Exercise 25.3: Multiple Choice

Choose the appropriate phrases from the choices below to complete the sentences.

1. ____________ make an effort to learn other languages because that is what enables countries to communicate openly.

   A. People should all　　B. It gives us the opportunity to　　C. It's unreasonable to

2. Smoking should be banned from public places because ____________ non-smokers to make them breathe in dangerous smoke.

   A. it's unethical to　　B. it's not good for society if　　C. it's unfair to

3. ____________ people are allowed total freedom of information because their minds could be corrupted by false news stories.
   A. It could have a bad effect on B. It's not good for society if C. It's unfair to
4. ____________ keep animals as pets because animals deserve to enjoy their native habitats.
   A. People should all B. It's important that people C. It's unethical to
5. ____________ to lie to people because we expect to be trusted and to be able to trust others.
   A. It's very unreasonable B. It's not necessary to C. It's vital to
6. ____________ the stability and safety of society that everyone is treated equally before the law.
   A. It's very important that B. It's vital for C. It's essential

EXTRA LANGUAGE POINT Techniques for Supporting Your Opinions
补充语言点 用来支持个人观点的技巧

现在我们来学习一些技巧，这些技巧可以帮助你支持自己的观点。

Here are some really useful techniques for supporting your opinions.

Examples

- For example…
- For instance…
- Let me give an example…

For example:

"*For example*, whenever I go to a bar there are always people smoking and I breathe in their smoke. This makes me a smoker even though I don't want to be."

Common sense

- Everyone knows…
- It's common knowledge that…

For example:

"*It's common knowledge that* birds do not enjoy being trapped in cages!"

Statistics

- Use numbers.
- Use figures to support an argument.

You don't have to know lots of complicated statistics, but if you do know some very general figures to back up what you want to say, then use them.

For example:

"Traffic should be reduced in Beijing. *Over 1,000* new cars go onto the roads every day. This is becoming a major problem."

Expert Opinion

- According to...
- To quote...
- The book says...
- I heard / read / saw somewhere that...

For example:

"*According to* many experts, global warming is not actually scientifically proven to exist!"

Exercise 25.4: Matching

Match sentences 1-5 with their supporting opinions types A-D.

1. The latest research says that more women smoke in the UK than men.
2. It is common knowledge that big cities are more expensive to live in than country towns.
3. To quote Robert Frost, "Forgive me my nonsense, as I also forgive the nonsense of those that think they talk sense."
4. I heard that almost 35% of 8th graders in the USA said they'd participated in musical activities in school.
5. Everyone knows that children are naturally naughty and need to be strictly disciplined.
6. Let me give you an example: only last week, I saw two young people helping an old lady across the street – therefore, I do believe that young people today are caring and kind.
7. Of course global warming is a problem! Global temperatures will rise between 1°C and 6 °C this century alone!
8. I don't think much more can be done to help the elderly. I remember reading somewhere that the population of almost every country is aging rapidly, so that soon the elderly will far outnumber the young – we won't be able to afford to do more for them.

A. Giving an example or personal anecdote to support an argument.
B. Stating that something is common sense to support an argument.
C. Using statistics to support an argument.
D. Stating expert opinion to support an argument.

For more practice, please go to: www.EQEnglish.com

Formula 26: Evaluating Two Different Opinions

AIMS 学习目标

In this lesson you'll master the Formula for Evaluating Two Different Opinions.

你将学会如何回答雅思口试第三部分的常见问题，比如：

- Why do some people think that university life is the best stage in life while others disagree?
- Give reasons why some people hold the opinion that it is acceptable to eat meat, while others insist on being vegetarians.
- Why are there many people in society who prefer to do sports in their free time, while there are others who would rather go shopping?
- Suggest reasons why some people prefer to travel in groups, yet others prefer to travel alone.

THE FORMULA 高分公式

To evaluate two different opinions, you should:

Answer Order

- Talk about which types of people hold which opinions.
- State why different people hold these opinions.

Language Steps

1. Talk about quantities of people and types of people in society. ("*The vast majority of working people* think..." / "*Most young students* believe..." / "*Many elderly people* are of the opinion that...")
2. Use transitional words and phrases to compare different opinions. ("Some people believe that city life is stressful, *while* others find it exciting." / "Many elderly people like to do calm leisurely sports, *yet* there are some who still enjoy strenuous exercise.")
3. Use adjectives and adjective phrases to say why people have different opinions. ("They think it is *more convenient* than..." / "They believe it is *more rewarding*..." / "They feel that it is *better for*...")

NATIVE SPEAKER WORDS 1 英语母语词汇 1

让我们来学习一些英语母语词汇，这些词汇对于回答该类型的问题非常有用，并且能够帮助你理解下面的答案范例。

Native Speaker Word	Part of Speech	Definition	Example Sentence
appealing 有吸引力的，引人注意的	adjective	something that is attractive or interesting	I can't understand why people like camping; sleeping in the middle of nowhere, with no showers or decent food isn't appealing to me!
footage 镜头，片段	noun	scenes from a film or recorded by a video camera, usually scenes from news reports or documentaries	The footage of the war in Vietnam was shocking! It was horrible to see so many people dying and suffering.
report 报告	verb	to recount or tell the facts of an event, often relating to newspaper, radio and TV news	The journalist reported the sad news of the disaster, while footage of the plane wreck was shown behind him. It was a moving moment.
launch 发射	verb	to take off (often used for rockets and spaceships)	When the rocket was launched everyone was amazed at the amount of smoke and fire from its engines.
astronaut 宇航员	noun	a spaceman; a person who travels in a spacecraft from earth into space and back again	You have to have a lot of skill and courage to be an astronaut – travelling into space is extremely dangerous.
spectator 观众	noun	similar to audience, but can also refer to people who watch other things, such as sports, fights etc (Audience only refers to people who watch performances, plays, movies etc.)	All the spectators were really impressed with the outdoor concert!
visual 视觉的，直观的	adjective	related to seeing (It is often used in contrast to "audio" – related to hearing – or things that you can only think of, but cannot see.)	I am a visual learner – I must see new words written down, otherwise I find them too hard to remember.
charm 魅力	noun	a quality that makes you attractive to someone or something	James Bond 007 is a successful spy not only because he is intelligent and resourceful, but also because of his charm – he can make any woman tell him everything he wants to know.
soothing 安抚的，使人宽心的	adjective	something that is relaxing or eases pain or tension	Some classical music is very soothing. It helps me wind down after a hard day at work.
distract 分散，使分心	verb	to make someone stop giving their attention to something	I hate it when I am trying to study and people play loud music or talk loudly. It really distracts me.

MODEL ANSWER 1 答案范例 1

阅读雅思考生Sophia的参考答案。

Interviewer Why do some people prefer listening to the news on the radio, while others prefer TV news?

Sophia Today, not many people like listening to the radio. Pretty much everyone has a television now. For most people televisions are very appealing because you can actually see real footage of what's being reported – for example, when I saw a report on the launching of a space rocket, I could actually see the rocket take off, the astronauts inside and all the spectators on the ground. So TV is a powerful source of news.

However, there are many people that don't share the same opinion. While some say the television is better, more visual and more modern, others feel the radio has a certain charm, and is more soothing and relaxing. It also depends on the lifestyle of the individual – many taxi drivers love listening to the radio because it is a very convenient way to hear news and plays without distracting them from driving.

NATIVE SPEAKER WORDS 2 英语母语词汇 2

让我们来学习一些英语母语词汇，这些词汇对于回答该类型的问题非常有用，并且能够帮助你理解下面的答案范例。

Native Speaker Word	Part of Speech	Definition	Example Sentence
Buddhist 佛教徒，和尚	noun	person who follows the Buddhist faith; a person who believes in the philosophy taught by the Buddha and / or his followers	There are many different Buddhist temples and shrines in China.
animal rights 动物权利		the belief that animals have certain rights that cannot be taken away, such as the right to not to be mistreated	Many years ago, people treated animals quite badly but I think that people nowadays are much more aware that animals should be treated well and now respect most animal rights.
movement 运动	noun	a group of people with a particular set of (usually political) aims	In the West the feminist movement was at its strongest during the 1970s, and it did succeed in winning more equality for women.
concerted effort 齐心协力，一致努力		a determined and serious attempt to do something	He was really worried that he might be fired, so recently he has been making a concerted effort to not be late, do a good job and go home later than usual.

续表

Native Speaker Word	Part of Speech	Definition	Example Sentence
ethics 道德，伦理	noun	set beliefs or social codes which promote good behaviour for the benefit of society, what we think of as "right" and "wrong"	Society's ethics are constantly changing, that's why lots of behaviour that was unacceptable to my parents' generation is now acceptable.
ethical 伦理的，道德的	adjective	something which is good moral behaviour or behaviour or beliefs which are good for society	Some people believe that eating meat is totally unethical because animals deserve the right to life.

MODEL ANSWER 2 答案范例 2

阅读雅思考生Mike的参考答案。

Interviewer Why do some people choose not to eat meat?

Mike That's an interesting question. In my country nearly everyone enjoys eating meat, though not in large quantities. However, some people, mainly Buddhists and young people who are members of animal rights movements, make a concerted effort not to eat meat for ethical reasons – they believe animals have the same right as us humans to live full, natural lives, so we humans should not eat animals. Although some scientists say it is important to eat meat for health reasons, others claim that if you eat the right vegetables and fruits, eating meat is not necessary to maintain a good standard of health.

LANGUAGE STEP 1 Quantities of People & Types of People 高分语言点 1 描述人物的数量和类型

让我们来看一下雅思考生Sophia和Mike是如何描述人物的数量和类型的。

Sophia Today, *not many people* like listening to the radio. *Pretty much everyone* has a television now. For *most people* televisions are very appealing because...However, there are *many people* that don't share the same opinion...It also depends on the lifestyle of the individual – *many taxi drivers* love listening to the radio because it is a very convenient way to hear news and plays without distracting them from driving.

Mike ...In my country *nearly everyone* enjoys eating meat, though not in large quantities. However, *some people*, mainly *Buddhists* and *young people who are members of animal rights movements*, make a concerted effort not to eat meat for ethical reasons...Although *some scientists* say it is important to eat meat for health reasons...

When evaluating two different opinions we should start by saying how many and what types of people hold those opinions.

Quantities of people

- nearly everyone
- almost everybody
- the (vast) majority of + types of people
- most + types of people
- a large percentage of + types of people
- some + types of people
- a few + types of people
- a handful of + types of people

Types of people – ages

- elderly people / retired people / the older generation
- working people
- office workers
- students
- adolescents / teenagers
- married couples

Types of people – behaviour

- very active people / sporty people / energetic people
- religious people
- animal lovers / food lovers
- English teachers
- lazy people

Types of people – specific

- People with + adjective noun combination
  "*People with creative talent* believe..."
  "*People with strong political views* think..."
  "*People with a lot of energy* like to..."

- People who have…
  "*People who have* an interest in art…"
  "*People who have* lots of free time…"
  "*People who have* their own pets…"

More examples:

"*Most people with a lot of energy* like to regularly play team and individual sports."

"*A handful of people who have lots of free time* actually decide to do volunteer work."

"*A large percentage of teenagers* have problems communicating properly with their parents and teachers."

Exercise 26.1: Gap Fill & Matching

Write the words below in the correct spaces and then match sentences 1-6 with sentences A-F.

a lot of	large percentage	most
political views	people with a lot of	vast majority

1. The ____________ of older people...
2. ____________ animal lovers...
3. ____________ students...
4. A ____________ of office workers...
5. People with strong ____________ think...
6. ____________ creative talent believe in...

A. ...tend to enjoy parties and social occasions.
B. ...teaching children about art and drama and philosophy.
C. ...don't really like to listen to dance music.
D. ...that the USA should never have invaded Iraq.
E. ...believe they should get paid overtime.
F. ...can't accept people doing cosmetic tests on dogs and cats.

LANGUAGE STEP 2 Transitional Words & Phrases
高分语言点 2 连接词和短语

让我们来看一下雅思考生Sophia和Mike使用了哪些连接词和短语。

Sophia ...*However*, there are many people that don't share the same opinion. *While* some say the television is better, more visual and more modern, others feel the radio has a certain charm, and is more soothing and relaxing. It *also* depends on the lifestyle of the individual...

Mike ...*However*, some people...make a concerted effort not to eat meat for ethical reasons...*Although* some scientists say it is important to eat meat for health reasons, others claim that if you eat the right vegetables and fruits, eating meat is not necessary to maintain a good standard of health.

When talking about different types of people and the opinions they have, you should use transitional words and phrases to link your ideas together.

Here are some of the most useful transitional words and phrases:

- while

  "Some people believe that city life is stressful, *while* others find the buzz and energy of living in a city exciting."

- yet

  "Some people are of the opinion that computer games can help children learn certain skills, *yet* other people think that they are just a waste of time."

- however

  "People who believe in animal rights, think that we should not wear leather shoes or animal skin clothes. *However*, people who think that we are superior to animals, believe we have the right to use them as we wish."

- although

  "*Although* some people hold the opinion that war is wrong, others believe that there are sometimes good reasons why countries should go to war."

  "Some believe that there are sometimes good reasons why countries should go to war, *although* others hold the opinion that war is wrong."

- conversely

  "The majority of people feel that living in an apartment is very convenient. *Conversely*, others believe that living in a house is a better option."

- on the one hand...on the other hand

  "*On the one hand*, there are old people that do a lot of exercise; *on the other hand*, there are many elderly people that prefer to sit and read, or play board games."

Exercise 26.2: Multiple Choice

Choose the appropriate transitional words or phrases from the choices below to complete the sentences.

1. ____________ some working people prefer to eat in restaurants each evening, there are others that don't mind cooking when they get back home after work.

   A. However B. Yet C. While

2. ____________, many animal lovers don't like the idea of pigs, cows, chickens etc being killed in a way which makes the animals suffer or feel scared, ____________, most farmers aren't cruel people, and they are just doing their jobs for the money they need.

   A. Although, but

   B. On the one hand, on the other hand

   C. However, still

3. ____________ many young people admire sports stars, there are others who don't really get very enthusiastic about these kinds of national heroes.

   A. Although B. However C. Conversely

4. A lot of people feel that living in a developing city is a thrilling experience, ____________ many commuters think it can be quite stressful and exhausting.

   A. yet B. on the one hand C. conversely

5. Many parents and students feel that education, from schooling to university, should be paid for by the government. ____________, others feel that it is the parents' responsibility to provide for their sons and daughters.

   A. While　　B. However　　C. Despite

6. Some do not believe in capital punishment because they think that it's wrong to take the life of another human, even if he is a criminal. ____________, others feel that some criminals, especially murderers, deserve to be killed.

   A. Although　　B. On the one hand　　C. Conversely

LANGUAGE STEP 3 Adjectives & Adjective Phrases to Say Why People Have Different Opinions
高分语言点 3 用形容词和形容词短语描述人们为何持有不同的观点

让我们来看一下雅思考生Sophia和Mike使用了哪些形容词和形容词短语来描述人们为何持有不同的观点。

Sophia ...For most people televisions are very *appealing* because you can actually see real footage of what's being reported...So TV is a *powerful* source of news...others feel the radio has a certain charm, and is more *soothing* and *relaxing*...many taxi drivers love listening to the radio because it is a very *convenient* way to hear news and plays...

Mike ...Although some scientists say it is *important* to eat meat for health reasons, others claim that if you eat the *right* vegetables and fruits, eating meat is *not necessary* to maintain a good *standard* of health.

When people weigh up two different opinions they often describe why these people have those opinions using adjectives or adjective phrases in the following structures.

Some people think / believe / enjoy / prefer X because it's + adjective

You may use the following adjectives and phrases:

- convenient
- important / necessary / vital
- interesting / fascinating / stimulating / exciting / inspiring
- beneficial
- healthy / better for you
- rewarding
- challenging
- informative
- unnecessary / unimportant / a waste of time

Examples:

"Many famous people believe it's really *convenient* to own a private aeroplane."

"A lot of young people today think it's very *rewarding* to go overseas for a year."

Some people think X is good / better / important / useful for + verb-ing

You may use the following verb-ing phrases:

- cultivating one's mind
- developing a greater sense of social responsibility
- teaching people to empathise with each other more
- maintaining social control
- keeping people happy and content
- establishing positive international relations
- keeping our natural environment cleaner
- contributing to making society a better place for poor people

Examples:

"They believe that this experience *is good for cultivating one's mind*."

"They consider learning more than one language as a good thing because it *is important for establishing positive international relations*."

Exercise 26.3: Gap Fill

Write the words and phrases below in the correct spaces.

better for
much wider variety
necessary for
it is very important that
because it's a very therapeutic hobby
rewarding and fulfilling
for establishing positive international relations
I think almost everyone agrees that it's important
energetic
more convenient
while younger people like
is a better place for relaxing
keep our natural environment cleaner

1. Some people prefer to go to the beach on holiday, rather than to the countryside, because, for them, the beach ____________.
2. Older people, like my grandmother, often enjoy knitting ____________, while younger people like to get into more ____________ hobbies in their free time.
3. A lot of people choose to use public transportation only because it helps ____________.
4. Many people argue we should all have more paid holidays. However, most of us think that ____________ the citizens of a developing country work especially hard to help the country grow.
5. Most countries believe that good communication is important ____________. Yet, there still exist a few countries that don't seem to want to co-operate or communicate openly.

6. There are a few young people today who believe that working for a charity organisation to help the poor is a ____________ experience. Yet, there are others that still feel that having a proper, well-paid job is ____________ gaining stability and a secure life.
7. Some people prefer to shop in small, more friendly local stores, while others like to shop in big supermarkets and malls because there's a ____________ of goods in stock and it's a lot ____________.
8. Quite a few adolescents in England don't eat meat because they say it's cruel to kill animals. Other people, however, feel that eating meat is ____________ maintaining a healthy diet and a strong body.
9. The older generation usually prefer quiet family gatherings, ____________ loud, crazy parties because these are great places to meet new friends!
10. ____________ to teach social responsibility in schools, because this is essential for making society a better place. However, there are some who firmly believe it is the parents' responsibility.

For more practice, please go to: www.EQEnglish.com

Formula 27: Agreeing and Disagreeing

AIMS 学习目标

In this lesson you'll master the Formula for Agreeing and Disagreeing.

你将学会如何回答雅思口试第三部分的常见问题，比如：

- Do you agree that famous people should be used to advertise products on television?
- Would you agree that people should have four-day working weeks and three-day weekends?
- Do you agree or disagree that office workers should all wear very formal clothes?
- Are you in agreement with the opinion that many young people today care too much about fashion and not enough about social responsibility?

THE FORMULA 高分公式

To agree and disagree, you should:

Answer Order

Decide what your opinion is about the question the examiner asks.

1. If you agree, you should:
   - State your agreement.
   - Give reasons why you agree.
2. If you only partially agree / disagree, you should:
   - Say to what extent you agree then state your disagreement.
   - Give reasons to support this.
3. If you totally disagree, you should:
   - State your strong disagreement politely.
   - Give reasons why you disagree.

Language Steps

1. Use agreement phrases. ("*I wholeheartedly agree!*" / "*I couldn't agree more!*" / "*I totally agree with you!*")
2. Use total and partial disagreement phrases. ("*I can agree with you to a point, but...*" / "*I can see your point, but...*" / "*I can agree to some extent, but have you considered...*")
3. Use cause and effect logic to support your opinion. ("I can't possibly agree, *because if we do X, then Y might happen.*" / "I'm sorry but I absolutely disagree. *If people continue to do X then it could be very bad for society...*")

NATIVE SPEAKER WORDS 1 英语母语词汇 1

让我们来学习一些英语母语词汇，这些词汇对于回答该类型的问题非常有用，并且能够帮助你理解下面的答案范例。

Native Speaker Word	Part of Speech	Definition	Example Sentence
constraint 约束，限制	noun	something which controls what you do by keeping you within particular limits	Due to financial constraints, the company could not afford to give the employees a pay rise this year.
stage 时期，阶段	noun	a period or time in life	John was at the stage in life when he really felt he wanted to get married and have children.
independent 独立的	adjective	not controlled or too influenced by other people; able to survive on one's own; self-sufficient	He enjoyed living in an apartment in Beijing on his own. He liked the independence and freedom this gave him.
unique 独特的	adjective	special, different from the usual, very rare	I would recognise your handwriting anywhere: it is really unique.

MODEL ANSWER 1 答案范例 1

阅读雅思考生Sophia的参考答案。

Interviewer Some people say that one's university years are the happiest time in life. Would you agree?

Sophia Yes, I couldn't agree more! I think that university life is probably the best stage in life because we are free from the constraints of home-life with our parents and we get the opportunity to discover the world for ourselves, much more independently than ever before. We can meet new people, study a variety of interesting subjects and learn to look after ourselves. So, I completely agree that this is by far the happiest time in our lives.

Interviewer But I've heard that many students find university life incredibly stressful and sometimes quite a tough experience?

Sophia Well, it depends on the person, but I don't think you're right in saying many students find it difficult. I am sure that some do, but the vast majority of people I know share my opinion that it's a unique and truly fantastic time in life.

NATIVE SPEAKER WORDS 2 英语母语词汇 2

让我们来学习一些英语母语词汇，这些词汇对于回答该类型的问题非常有用，并且能够帮助你理解接下来的答案范例。

Native Speaker Word	Part of Speech	Definition	Example Sentence
celebrity 名人	noun	a famous person, usually in entertainment (such as movie stars, singers, sports players; does not refer to famous politicians, businessmen etc)	Maggie Cheung became a big celebrity after her first Wang Kar Wai movie *As the Tears Go By* (1988).
deodorant 除臭剂	noun	a substance that you put on your body to prevent or hide unpleasant smells	He sweats a lot and did not put on any deodorant today, so he smells pretty bad!
make 品牌	noun	the brand, or name of the company that produces a particular product	There are many different makes of car, including BMW, Chrysler and VW.
unethical 不道德的	adjective	not conforming to social codes which are good for society	His behaviour is unethical – it is wrong to treat his family in that selfish way!
fast-paced 快节奏的，快速的	adjective	something that moves or develops quickly	Life in Guang Zhou is very fast-paced; everyone is rushing everywhere and nobody seems to slow down and relax.
take advantage of 利用		to benefit from; to use; to utilise for your own ends	He took advantage of his mother's generosity by constantly asking her to give him more money.
impose regulations on 对……加以管制		to put controls on something (used when a government or authority makes and enforces laws or rules to control people's actions)	After the riots in London, the police imposed stricter regulations on demonstrations in the city centre.
ensure 确保	verb	to make sure something is certain to happen, to guarantee	The airline is taking steps to ensure higher levels of safety on the aircraft.

MODEL ANSWER 2 答案范例 2

阅读雅思考生Mike的参考答案。

Interviewer Many believe that famous people should not be used in advertisements to sell products. Do you agree?

Mike No, I can't agree with that. I firmly believe that everyone, whether they are famous or not, has the freedom to advertise what they want. Just because Jackie Chan is a celebrity, why should this stop him advertising a deodorant or a make of camera?

Interviewer I see your point, but some people would disagree and say that advertising companies are using his public image as a famous star as a way to convince people in society to buy their product. Is that not unethical?

Mike OK, but it seems to me that many people, especially younger people, are very vulnerable, particularly in today's fast-paced competitive society, and big companies are taking advantage of them to make money from them. However, I don't think this is solely the responsibility of a famous star who advertises a product – I think the government should impose stricter regulations on advertising agencies to ensure that the information is honest and fairly presented.

LANGUAGE STEP 1 Agreement Phrases 高分语言点 1 同意的表达方法

让我们来看一下雅思考生Sophia用了什么表达方法来赞同某人的观点。

Interviewer Some people say that one's university years are the happiest time in life. Would you agree?

Sophia *Yes, I couldn't agree more!...*

Notice how Sophia expresses total agreement with the examiner's question by saying "*Yes, I couldn't agree more!*". This is a very native speaker way to say that you agree 100% with the other person.

Look at this list of similar agreement phrases:

- Yes, I agree wholeheartedly.
- I completely agree.
- I couldn't agree more!
- Sure, I, too believe that's true / the case.
- Yes, I share the same opinion.

Now look at these agreement phrases in the context of IELTS tests. Notice how the student not only expresses his agreement, but continues to elaborate on the point and gives reasons to support his agreement:

Interviewer Well, some people would argue that the best stage in life is after retirement, because life is relaxed and predictable.

Donald *Yes, I totally agree.* After a person has retired, they have gone through the challenges of their life and can finally sit back and watch life with a more relaxed attitude.

Interviewer Many say that parents should give their sons and daughters the freedom to choose their own majors. Do you agree?

Donald *Yes, I agree wholeheartedly on that point.* Too many parents think they know best what their sons and daughters should choose to study in university. This means many young people study subjects they don't like, so they don't study with passion or enthusiasm.

> 小贴士 在考试中如果你完全赞同考官的观点，你可以表示赞同，然后描述你为什么赞同并且举例说明。

Exercise 27.1: Gap Fill

Write the agreement phrases below in the correct spaces.

completely agree with   couldn't agree   agree   believe that's true

1. A: Today a lot of people feel that smoking should be banned in all public places. Do you agree?
   B: I ____________ wholeheartedly that smoking should, indeed, be prohibited in public. It's not fair that non-smokers should have to breathe in toxic smoke.
2. A: Do you agree that children should wear school uniforms?
   B: I ____________ more! Children should wear uniforms not only so that they are all "equal" when at school but also for safety purposes.
3. A: Do you agree or disagree with the view that everyone should get a university education?
   B: Sure, I ____________. A university education is beneficial for anyone, regardless of their ability or background.
4. A: Many people say that historic buildings should be carefully preserved and protected. Do you agree?
   B: Yes, I ____________ that view. Historic buildings are vital for allowing us to remember our own history and culture; they remind us who we really are.

LANGUAGE STEP 2 Total & Partial Disagreement Phrases
高分语言点 2 完全不赞同和部分不赞同的表达方法

让我们来看一下雅思考生Mike用了哪些方法表达自己不赞同某事。

Interviewer Many believe that famous people should not be used in advertisements to sell products. Do you agree?

Mike *No, I can't agree with that…*

Interviewer *I see your point, but* some people would disagree and say that advertising companies are using his public image as a famous star as a way to convince people in society to buy their product. Is that not unethical?

Mike *OK, but it seems to me* that many people, especially younger people, are very vulnerable, particularly in today's fast-paced competitive society, and big companies are taking advantage of them to make money from them…

Partial disagreement

If you don't agree with what the interviewer says, it's polite to say that you can understand the other person's opinion but you don't agree with it.

Look at this list of partial disagreement phrases:

- I can see your point, but...
- I can see what you're saying, but...
- I agree up to a point, but...
- I understand what you're saying, but I don't really agree because...
- OK, but have you considered...
- Some may hold that opinion, but I'm afraid I disagree because...

Now look at these partial agreement phrases in the context of IELTS speaking tests. Again, notice how the student not only expresses his disagreement, but continues to elaborate on the point and gives reasons to support his disagreement:

Interviewer Some parents do not accept that their sons and daughters, when in university, go to bars and night clubs on weekends. Do you agree?

Donald *Ermmm...I can agree to a point, but* I do believe that many parents here are too strict and too traditional. Whilst young people should respect their parents to a certain point, parents should also understand that life is different now to when they were young.

Interviewer But, many people would argue that young people are not responsible enough for themselves, so they need their parents to stop them from getting into danger or into trouble.

Donald *I can see what you're saying, but I don't totally agree.* I think that when we're in university we have reached an age where we should be able to make decisions for ourselves.

Total disagreement

It's also very useful to be able to express total or strong disagreement when you want to be assertive – without, however, sounding rude. When you do this, it's even more important to give good reasons why you do not agree.

Look at these total disagreement phrases:

- I absolutely disagree, because...
- I'm sorry, but I can't agree with that because...
- I can't possibly agree with that because...
- I can't share your opinion on this issue, to be honest, because...

Now look at these total disagreement phrases in the context of IELTS speaking tests. Again, notice how the student not only expresses his disagreement, but continues to elaborate on the point and gives reasons to support his disagreement:

Interviewer Do you agree that humans should not be allowed to eat animals?

Donald *I can't possibly agree with that because* humans need to eat meat, at least occasionally, to stay healthy. If we don't eat meat, we don't grow up so fast or strong and we will frequently be under the weather and suffer from minor complaints like colds and coughs.

Interviewer But many scientists say that's not true, humans can be equally healthy if they have a completely vegetarian diet.

Donald *I absolutely disagree because* I have had a few vegetarian friends over the years and they haven't been as healthy as my meat-eating friends.

Exercise 27.2: Multiple Choice

Choose the appropriate disagreement phrase from the choices below to complete the sentences.

1. Interviewer: I think that most teenagers today are very lazy about their studies. Do you agree?
   David: ____________ I don't entirely agree with you. A lot of teenagers do lack interest and motivation in their studies. But I don't think that it is because they are lazy – I think it's because their classes are boring!
   A. I can see your point
   B. I can see what you're saying, but
   C. I can't possibly agree with that because
2. Interviewer: A lot of people are of the opinion that train travel is preferable to flying? Would you agree?
   David: ____________, because many feel that train travel is a more romantic way to get around a country. However, I disagree; travelling by plane is much more convenient and efficient.
   A. I absolutely disagree
   B. I understand what you're saying
   C. I can understand why some people might think that
3. Interviewer: Some people think it's OK to hunt animals for sport. Do you agree or disagree?
   David: ____________ hunting is very cruel and painful for animals. I strongly believe we should not get enjoyment from the pain or suffering of other living things.
   A. I can possibly agree with that because
   B. I can't share your opinion on this issue, to be honest, because
   C. I can't possibly agree with that because
4. Interviewer: Some people think that every week all workers should have three-day weekends. What do you think?
   David: Ha ha...that would be wonderful! I can see why some hold that opinion,

____________ if we all had three-day weekends I don't think a country would develop and maintain a healthy economy.

A. but I'm afraid I disagree because

B. but have you considered

C. but I absolutely disagree because

5. Interviewer: Many animal rights activists believe that all zoos should be closed and the animals returned to the wild. Do you agree?

   David: ____________ without a safe enclosure many of these animals would soon die, and their species become extinct? Besides, most of these animals grew up in zoos, and so don't actually know how to look after themselves.

   A. I can't share your opinion on this issue, because

   B. I'm sorry, I can't agree with that because

   C. OK, but have you considered

6. Interviewer: Do you agree that healthcare should be provided free to everybody?

   David: ____________ I think rich people or the comfortably off should pay for their own healthcare, and not rely on the other taxpayers. It should mainly be provided free to the poor.

   A. I absolutely disagree, because

   B. I'm sorry, but I can't agree with that because

   C. I agree up to a point, but

LANGUAGE STEP 3 Cause & Effect Logic
高分语言点 3 表达因果关系

As you will have noticed in Language Steps 1 and 2, it is vitally important that, whatever your opinion, you support your point with reasons and say why you think that way.

Native English speakers will often use the logic of cause and effect to support their opinions. This means that you say what will or what would happen under the circumstances being proposed.

For example, we shouldn't just say "The rainforests should all be protected..." as this is not a very strong argument. It would be much better to say: "The rainforests should all be protected because otherwise global warming will get much worse and many animal species will be killed." This is a much more powerful and convincing statement.

Look at a few more examples of cause and effect logic supporting opinions:

Opinion	Cause & Effect Logic
I can't agree with that	because if we don't take care of the natural environment then we'll regret it in the future.
I completely agree that sports players' salaries should be reduced	because sports are ruined when there is too much money involved and teams start to resemble businesses.
I absolutely disagree with you	for if we don't invest in alternative energy the pollution will reach a dangerous level.
I can't possibly agree	that we should give children more holidays as it will have a detrimental effect on their studies.
I agree with you to a point	since I think it is unfair that some people can't go to university just because they can't afford it, but then again the country can't pay for everyone to go as we'd run out of money!
I really don't agree that women should always stay home and look after the children	because today women also have the right to earn money for the family.

Exercise 27.3: Matching

Match opinions 1-5 with cause & effect logic sentences A-E.

1. I disagree. If we keep paying workers too little…
2. I couldn't agree more. Because if we don't plant more trees and flowers in our city…
3. I'm sorry, but I hold a different opinion. It's very important to spend a lot of money on the military…
4. No, I don't agree that traditional culture is always a good thing;...
5. Yes, I totally agree that parents should send their children to kindergartens;...

A. …so the country can keep strong and defend itself if necessary.

B. …some traditions hold a country back from developing properly and bring much suffering.

C. …it won't be a bright and pretty environment for us all to live in and this will inevitably affect the happiness and spirit of its inhabitants.

D. …if they don't then children won't learn to get along with other children harmoniously.

E. …they will lose their loyalty to the company.

EXTRA LANGUAGE POINT Rhetorical Questions
补充语言点 反问句

让我们来看一下雅思考生Mike是如何使用反问句的。

Mike No, I can't agree with that. I firmly believe that everyone, whether they are famous or not, has the freedom to advertise what they want. *Just because Jackie Chan is a celebrity, why should this stop him advertising a deodorant or a make of camera?*

Sometimes, native speakers will use a rhetorical question, usually at the end of their statement, to express disagreement. A rhetorical question is a question form, but does not actually require the other person to answer. It is used as a challenge or for persuasive effect when we are disagreeing.

In the model answer extract above, notice how Mike makes his point, then ends with the question: "*Just because Jacky Chan is a celebrity, why should this stop him advertising a deodorant or a make of camera?*" Mike is actually saying: "Just because Jacky Chan is a celebrity, it doesn't mean he should not advertise things."

Look at the examples of rhetorical questions and what they actually mean in the table below.

Rhetorical Question	Meaning
Do you really think that it is fair to stop children playing computer games?	I don't think it is fair at all, that people stop children playing computer games.
How can anyone possibly suggest old age is the best time in life?	Old age is undoubtedly not the best time in life!
Given the facts I've just mentioned, how could anyone justify capital punishment?	There is no way capital punishment can be justified.
How can anyone possibly argue that exercise is bad for the health?	Everyone knows that exercise is good for everyone.

Exercise 27.4: Matching

Match rhetorical questions 1-5 with their more direct meanings A-E.

1. Considering what I've just said, how can anyone claim university life is the easiest time in life?
2. They are doing everything they can. What more could our government do to help the farmers?
3. Given these facts, how can anyone argue that testing cosmetics and medicines on innocent animals is a fair thing?
4. Given the amount of work they do, why should construction workers live in such bad

conditions and get paid so little?

5. Just because my skin is a different colour, does that mean I should be treated differently?

A. People that work on building sites deserve to be paid more and treated better.
B. I don't think I should be treated differently to other people.
C. In my opinion, there is no justification for animal testing.
D. I don't agree that life as a student is at all easy. I think it's quite a tough time.
E. I believe that they're doing everything they can to help countryside people.

For more practice, please go to: www.EQEnglish.com

Formula 28: Talking About Advantages and Disadvantages

AIMS 学习目标

In this lesson you'll master the Formula for Talking About Advantages and Disadvantages.
你将学会如何回答雅思口试第三部分的常见问题，比如：

- What are the advantages and disadvantages of buying and using a motor car?
- Tell me about the advantages of keeping pets like dogs and cats in the home.
- Describe some of the disadvantages of big city life.

THE FORMULA 高分公式

To talk about advantages and disadvantages, you should:

Answer Order

There are three types of questions the examiner is likely to ask you:

1. What are the advantages of X?
   - Talk about two or three advantages of X and give reasons and examples.
2. What are the disadvantages of X?
   - Talk about two or three disadvantages of X and give reasons and examples.
3. What are the advantages and disadvantages of X?
   - Talk about two advantages and disadvantages of X and give reasons and examples.

Language Steps

1. Use introducing advantages phrases. ("*One of the main advantages of X is...*" / "*Another major advantage is...*" / "*A good thing about X is...*")
2. Use introducing disadvantages phrases and highlighting bad points phrases. ("*One principal drawback of X is...*" / "*One big disadvantage is...*" / "*...X is detrimental to one's health...*" / "*X is unsuitable for...*")
3. Use transitional words and phrases properly to weigh up advantages and disadvantages of something. ("*While* plane travel is very convenient, it can be very expensive." / "*On the one hand*, fast food can be great when you are in a rush; *on the other hand*, it is not very good for your health.")

NATIVE SPEAKER WORDS 1 英语母语词汇 1

让我们来学习一些英语母语词汇，这些词汇对于回答该类型的问题非常有用，并且能够帮助你理解下面的答案范例。

Native Speaker Word	Part of Speech	Definition	Example Sentence
stressful 有压力的	adjective	describing something that can make someone worried or experience a lot of tension	His day job is very stressful; he has too much work to do in too short a time.
manage your time 管理你的时间		to be very organised with your work tasks, your hobbies and interests and your free time	Sarah is very efficient; she works really hard, but also makes enough time to go to the gym, paint and do all sorts of other hobbies. She manages her time very well.
routine 惯例，常规，例行公事	noun	the general schedule or order in which you do things in a day	Her daily routine is fairly normal: she wakes up, has a shower, gets dressed, goes to work, returns home, has dinner, then watches movies with her boyfriend.
smart 正式的	adjective	presentable, well-dressed	Jason is very smart this week – he has been wearing a suit to work every day.
work-from-home job 在家办公		a job where you don't have to go to a workplace or office but work at home	The advantage of being a writer is that it is a work-from-home job.

MODEL ANSWER 1 答案范例 1

阅读雅思考生Sophia的参考答案。

Interviewer What are the advantages of doing a job where you can work from home?

Sophia One of the main advantages of working from home is the amount of freedom you have. You don't have to worry about travelling to work on public transport, which can be very stressful, and you can often manage your time more efficiently according to your own routine. Another good thing about working from home is that you don't have to get changed into smart clothes or uncomfortable office shoes.

Interviewer Are there any disadvantages to working from home?

Sophia Yes, many work-from-home jobs don't pay as well as full-time jobs in a workplace. A lot of work-from-home jobs are part-time or offer a few hours' work per day, rather than standard salaries that pay a fixed amount every month. So, they are not as secure and stable as most other jobs.

NATIVE SPEAKER WORDS 2 英语母语词汇 2

让我们来学习一些英语母语词汇，这些词汇对于回答该类型的问题非常有用，并且能够帮助你理解下面的答案范例。

Native Speaker Word	Part of Speech	Definition	Example Sentence
poorly-paid 低收入的	adjective	describing low-paid, paid little money	Working as a waiter or waitress is often very poorly-paid.
physical 体力的，身体的	adjective	describing something which involves or is related to using your body	The advantage of physical work is that you can exercise your body at the same time as working.
open air 户外，野外		outside, not in an enclosed space, usually with a sense of freedom	I'm going camping in the countryside this summer; it's going to be great to spend so much time in the open air.

MODEL ANSWER 2 答案范例 2

阅读雅思考生Mike的参考答案。

Interviewer What are the advantages and disadvantages of working outdoors?

Mike That's a good question! I think it really depends on what kind of job you have outdoors. In general, most outdoor jobs are quite physical, so I think that they can help people keep fit and healthy and strong as well as being outside in the open air. On the other hand, it can be awful to work outside because you may have to work in terrible weather conditions like rain, snow and extreme cold. Outdoor work in my country is generally quite poorly-paid, so that's certainly another disadvantage.

LANGUAGE STEP 1 Introducing Advantages Phrases 高分语言点 1 描述优点的表达方法

让我们来看一下雅思考生Sophia是如何描述优点的。

Sophia *One of the main advantages of working from home is* the amount of freedom you have...*Another good thing about working from home is* that you don't have to get changed into smart clothes or uncomfortable office shoes...

When you introduce the advantages of something, you should use a variety of expressions so that you really sound like a native.

Here are some really common and useful introducing advantages phrases:

- one of the main advantages of
- one of the main benefits of
- one of the major strong points of
- the great advantage of
- a key advantage of
- a really / very good thing about
- another good thing about
- another advantage of
- one more great thing about

All of the above phrases can be completed with the following:

- verb-ing / noun is you can...
- verb-ing / noun is that you're able to...
- verb-ing / noun is you don't have to...
- verb-ing / noun is you don't need to...

Look at the table below for examples of the above phrases combined:

Introducing Phrase	Object / Activity	Advantage
The main advantage of	cycling to work	is that you don't pollute the air.
Another key advantage of	riding your bike	is that it's a good form of exercise.
One of the major strong points of	eating in restaurants	is you don't have to do the washing-up.
One more great thing	about eating out	is you can taste a wide variety of different dishes.
A very good thing about	mobile phones	is you can get in touch with anyone, anytime.
The great advantage of	the electronic dictionary	is that it's so light and portable so you can carry it everywhere.

Exercise 28.1: Matching

Match the introducing phrases with the objects / activities and their advantages.

Introducing Phrase	Object / Activity	Advantage
The main advantage of	living in the countryside	is you can travel to work quickly and cheaply.
The good thing about	working in an office	is that you can take peaceful walks and breathe fresh air.
One of the main benefits of	having regular holidays	is that you are able to keep up with the latest fashions, go to clubs, bars and restaurants.
A major advantage of	living in cities	is you can sit in a comfortable chair all day and drink tea!
A key advantage of	taking the sub-way	is that you can give the mind and body a rest from the stress of work.

EXTRA LANGUAGE POINT 1 Positive Adjectives
补充语言点 1 表示积极意义的形容词

让我们来看一下雅思考生Sophia和Mike用了哪些表示积极意义的形容词。

Sophia ...Another *good* thing about working from home is that you don't have to get changed into *smart* clothes or uncomfortable office shoes...A lot of work-from-home jobs are part-time or offer a few hours' work per day, rather than *standard* salaries that pay a *fixed* amount every month. So, they are not as *secure* and *stable* as most other jobs.

Mike That's a *good* question!...In general, most outdoor jobs are quite physical, so I think that they can help people keep *fit* and *healthy* and *strong* as well as being outside in the open air...

When talking about why something has certain advantages or strong points, you should use positive adjectives to help support your claims.

Look at the following table of useful positive adjectives:

Activities	Objects	Habits / Customs	Laws
rewarding	practical	socially beneficial	reliable

续表

Activities	Objects	Habits / Customs	Laws
challenging	environmentally friendly	sensible	impartial
inspiring	sophisticated	educational	just
refreshing	good for society	culturally rich	sound
healthy	aesthetically pleasing	provides a sense of community	supportive
exhilarating	convenient	familial	fair
interesting	portable	atmospheric	can help maintain social stability

Examples:

"The main advantage of the laptop computer is that it is *portable*."

"The one good thing about the new advertising laws is that they protect the consumer and so I think they are *just* and *sensible*."

"The major advantage of keeping our national customs is that they can *provide us with a sense of community* and identity."

LANGUAGE STEP 2 Introducing Disadvantages & Highlighting Bad Points Phrases 高分语言点 2 描述缺点或不利的表达方法

让我们来看一看下面的表达方法。

To introduce disadvantages or highlight bad points about X, you should first use some of the following phrases:

- the main disadvantage of
- a / the bad thing about
- a major disadvantage of
- one drawback of
- a / the one bad point about / of
- another disadvantage of

Then use one of the following:

- verb-ing / noun is you can / might / may / could
- verb-ing / noun is that it can / might / may / could / is possible that it may

Then use one of the following:

- to damage / harm
- to cause illness / health problems / stress / harm to

- to get damaged / get stolen / get broken easily / get cheated by / get addicted to / get obsessed with / get bored with / get frustrated by
- to not be so good for
- to be problematic for
- to be inconvenient because / for
- to be confusing
- to give a bad impression of somebody / something to somebody

Examples:

"The main disadvantage of working outside is that it might cause health problems in winter."

"The bad thing about owning an expensive bike is that it could get stolen."

"One drawback of being a computer programmer is that the work can be quite confusing sometimes."

"The one bad point about being outspoken and confident in class is that some people may think you are arrogant."

Exercise 28.2: Gap Fill

Write the words below in the correct spaces.

annoying	can get stressful
can give a very bad impression to others	can get complicated
get bothered by	inconvenient for
might get bored	bored
might get stolen	not good for
the bad thing	the disadvantage of
too obsessed with	

1. A big disadvantage of student life is that it ____________ near exam time.
2. A major disadvantage of being very rich is that you might get ____________ money and possessions, and this ____________.
3. A bad thing about parties is that you ____________ with crazy drunken people, and this is very ____________ if you want to relax and have an intelligent conversation.
4. One drawback of being a celebrity is that you might ____________ the media all the time, and this is ____________ your private life.
5. ____________ living in the suburbs is that it can be ____________ using public transport to commute into town.
6. ____________ about owning a bicycle is that it ____________ if you lock it up in some areas of the city.
7. Although it is a challenging profession, the bad part about being an engineer is that with some projects it ______________________ at times. This means it can be a tiring job.

EXTRA LANGUAGE POINT 2 Negative Adjectives
补充语言点 2 带有负面意义的形容词

让我们来看一下雅思考生Mike用了哪些带有负面意义的形容词。

Mike …On the other hand, it can be *awful* to work outside because you may have to work in *terrible* weather conditions like rain, snow and extreme cold. Outdoor work in my country is generally quite *poorly-paid*, so that's certainly another disadvantage.

When talking about disadvantages or drawbacks it's good to use a range of adjectives to help explain what these are.

Activities	Objects	Habits / Customs	Laws
dull / boring	not user-friendly	out-dated	unfair
tiring / exhausting	overly-complicated	old-fashioned	overly-restrictive
time-consuming	unattractive	a little ridiculous	oppressive
difficult	fragile	unhealthy	narrow-minded
repetitive	impractical	environmentally unfriendly	discriminatory
poorly-paid	poorly-made	anti-social	vague
unstable	over-priced	annoying	a little harsh
counter-productive	low-quality	a bit sexist	unjust

Examples:

"The disadvantage of the new subway system is the cards – they are all disposable and made of plastic and therefore this is quite *environmentally unfriendly*."

"The drawback of going to the gym is that it's quite *exhausting* after you've done a long day's work."

"The bad thing about the legal system there is that sometimes the laws are very *oppressive*."

LANGUAGE STEP 3 Transitional Words & Phrases
高分语言点 3 连接词和短语

让我们来看一下雅思考生Sophia和Mike使用了哪些连接词和短语。

Sophia …A lot of work-from-home jobs are part-time or offer a few hours' work per day, *rather than* standard salaries that pay a fixed amount every month. *So*, they are not as secure and stable as most other jobs.

Mike ...people keep fit and healthy and strong as well as being outside in the open air. *On the other hand*, it can be awful to work outside because you may have to work in terrible weather conditions like rain, snow and extreme cold...

Sometimes the interviewer will ask you about the advantages and disadvantages at the same time. You should try to show that there are good points and bad points, weighing them up with a transitional word or phrase.

Look at the following transitional words and phrases:

- although
- however
- while
- yet at the same time
- while at the same time
- having said that
- then again
- on the one hand...on the other hand

Examples:

"The main disadvantage of eating in restaurants is that it's expensive, *although* it can be exciting and fun to eat out every now and again."

"A great thing about computers is that you can buy a computer now that was state-of-the-art only a few months ago quite cheaply. *Then again*, this means that the computer you buy now will soon be out-dated."

"The telephone is incredibly useful, *while at the same time* it can be quite annoying when you want to be left alone."

"Being into fashion can be a really good thing, *yet at the same time* it can sometimes be a bit silly if people spend too much time thinking about fashion."

"Going to see sports games can be fun and exciting and exhilarating. *Having said that*, it can be annoying to be in a crowded stadium with lots of people."

"*On the one hand* contact sports are a great way to exercise, but *on the other hand* they can be quite dangerous."

Exercise 28.3: Matching

Match sentence halves 1-7 with sentence halves A-G.

1. One drawback of having holidays in the countryside is that there are lots of mosquitoes in the early summer...
2. While there are many disadvantages to getting old, like suffering poorer health, for example...

3. The good thing about hot, sunny weather in my town is that you can go to the beach and relax in the sunshine...
4. On the one hand, working for a small company means that you don't get all the benefits and security you get when you work for a large firm...
5. The advantage of the motor car is that it's good for getting to work when you live far from the city centre...
6. The one bad thing about having visitors to your home, is that you have to wash a lot of dishes after they leave!...
7. The key advantage of going abroad to study is to improve one's academic experience and one's education,...

A. ...However, the bad thing is that it's fairly humid and uncomfortable if you have to work long hours outside.

B. ...Yet at the same time this contributes to a lot of air pollution.

C. ...Having said that, it's fairly easy to buy mosquito repellent, and it certainly is worth getting out of the city and enjoying natural beauty.

D. ...On the other hand, you tend to get more opportunities for promotion and are given more responsibility.

E. ...Then again, the great thing about receiving guests is the conversation and laughter that we all have when we eat and drink with friends.

F. ...it's also a very peaceful and contemplative stage in life.

G. ...although it can still be difficult to find a job when you return to your country.

For more practice, please go to: www.EQEnglish.com

Formula 29: Expressing Importance and Priority

AIMS 学习目标

In this lesson you'll master the Formula for Expressing Importance & Priority.
你将学会如何回答雅思口试第三部分的常见问题，比如：

- What are the most important things to bear in mind if you are planning an overseas trip?
- Which subjects, sports, activities or lessons do you believe to have the highest priority in a child's education?
- What environmental concerns today should be addressed most urgently?

THE FORMULA 高分公式

To express importance & priority, you should:

Answer Order

- Say how important you think X is.
- Compare the importance of X with other things.
- Explain why you think this.

Language Steps

1. Use native speaker importance phrases and adverbs of degree to introduce your opinion. ("Yes, computers *play a big role* in our lives." / "Indeed, this is an *important issue* for our country today." / "I think economics is *especially important* in today's society.")
2. Use comparatives and superlatives to say why one thing is more important than another. ("Personality is *more important than* physical appearance." / "It's *more valuable* to teach children maths *than* art.")
3. Use expressions to say why something is important. ("Gymnastics is *essential for* maintaining a supple body." / "Reading is *crucial for* developing good vocabulary.")

NATIVE SPEAKER WORDS1 英语母语词汇1

让我们来学习一些英语母语词汇，这些词汇对于回答该类型的问题非常有用，并且能够帮助你理解下面的答案范例。

Native Speaker Word	Part of Speech	Definition	Example Sentence
drama 戏剧，话剧	noun	a performing art involving acting, especially a school subject	Drama classes are really fun. We are putting on the Shakespeare play *A Midsummer Night's Dream* and I'm going to be acting the role of Theseus.
sound 可靠的，合理的，正确的	adjective	good, of high quality, reliable	He has a sound knowledge of maths and science. I am sure he will get a good job.
establish a career 开创事业		to find a secure career or profession that you feel comfortable with	He was studying hard because he wanted to establish a career in medicine.
promote 提升，促进	verb	to be good for; to encourage the development of	It's common knowledge that regular exercise promotes good health.
express oneself 表达自己的想法		to communicate what you are thinking or feeling in speech or writing	I am not good at expressing myself sometimes; I know what I want to say, but I don't seem to be able to explain myself well.
valuable 有价值的，重要的，宝贵的	adjective	having value, importance, significance, benefit (not only used for monetary value)	I think that living and working in a foreign country is a very valuable learning experience.
not to be neglected 不容忽视的		an expression used to say that something is important and should not be left out or forgotten about while considering an issue	While I believe personality is more important than physical appearance, being clean and presentable is something that is not to be neglected.

MODEL ANSWER 1 答案范例 1

阅读雅思考生Sophia的参考答案。

Interviewer Which is more important in a child's school education: academic subjects, learning teamwork through sporting activities, or learning about art and drama?

Sophia That's a tough question, because so much depends on the individual pupil. As a general rule I think that academic subjects are the most important part of a child's education. Children need to have a sound academic basis in order to progress successfully onto further education and establish a career in the future, for this is what society requires.

Having said that, I do feel that sporting activities should play a role in a child's school education, not only because this promotes good health, but also because learning to work in a team is considerably important. For this reason, I feel that team sports are certainly more valuable than individual sports in a child's education.

Learning about art and participating in drama activities, though not as important as academic pursuits and sports, in my opinion, is also fairly important for helping young people develop more creative skills as well as learning to express themselves. So I have to say that although I feel academic studies and learning teamwork through sports are more important, learning about art and drama should not be neglected.

NATIVE SPEAKER WORDS 2 英语母语词汇 2

让我们来学习一些英语母语词汇，这些词汇对于回答该类型的问题非常有用，并且能够帮助你理解下面的答案范例。

Native Speaker Word	Part of Speech	Definition	Example Sentence
extent 范围，程度	noun	the length, amount or distance, the area something covers	The extent of the damage to the building after the storm was enormous.
take precedence over 比……重要，优先于		to be more important than something; to have greater priority than something	Oral fluency should take precedence over grammar when teaching English to business students.
controversial 有争议的	adjective	a subject that can cause disagreement, discussion or debate because many people have different opinions about it	After the Sichuan earthquake, the actions of a teacher – Fan Pao Pao – became very controversial. Everyone was talking about whether what he did was right or wrong.
pose a dilemma to 造成困境		to create a situation where there are two choices or decisions to be made and it is very hard to decide which is the best	The crisis posed a dilemma: should the government put more money into saving the natural environment or try to boost the economy first?
environmental concerns 环境问题		problems related to the pollution or the damage of the natural environment	Many environmental concerns have been addressed by our government in the past few years, but still there is a long way to go.
reduce 减少	verb	to make something smaller in size, amount or degree	The government has recently reduced the tax on motor cars by 17%.

续表

Native Speaker Word	Part of Speech	Definition	Example Sentence
come at a cost 付出代价		to cost a lot of money to do something, to put into action	Economic development comes at a cost – the price you pay is the environmental damage that comes as a result.
put greater emphasis on 着重，强调，把重点放在……		to think one thing is more important than another thing, to emphasise one thing rather than another	The Western education system puts a greater emphasis upon learning skills and developing abilities rather than remembering lots of information and passing exams.
manufacturer 制造商，厂家	noun	the company that makes products	The manufacturers of electronic goods are suffering from economic problems this year.
emissions regulations 排放法规		the rules that governments make to control the amount of toxic gases or chemicals that are released by factories	It's very hard for the authorities to get factories to comply with the government's emissions regulations.

MODEL ANSWER 2 答案范例 2

阅读雅思考生Mike的参考答案。

Interviewer Today in society, environmental concerns often feature in the news. To what extent do you believe the economic development of a country should take precedence over protecting the environment?

Mike Well, that's quite a controversial issue at the moment. It's hard to say, whilst environmental concerns are indeed important, this question poses a bit of a dilemma to most governments – protecting the natural environment and reducing air and water pollution are incredibly important if a country is to progress, develop and maintain a healthy population. However, protecting the environment also comes at a cost: it is expensive to ensure that factories and car manufacturers comply with certain emissions regulations, and to be able to do this the country must make money and spend that money wisely.

Now that I think about it, in the short term I believe that economic development is more important than environmental concerns because this enables a country to become strong enough to address environmental issues in the long term. Once a country is richer and more developed, it should then put greater emphasis upon protecting the environment.

LANGUAGE STEP 1 Importance Phrases & Adverbs of Degree
高分语言点 1 描述重要性的短语和程度副词

让我们来看一下雅思考生Sophia和Mike是如何描述某件事情的重要性的。

Sophia ...As a general rule I think that academic subjects are *the most important part of* a child's education...Having said that, I do feel that sporting activities should play a role in a child's school education...Learning about art and participating in drama activities...is also *fairly important* for helping young people develop more creative skills as well as learning to express themselves...

Mike Well, that's quite a *controversial issue* at the moment...protecting the natural environment and reducing air and water pollution are *incredibly important* if a country is to progress, develop and maintain a healthy population...

Importance phrases

When you are asked how important something is, it's best to begin by using an importance phrase such as the following:

- X should play a role
- X plays a big role in our lives
- X is an important part of our lives
- X is a controversial issue / question
- X is an important issue / question
- X is a top priority

Examples:

"Yes, computers *play a big role in our lives*..."

"I think it*'s an important issue* today..."

"Entertainment *has always been an important part of our lives*..."

"Friendship is something we should always *take very seriously*..."

"Being responsible at work *is a top priority* in life..."

Adverbs of degree

When you begin to talk about how important or valuable something is, it's good to use a variety of native speaker adverbs of degree, such as:

- to some extent important
- important to a point
- quite important
- fairly important
- very important
- especially important
- particularly important
- considerably important
- incredibly important

Examples:
"I think that art is *very important* in life."
"I don't think learning history is *particularly important* for people."
"*To some extent* fashion is *important*."
"Being able to do mathematics is *important to a point*, but..."
"Being a good speaker is *fairly important* in life."
"Diplomacy is *especially important* in today's society."
"Learning to read and write is *incredibly important* for every person in society."

小贴士

副词 completely 和 absolutely 几乎总是与表示否定意义的 unimportant 连用，比如：
"Age is *completely unimportant* when I think about my ideal husband."
"Being interested in fashion is *absolutely unimportant*! I think it is ridiculous and superficial!"
"I think it is *totally unimportant* if a husband or wife are of different social backgrounds. Care and love are the highest priority in a relationship."

Exercise 29.1: Multiple Choice & Matching

Choose the appropriate words from the choices below and then match sentences 1-5 with sentences A-E.

1. When you are planning to set up a new apartment for the first time it is ____________ important...
   A. absolutely B. particularly C. completely
2. When you are planning to travel overseas to another country it is ____________ buy a good guidebook...
   A. totally unimportant to B. absolutely essential to C. a matter of life and death to
3. You must follow three ____________ rules when you go into some temples and sacred places...
   A. incredibly important B. totally important C. not very important
4. Learning to respect our fellow workers, neighbours, and even strangers in the street should always be a ____________ if...
   A. especially important B. thing of little importance C. top priority
5. I think that teaching children to paint and draw in schools is important ____________ but not of great importance...
   A. to some extent B. at some extent C. on some extent

A. ...I think that other subjects should be given precedence over art and music.
B. ...we want to maintain a friendly and happy society.

C. ...to get some practical things like kitchen equipment and bathroom accessories.

D. ...Firstly, you must take off your shoes; secondly you must remove your hat; and thirdly you mustn't take photos.

E. ...and learn some basic phrases like "please" and "thank you" in that language.

EXTRA LANGUAGE POINT 1 Time Buying Phrases & Backtracking
补充语言点1 争取时间的短语和表达对观点的回顾和调整

让我们来看一下雅思考生Sophia和Mike用了哪些表达方法为自己争取更多的时间以及他们是如何回顾和调整自己之前的观点的。

Sophia *That's a tough question*, because so much depends on the individual pupil... *Having said that*, I do feel that sporting activities should play a role in a child's school education...

Mike *Well, that's quite a controversial issue at the moment. It's hard to say*, whilst environmental concerns are indeed important, this question poses a bit of a dilemma to most governments...*Now that I think about it*, in the short term I believe that economic development is more important than environmental concerns because this enables a country to become strong enough to address environmental issues in the long term...

Time buying phrases

Notice how Sophia and Mike use native speaker time buying phrases in introducing their answers. "Buying time" is a useful skill because it can give you a few more valuable seconds while you think about what your opinion is and how to express it.

So, if the question the interviewer asks is something which is a little controversial, or subject to different opinions you can "buy yourself some time" with:

- That's a tough question...
- Mmm, that's an interesting point...
- Let me think for a second...
- Let me see...
- I have to say that...
- It's hard to say...
- Actually...
- In fact...
- You see...
- Well,...

Backtracking

Sometimes, native speakers will think back at what they have just said, and change their opinion slightly or add an extra, slightly contrasting point. It's completely acceptable to do this, you won't lose points for backtracking because natives do it all the time!

You can backtrack with:

- Having said that...
- Now that I think about it, I guess...
- Come to think of it...

LANGUAGE STEP 2 Comparatives & Superlatives
高分语言点 2 比较级和最高级

让我们来看一下雅思考生Sophia和Mike是如何使用比较级和最高级的。

Sophia ...As a general rule I think that academic subjects are *the most important* part of a child's education...I feel that team sports are certainly *more valuable than* individual sports in a child's education. Learning about art and participating in drama activities, though *not as important as* academic pursuits and sports...although I feel academic studies and learning teamwork through sports are *more important*, learning about art and drama should not be neglected.

Mike ...in the short term I believe that economic development *is more important than* environmental concerns because this enables a country to become strong enough to address environmental issues in the long term. Once a country is *richer* and *more developed*, it should then put *greater* emphasis upon protecting the environment.

Comparing importance or priority

When you are discussing how important something is or how high a priority something should be given, most native speakers will use the following comparative structures:

- X is more convenient than Y because...

"I am convinced that *watching DVDs is much more interesting and convenient than watching films* in the cinema *because*..."

- X (should have) has a higher priority than because...

"I believe *science should have a higher priority than art* in schools *because*..."

- X is more important than Y because...

"I hold the opinion that *keeping healthy is more important than just hanging out with friends and having fun because*..."

- X is undoubtedly of greater importance than Y because...

"I feel that *quality education is undoubtedly of greater importance than economic development because*..."

- X is certainly in need of more attention than Y because...

"For me, *slowing down global warming is certainly in need of more attention than saving* particular species of *animals because*..."

- X should take precedence over Y because...

"*Spending money improving our hospitals should take precedence over spending money renovating historic buildings.*"

Another way of expressing that one thing is more important than another is by saying:

- Before doing X, we should do Y.

"*Before spending more money on education, we should try to raise the standard of living* of the countryside population."

If the two things you are comparing have the same importance or priority, you can use:

- X is equally as important as Y because...

"*Developing the economy is equally important as saving the environment because*..."

Superlatives

It's also useful to use the superlative as Sophia did in the beginning of her answer:

"As a general rule I think that academic subjects are *the most important part* of a child's education."

"The way I see it, looking after the ordinary people is *the highest priority* of the state."

Exercise 29.2: Gap Fill

Write the words below in the correct spaces.

before thinking
have a higher priority
more important
should try to
than
equally as important as
in need of more attention than
much more valuable
take precedence over
undoubtedly of greater importance than

1. I believe that learning to use a computer is __________ than anything else if you want to get ahead in a good career in accounting.
2. Teaching children to respect and listen to others and be good citizens should __________ than pushing them to learn about politics and history.
3. Getting regular physical exercise is __________ learning about art or music in school. Health is the most important thing we have.
4. When it comes to environmental concerns, big city air pollution is without doubt __________ other environmental issues like noise pollution or damage to historical buildings.
5. Spending tax-payers' money to improve the standards of countryside schools should __________ trying to build huge expensive shopping malls to make our big cities look modern!

6. ___________ about a person's physical appearance and beauty, we ___________ get to know them and look into their heart and personality.
7. Learning languages is ___________ learning to do mathematics, learning about history, or learning about politics; it really depends what you want to do in the future.
8. Everyone would agree that when you give gifts giving a home-made gift from the heart is ___________ and meaningful ___________ an expensive present.

LANGUAGE STEP 3 Expressions to Say Why Something Is Important
高分语言点 3 描述为什么某件事情很重要

让我们来看一下雅思考生Sophia如何描述为什么某件事情是很重要的。

Sophia ...Having said that, I do feel that sporting activities should play a role in a child's school education, not only because *this promotes good health*, but also because learning to work in a team is considerably important...Learning about art and participating in drama activities...is also fairly *important for helping young people develop* more creative skills as well as learning to express themselves...

Of course, after you have expressed how important something is in relation to something else, you should support your claim with reasons, saying why it is important.

- X is important / necessary / crucial / useful / good + for + verb-ing

"...because caring for the environment is *necessary for helping* people keep healthy."
"Physical exercise is *useful for keeping* fit and healthy and happy."
"Doing adventure sports is *good for breathing* fresh air and *experiencing* nature."
"The upkeep of historic buildings is *important for building* national identity."
"Disciplining children is absolutely *essential for teaching* them respect for others."
"Eating a balanced diet with lots of fruit and vegetables is *crucial for staying* in good shape."

Or you can use:

- activity verb-ing + promotes + noun

"*Giving gifts* on special occasions *promotes good feeling* amongst friends and family."
"*Donating money* to charity on a regular basis *promotes the development* of a caring and unselfish community spirit."
"*Offering employees* good salaries and fair holidays *promotes a happy and warm working environment*."

Exercise 29.3: Matching

Match sentences halves 1-5 with sentences halves A-E.

1. Friends are more important than anything else in life...

2. Souvenirs and handicrafts are very important for…
3. Giving expensive gifts is sometimes important and is certainly…
4. Being able to cook well is very important for…
5. Today, speaking more than one language is good for…

A. …becoming an independent young person if you move away from home.
B. …opening up greater, more international career opportunities.
C. …giving tourists an insight into the local culture of a place of interest.
D. …because they are necessary for fun, laughter and sharing your feelings in times of need.
E. …essential for developing good business relationships in some countries.

EXTRA LANGUAGE POINT 2 Sequencing
补充语言点 2 描述先后次序

让我们来看一看下面的例句是如何表达先后次序的。

Another way to express degree of importance is to list “priorities” or “sequence”. This is quite simple. You can list two or three things and put them in order of importance as in the following example:

“Well, I think that, when you go on a long journey with a friend, *the first thing* that you should consider in planning the trip is the amount of time you have and the distance you hope to travel in that time. *Secondly*, you should think about what kind of things you want to see, and *thirdly* you need to think about your budget for travel, food and accommodation.”

Look at these variations:

- Firstly / the first thing you / we / they should consider is...
- Secondly / the second consideration should be...
- Thirdly / the third thing that you / we / they must do is...

For more practice, please go to: www.EQEnglish.com

Formula 30: Proposing Solutions to Problems

AIMS 学习目标

In this lesson you'll master the Formula for Proposing Solutions to Problems.
你将学会如何回答雅思口试第三部分的常见问题，比如：

- Think about restaurants and customer services in your town or city. What kind of problems are there? How would you suggest they improve?
- What are the main environmental problems facing the world today? How could they be addressed?
- What are the drawbacks of travelling in your country as a foreigner? How could tourist companies as well as individuals go about surmounting these problems?

THE FORMULA 高分公式

To propose solutions to problems, you should:

Answer Order

- Identify the problems.
- Suggest solutions.
- Suggest definite actions that should be taken.

Language Steps

1. Use phrases to identify problems. ("The system is *rife with problems*." / "The *main problem* with X is...")
2. Use phrases to suggest solutions. ("They should *make an effort to*..." / "We must *pay more attention to*..." / "You could *spend more money on*...")
3. Use phrases to express definite actions. ("They should *prohibit* people from..." / "They could *get rid of* poor workers." / "We could *impose strict regulations on*...")

NATIVE SPEAKER WORDS1 英语母语词汇1

让我们来学习一些英语母语词汇，这些词汇对于回答该类型的问题非常有用，并且能够帮助你理解下面的答案范例。

Native Speaker Word	Part of Speech	Definition	Example Sentence
up-to-date 最新的，现代的	adjective	modern, recent or containing the latest information	I like to stay up-to-date with the international news so I know what's going on in the world.
hygiene 卫生	noun	the degree to which people keep themselves and their surroundings clean	The hygiene standards in some restaurants in my hometown are really not very good – you sometimes get sick after eating there.

MODEL ANSWER 1 答案范例 1

阅读雅思考生Sophia的参考答案。

Interviewer What kind of problems do students sometimes have in university, and what could be done to address them?

Sophia Well, firstly, I think the main problem is that the classes are exceedingly boring. In more active and modern classes students are more interested, work harder and learn faster. I believe that teachers should be made to go on more up-to-date, modern training courses. Secondly, I think that the restaurants and canteens on campus have a very poor standard of food and don't offer much variety. They could pay more attention to hygiene and to making the menus more interesting.

NATIVE SPEAKER WORDS 2 英语母语词汇 2

让我们来学习一些英语母语词汇，这些词汇对于回答该类型的问题非常有用，并且能够帮助你理解下面的答案范例。

Native Speaker Word	Part of Speech	Definition	Example Sentence
be rife with problems 问题重重		to be full of problems	His body is rife with problems: he's overweight, balding, has heart problems, and he's got a bad back.
bus lanes 公交专用车道	noun	the parts of the road or avenue which are only for public buses to travel on	There aren't enough bus lanes in Beijing, but the authorities are building more and more every day.

续表

Native Speaker Word	Part of Speech	Definition	Example Sentence
extend 扩大	verb	to make bigger or longer or more extensive	We are extending the university campus, so that we can build new tennis courts and a sports stadium.
measure 措施，方法	noun	a step or a means of solving a problem	We need to take measures to improve the conditions in local hospitals.

MODEL ANSWER2 答案范例2

阅读雅思考生Mike的参考答案。

Interviewer How would you suggest that the government improve the transport system in your city?

Mike The transport system is rife with problems: there are too many cars on the roads, there are not enough bus lanes and the subway system is not extensive enough.

There are a few measures that can be taken to improve the transport system. The most important thing is to build more roads and be very careful where those roads are built. Then, when there are more and better roads, they can make more bus lanes and extend the subway lines. These are big projects and may take some time, but are necessary if transport problems are going to be solved.

Interviewer What should we do to deal with the problem of environmental pollution?

Mike That's a good question, and a very important one today. Well, there are a lot of environmental problems facing us today. I think the most important issues are water and air pollution. The authorities should make more effort to address the issue of water pollution by putting pressure on factories to stop pumping their chemical waste into rivers and lakes. Another measure would be to encourage people to only buy products from companies that respect the environment.

LANGUAGE STEP 1 Phrases to Identify Problems
高分语言点1 指出问题的表达方法

让我们看一下雅思考生Sophia和Mike是如何指出问题的。

Sophia Well, firstly, *I think the main problem is that* the classes are exceedingly boring…

Mike The transport system *is rife with problems*: there are too many cars on the roads, there are not enough bus lanes and the subway system is not extensive enough…

Well, *there are a lot of* environmental *problems* facing us today. I think the most important issues are water and air pollution…

Notice how both Sophia and Mike identify the problems under discussion. Here are some other *phrases to identify problems*:

- There're a lot of problems with X.
  "*There're a lot of problems with the national football team.*"
- One major concern (with X) that needs addressing is Y.
  "*One major concern with the aging population that needs addressing is* how we are going to pay for all of those pensions."
- The biggest problem with X is Y.
  "*The biggest problem with professional sports is that teams become businesses* rather than playing for the love of the sport."
- The main reasons behind X are Y and Z.
  "*The main reasons behind desertification are agricultural misuse and rising global temperatures.*"
- The main issue many people have with X is Y.
  "*The main issue many people have with warfare is that they feel it is immoral.*"
- Most people believe that X is the main problem.
  "In regard to the spread of AIDS in Africa, *most people believe that the Pope's teachings about the use of condoms is the main problem.*"

Exercise 30.1: Multiple Choice

Choose the appropriate phrases to identify problems from the choices below to complete the sentences.

1. ____________ many people have with football stars is the amount of money they get paid.
   A. The main reasons behind B. The main issue C. One major concern
2. ____________ that rising house prices is the main reason behind the financial crisis.
   A. There're a lot of problems B. One major concern that needs addressing is
   C. Most people believe
3. ____________ I have about our schools is the very poor quality of teachers they employ.
   A. The biggest problem B. A major concern C. The main reason
4. ____________ our transport system is the sheer quantity of cars that go on the roads each day.
   A. The biggest problem with
   B. Most people believe that
   C. The main reasons behind

5. ____________ petty crime in my country are poverty and the wealth gap behind rich and poor.
   A. There are a lot of problems
   B. The biggest problem with
   C. The main reasons behind
6. ____________ the labour laws in many countries.
   A. There are a lot of problems with
   B. The biggest problem with
   C. Most people believe that

LANGUAGE STEP 2 Phrases to Suggest Solutions
高分语言点 2 提出解决方法的短语

让我们来看一下雅思考生Sophia和Mike是如何提出自己的解决方法的。

Sophia ...I believe that teachers *should be made to* go on more up-to-date, modern training courses. Secondly, I think that the restaurants...*could pay more attention to* hygiene and to making the menus more interesting.

Mike ...when there are more and better roads, *they can make* more bus lanes and extend the subway lines...The authorities *should make more effort to* address the issue of water pollution by putting pressure on factories to stop pumping their chemical waste into rivers and lakes...

Imagine if the interviewer asked you these questions:
"What do you think the government should do to deal with this problem?"
"What can be done to improve the conditions in the countryside?"
"How can we try to solve this problem?"

To answer such questions, you should use modal verbs such as "could", "ought to" and "should", as in the following phrases to suggest solutions:

- could spend more money on
- should pay more attention to
- ought to make an effort to
- can provide more
- could try harder to
- should take measures to
- ought to take steps to

Look at the way native speakers use these phrases to answer the above types of question:

"One thing that they *could do is to make an effort to* provide farmers with more access to better medical care."

"I believe we *should take steps towards* dealing with the problem of water pollution."

"I believe that young people *ought to pay more attention to* how they behave towards old people in public."

"I am sure that we *should try harder to* solve the current traffic problems."

"We *should* certainly *take measures to* improve the customer services in this country."

"The British government *could spend more money on* public transport, to reduce the cost of travel."

"Hospitals *could provide better* and *more* customer-centred care."

Exercise 30.2: Gap Fill

Write the words below in the correct spaces.

could spend more money on　　ought to provide　　ought to try harder to
pay more attention to　　should make a real effort to address
take measures to　　to take steps to

1. I feel that the police really ought ____________ reduce the number of traffic accidents.
2. To encourage poorer students to attend university, universities and educational organisations ____________ more scholarships.
3. We ____________ deal with corruption amongst businessmen.
4. Because environmental concerns are the most pressing issues facing society today, I feel we ____________ these issues before moving on to worrying about urban planning.
5. I strongly believe that we should ____________ taking care of animals in danger of distinction.
6. It is absolutely necessary that we ____________ improve the quality of food products sold in our national supermarkets.
7. Some people believe that the Egyptian government ____________ alleviating rural poverty.

LANGUAGE STEP 3 Phrases to Express Definite Actions
高分语言点 3 描述具体的解决方案

让我们来看一下雅思考生Sophia和Mike是如何描述具体的解决方案的。

Sophia ...I believe that teachers *should be made to* go on more up-to-date, modern training courses...

Mike ...The authorities should make more effort to address the issue of water pollution *by putting pressure on* factories to stop pumping their chemical waste into rivers and lakes. Another measure would be *to encourage people* to only buy products from companies that respect the environment.

Look at these verbs and phrases that native speakers use to propose concrete actions to solve problems:

- to get rid of
- to abolish
- to clean up
- to spend money on
- to impose tighter regulations on
- to put pressure on
- to encourage people to
- to repair
- to renovate

These verbs and phrases can be used in two ways.

- should + verb / phrase

The above verbs and phrases can be used with the structure should + verb / phrase, as in the following examples:

"I strongly believe the authorities *should put pressure on* factory owners to reduce emissions."

"I am of the opinion that they *should clean up* the poorer ends of town."

"I think they *should impose tighter regulations on* the DVD sales."

"I really believe they *ought to spend more money on* improving the school facilities."

"I am convinced that they *should abolish* certain out-dated laws in this country."

"Do you feel that it is advisable to *get rid of* all cigarette advertisements in public places?"

"One step would be to *encourage people to* stop buying products from manufacturers that damage the environment."

- by + verb-ing

These phrases can be used with the structure by + verb-ing.

"They could improve the situation *by imposing tighter regulations on*..."

"They could improve things *by cleaning up* the most polluted areas of..."

"We could fix this problem *by putting pressure on* local governments to..."

"We could take measures to solve this problem *by spending more money on* education and less on arms..."

"We can make it a lot better *by repairing* the damage and *by renovating* the building..."

Exercise 30.3: Multiple Choice

Choose the appropriate phrases to express definite actions from the choices below to complete the sentences.

1. The law that university students are not allowed to get married should be ____________ because it is an unfair law.

A. cleaned up B. put pressure on C. abolished

2. I am of the opinion that governments ought to ____________ public health care and less on defense.

A. abolish B. spend more money on C. clean up

3. Many people feel that we should ____________ to be more culturally aware when we visit tourist sites in foreign countries.

A. get rid of people B. encourage people C. spend more money

4. I think the only solution to the problem of contaminated food would be to ____________ on the factories and companies that produce food products.

A. abolish B. clean up C. impose tighter regulations

5. If we want to improve the conditions in most Egyptian cities I think we will have to ____________ some of the corrupt officials that take a lot of tax payers' money and put it into their own pockets.

A. get rid of B. impose stricter regulations C. encourage people

6. I believe developing countries should ____________ developed countries to have more representation at international organisations such as the G8, UN and the IMF.

A. clean up B. impose tighter regulations on C. put pressure on

For more practice, please go to: www.EQEnglish.com

Formula 31: Speculating About Future Events and Outcomes

AIMS 学习目标

In this lesson you'll master the Formula for Speculating About Future Events & Outcomes.

你将学会如何回答雅思口试第三部分的常见问题，比如：

- Describe some of the major changes you think will happen in your country in the next 20 years.
- Do you think that people in the future will have solved many of the environmental and social problems that we are still facing today?
- What future predictions would you make about how technology in the future will develop and how it will affect the daily lives of humans?

THE FORMULA 高分公式

To speculate about future events and outcomes, you should:

Answer Order

- State present conditions.
- Predict future outcomes.
- Talk about what will happen in the future IF we take certain steps.

Language Steps

1. Use common present conditions & future outcomes phrases. ("*Given that* the level of unemployment is high I don't think many people *will find* jobs." / "*Taking into consideration* the current situation, I think John *will succeed*.")
2. Use the future perfect tense accurately with time phrases. ("*By the year 2030* scientists say that all ice caps *will have melted*." / "*In about 20 years* another 34 species of animals *will have died out*.")
3. Use the future continuous tense to predict and talk about continuous, uncompleted future actions. Know when to use the future continuous and future simple. ("By next century I believe that humans *will be living* much better, happier lives." / "In the future we *may be all travelling* around in flying cars!")

NATIVE SPEAKER WORDS 1 英语母语词汇 1

让我们来学习一些英语母语词汇，这些词汇对于回答该类型的问题非常有用，并且能够帮助你理解下面的答案范例。

Native Speaker Word	Part of Speech	Definition	Example Sentence
rate 比率，速度	noun	the speed at which something happens or changes	After the Wall Street crash of 1929 the unemployment rate increased dramatically as a result of the economic problems.
alarming 令人担忧的，惊人的，吓人的	adjective	shocking, worrying, surprising	The amount of mosquitoes in the garden this year is alarming!
global warming 全球变暖		the increase of the temperature of the earth's surface – believed to be a danger related to pollution	Most people today are of the opinion that carbon dioxide emissions are the main cause of global warming.
melt 融化	verb	to turn from something solid into a liquid due to heat	The ice cream melted because it was so hot outside. They should have put it in the fridge.
ice caps 冰冠，冰帽		thick layers of ice that permanently cover areas at the north and south pole	The ice caps have been melting for years and years as the earth's temperature has been increasing.

MODEL ANSWER 1 答案范例 1

阅读雅思考生Sophia的参考答案。

Interviewer What do you think your country will be like in about 20 years time?

Sophia Well, it's hard to predict because things change so fast sometimes, and unexpected things happen. Mmm, I think that given the current rate of development, China will be a very strong and modern country in quite a short time. At the moment the cities are becoming more and more modern, people are constructing more and more office blocks, and traditional residential areas are disappearing at an alarming rate. Taking all these facts into consideration I have no doubt that China will be a safer, cleaner and more beautiful and convenient place to live in the future.

Interviewer Let's talk about our planet. Some people are not hopeful about the future of earth. What do you think will happen to the world in the future?

Sophia Well, that's another tough question. A lot of scientists are suggesting that due to global warming, it is very likely that we will face serious problems in the next

30 years. They say that by the year 2030 the ice caps will have melted and we will be paying the price for the damage we did to the environment. Some say that we will possibly be living a very different lifestyle and others even suggest we may be living on other planets by then!

NATIVE SPEAKER WORDS 2 英语母语词汇 2

让我们来学习一些英语母语词汇，这些词汇对于回答该类型的问题非常有用，并且能够帮助你理解下面的答案范例。

Native Speaker Word	Part of Speech	Definition	Example Sentence
transform 转变	verb	to change from one thing / state into another	Caterpillars transform into butterflies.
dramatically 突然地，显著地	adverb	suddenly, noticeably	The weather changed dramatically: one minute it was beautiful and sunny and the next minute it was pouring down with rain!
wristwatch 手表	noun	a timepiece which is worn on the wrist	Making a good wristwatch is a fine art. That's why many high quality watches are very expensive.
activate 发动，激活	verb	to cause something to start	He pressed the button and activated the machine. It made a loud noise as the engine started.
voice control 声控		an electronic feature that enables a user to speak into a device instead of typing or pushing buttons	He always uses the voice control function on his mobile phone; he just speaks the name of the person he wants to call and the telephone recognises the name and dials the number!

MODEL ANSWER 2 答案范例 2

阅读雅思考生Mike的参考答案。

Interviewer Can you describe some of the changes you think will happen in the future because of technological developments?

Mike Yes, I've thought about this a lot recently, actually. I believe that technology will continue to transform our lives dramatically. For instance, I am quite sure that cell phones will be like wristwatches and will be activated by voice control, rather than pressing buttons to input numbers. I am also convinced that technology will contribute enormously to advances in the medical industry. For example, I think that in about 50 years we will have found a cure for cancer and other serious diseases.

LANGUAGE STEP 1 Present Conditions & Future Outcomes Phrases
高分语言点 1 描述现在状况以及未来结果的短语

让我们看一下雅思考生Sophia是如何描述现在的情况以及将来可能发生的结果的。

Sophia …I think that *given the current rate of development, China will be a very strong and modern country in quite a short time*. At the moment the cities are becoming more and more modern, people are constructing more and more office blocks, and traditional residential areas are disappearing at an alarming rate. *Taking all these facts into consideration I have no doubt that China will be a safer, cleaner and more beautiful and convenient place to live in the future*…A lot of scientists are suggesting that *due to global warming, it is very likely that we will face serious problems in the next 30 years*…

Notice that in talking about future "predictions", Sophia describes what the present conditions are, and what future outcomes these may lead to.

Let's look at these similar structures native speakers use:

- given the + noun + future predication
- taking into consideration + noun + future prediction

Look at the following examples in the table and see how each of the parts of the sentence fit together.

Opener	Noun	Future Prediction
Given the	current situation	I am sure that the financial crisis will end in a few years.
Taking into consideration	the problems we are facing	I think we will have to take drastic measures to change things.
Taking into account	the amazing technological advances this century	I am sure we will be living on other plants in a short time.

Or you can use these structures:

- given that + phrase with verb + future prediction
- considering that + phrase with verb + future prediction
- since + phrase with verb + future prediction

Again, look at examples of these structures in the table below:

Opener	Verb Phrase	Future Prediction
Given that	they are making so much effort	I am sure they will clean up the city before all the tourists come.

续表

Opener	Verb Phrase	Future Prediction
Considering that	they have been working so hard	I have no doubt they will all get the scholarships.
Since	they are currently putting more money into education	I think that in 10 years most of the schools will be very modern.

Exercise 31.1: Gap Fill & Matching

Write the phrases below in the correct spaces, and then match sentence halves 1-5 with sentence halves A-E.

are reforming the labour laws
are spending a lot of money
taking into consideration
the current rate of international development
we are constantly improving our education standards

1. Given ______________________________...
2. ______________________________ the state of the economy in the Middle East...
3. Given that ______________________________...
4. Given that the authorities ______________________________ on restoring old buildings...
5. Since they ______________________________...

A. ...I think we will see a great improvement in working conditions in the next few years.
B. ...I am sure there will be less poverty in the world by 2020.
C. ...I think it will be in trouble after about 50 years and everyone stops using oil.
D. ...I believe the future for our country will be a bright one.
E. ...I believe that we will have an even greater tourist industry in the coming few years.

LANGUAGE STEP 2 The Future Perfect & Time Phrases
高分语言点 2 将来完成时和时间短语

让我们来看一下雅思考生Sophia和Mike是如何使用将来完成时以及时间短语的。

Sophia ...They say that *by the year 2030* the ice caps *will have melted* and we will be paying the price for the damage we did to the environment...

Mike ...I am also convinced that technology will contribute enormously to advances in the medical industry. For example, I think that *in about 50 years we will have found* a cure for cancer and other serious diseases.

Like Mike and Sophia, to predict future outcomes you should use the future perfect tense. The future perfect is used to talk about things that will have been completed or finished at or by a certain point in the future.

The structure of the future perfect is will + have + past participle.

Examples:

"I *will have eaten* my dinner by 5 p.m."

"We *will have solved* many environmental problems in..."

We can use the future perfect with the following time phrases:

- in the future
- in the next few years
- in about 40 years
- in the next two decades
- in a short time
- in only a couple of years
- in our lifetime
- by the year 2055
- by 2030
- by next century
- by the time we + action / state

小贴士

in 后面接时间段，而 by 后面接具体的时间点。

Take a look at the following examples, which combine the future perfect and time phrases:

"They say that *by the year 2030* the ice caps *will have melted*."

"Some believe that *by the time* we are old mankind *will have cut down* all the rainforests on earth."

"Some scientists say that *by the late 2050s* man *will have built* cities on the moon."

"Many believe that *in only a few years* another 200 species of endangered animals *will have become extinct*."

"I am pretty sure that *in 100 years* we *will have succeeded* in finding a cure for cancer."

Exercise 31.2: Multiple Choice

Choose the appropriate future perfect form or time phrase from the choices below to complete the sentences.

1. Some people believe that ____________ 20 years we ____________ aeroplanes that can go around the world in only a few hours.

   A. in the future, will invented

   B. in the next, will have invent

   C. in about, will have invented

2. I am convinced that ____________ the 22nd century humankind ____________ all the animal lives on the planet.
   A. by, will destroyed
   B. by, will have destroyed
   C. in about, will be destroyed
3. I am quite sure that ____________ our government ____________ most transport problems facing the nation.
   A. in a very short time, will have solved
   B. in the future, will having solved
   C. in only a couple of years, will have solve
4. A lot of medical research has been done in recent years. I think that ____________ scientists ____________ cures for most known diseases.
   A. in a short time, will have find
   B. by next century, will have discovered
   C. in the next few years, will discovered
5. A lot of my friends believe the world is getting worse and worse, but I don't agree. I think that in just ____________ or two ____________ solved the problem of world poverty.
   A. our lifetime, we will had
   B. a short time, we would have
   C. a decade, we will have

LANGUAGE STEP 3 The Future Continuous
高分语言点 3 将来进行时

让我们来看一下雅思考生Sophia是如何使用将来进行时的。

Sophia ...They say that *by the year 2030* the ice caps will have melted and *we will be paying* the price for the damage we did to the environment. Some say that *we will possibly be living* a very different lifestyle and others even suggest *we may be living* on other planets by then!

Notice how Sophia talks about what things they think people will be doing in the future as continuing "future" actions, as opposed to "finished" actions. The future continuous is used to talk about something that we think will happen in the future and will continue to happen for a period of time, rather than a sudden or a finished event in the future.

The structure of the future continuous is will + be + verb-ing.
Examples:
"The Chinese countryside *will be developing* for many years to come."
"By 2015 I *will be studying* in England."

We can also use the future continuous with the following time phrases:

- in the future
- in the next few years
- in about 40 years
- in the next two decades
- in a short time
- in only a couple of years
- in our lifetime
- by the year
- by 2030
- by next century
- by the time we + action / state

Examples:

"I believe that *in about 50 years we will be living* on the moon."

"I think that *in about 100 years we will be driving* flying cars like we see in the movies."

"Some people are convinced that *by the 22nd century* humans *will be living* on the moon."

"Many are of the opinion that *in only a short time* everyone in the world *will be using* a home computer."

小贴士

我们不可以说 we will be having 或者 we will be knowing, 因为这些动词是描述状态的动词（state verbs）和感官动词（sense verbs），而不是行为动词，因此它们没有进行时态。以下是一些感官动词和状态动词：

realise ——不可以说 will be realising
know ——不可以说 will be knowing
love ——不可以说 will be loving
want ——不可以说 will be wanting
believe ——不可以说 will be believing

Exercise 31.3: Sentence Completion

Complete the sentences below by writing the correct future continuous forms of the words in brackets.

1. Some believe that in a few years we ____________ (pay) the price for the damage we have inflicted upon the natural environment.
2. I think that in one or two decades people ____________ (use) mobile phones inserted into their brains.
3. Because fashion is constantly changing, many people think that in the future people (wear) ____________ very different clothes than we wear today.
4. Due to the increasing levels of air pollution, many are sure that in only 10 years or so we ____________ (have to wear) special masks when we go outside.

5. A lot of my colleagues are of the opinion that in only a short time everyone in the world ____________ (have) a home computer and a mobile telephone.
6. Many people think that it is not fair that London ____________ (host) the Olympic Games again in 2012.
7. In the near future we ____________ (all drive) around in environmentally friendly cars which do not pollute the atmosphere.
8. I believe that if we continue to invite artists and musicians from all over the world to our country, everyone ____________ (love) art and music.

EXTRA LANGUAGE POINT Expressing Likelihood with the First Conditional
补充语言点 用第一条件句描述事件的可能性

让我们来看一看下面的例句中是如何使用第一条件句来描述事件的可能性的。

Another extremely useful way of predicting future outcomes is to use the first conditional. Remind yourself of its structure:

- if + present verb + will + present verb

"*If* we *continue* to treat the planet in this way, we *will be* in serious trouble in the future."

"*If* we *don't address* the current traffic problems soon, we *will face* serious problems in the near future."

To make your predictions sound more like a native speaker, you can use the following types of "likelihood" expressions in your first conditional sentences.

- it is likely / quite likely / highly likely / extremely likely
- it is probable / quite probable / highly probable
- it is possible / quite possible

Examples:

"*If* we *continue* to treat the planet in this way *it is very likely* that we *will be* in serious trouble in the future."

"*If* we *don't address* the current traffic problems soon, *it is highly probable* that we *will face* serious problems in the near future."

Remember that we can also reverse the first conditional structure.

Examples:

"*It is extremely likely* that people *will be* a lot more open-minded in the future *if* our society *continues* to welcome art and culture from all over the world."

"*It is quite possible* that the world *will be* a really clean and harmonious place in the future *if* we *take* measures to take care of our planet."

For more practice, please go to: www.EQEnglish.com

Appendices 附录

Top 10 Do's and Don'ts for the IELTS Speaking Test
雅思口语考试的"十要"和"十不要"

We've put together our top 10 **do's** and **don'ts** so that you can avoid all those mistakes that other candidates make.

1. **Do** develop your answers, don't just say "yes" or "no".

By adding a little extra information, reasons and examples to support opinions, you will score higher.

2. **Do** remember that it's not a test of your knowledge.

You don't have to know facts about the topics the examiner asks you; you just have to talk about your opinion and impressions.

3. **Do** listen carefully to the whole question the examiner asks, not just the first few key words.

Don't just "guess" what the examiner is going to say from the first few words. Make sure you listen carefully so your answer is relevant.

4. **Do** ask for clarification occasionally if you need to.

If you don't understand, don't be afraid to ask the examiner to rephrase or repeat a question.

5. **Do** include personal anecdotes and "stories" into your Part Two monologue.

It gives your talk a more authentic and colourful feel, and helps to hold the examiner's interest.

6. **Don't** learn or memorise set answers to questions.

It's very easy to spot a student who is reciting memorised full answers. The examiner will certainly lower your score or move on to another question.

7. **Don't** ask the examiner to change the topic if you don't feel comfortable with it.

You have to talk about the topic he or she selects — those are the rules.

8. **Don't** shout or speak really loudly at the examiner.

Speak at a normal, natural volume and pace you feel comfortable with.

9. **Don't** worry if the examiner stops you and moves you on to another question.

The examiner has to keep to certain times for each part of the test so he or she may jump in and interrupt you a few times.

10. **Don't** go to the test without being clean and fresh.

An examiner can feel very uncomfortable if a student smells unpleasant or has bad breath.

Verbs Most Commonly Misused by IELTS Candidates

雅思考生易混淆的动词

我们对雅思口语考试做了大量的研究和分析，发现下列 60 个不规则动词经常被考生误用。

要想在雅思口试中获得高分，就必须正确地使用这些动词——确保考生知道这些动词的不同形式，这样就不会犯错！

Base Form	Past	Past Participle
is / are	was / were	been
become	became	become
begin	began	begun
break	broke	broken
bring	brought	brought
build	built	built
buy	bought	bought
catch	caught	caught
choose	chose	chosen
come	came	come
cut	cut	cut
do	did	done
draw	drew	drawn
drink	drank	drunk
drive	drove	driven
eat	ate	eaten
fall	fell	fallen
feed	fed	fed
find	found	found
fly	flew	flown
forget	forgot	forgotten
get	got	gotten
give	gave	given
go	went	gone
have	had	had
hear	heard	heard
hide	hid	hidden
hit	hit	hit
hold	held	held
keep	kept	kept

Base Verb	Past	Past Participle
know	knew	known
lay	laid	laid
leave	left	left
let	let	let
lose	lost	lost
make	made	made
mean	meant	meant
meet	met	met
pay	paid	paid
put	put	put
read	read	read
ride	rode	ridden
run	ran	run
say	said	said
see	saw	seen
sell	sold	sold
send	sent	sent
sleep	slept	slept
stand	stood	stood
swim	swam	swum
take	took	taken
teach	taught	taught
tell	told	told
think	thought	thought
try	tried	tried
understand	understood	understood
wake	woke	woken
wear	wore	worn
welcome	welcomed	welcomed
write	wrote	written

Answer Key 练习答案

Part One

Formula 1

Exercise 1.1: Error Correction

1. I prefer to go to the cinema rather than watch DVDs at home.
2. My sister prefers writing letters to writing emails.
3. I prefer to talk with friends on the phone rather than use QQ.
4. I much prefer to live in a town rather than a big city. (correct)
5. My mother prefers shopping at the market rather than in supermarkets.
6. My friends generally prefer to send text messages rather than talk on the phone.

Exercise 1.2: Gap Fill

1. better 2. more independent 3. cheaper 4. more fun
5. faster 6. not as comfortable 7. convenient 8. peaceful

Exercise 1.3: Gap Fill

1. Needless to say 2. actually 3. Besides 4. also 5. fact

Formula 2

Exercise 2.1: Word Order

1. I usually eat steamed buns. / Usually I eat steamed buns.
2. I almost never do exercise.
3. He hardly ever gets home early.
4. She never reads novels.
5. My father always rides a bike.
6. I sometimes read a magazine during lunch. / Sometimes I read a magazine during lunch.
7. Normally I watch TV with my parents. / I normally watch TV with my parents.
8. I rarely play computer games.
9. I often go cycling on the weekend.

Exercise 2.2: Gap Fill

wake up; watch; eat; go out; meet up; play; have; hang out with; lie; watch

Exercise 2.3: Error Correction

1. I often go to my sister's house for lunch on / at the weekend.
2. On holiday, I usually get up at 4 p.m. in the afternoon.
3. I always go for a jog in the evening, when it is cool.
4. Normally, I go to bed at 11 p.m. / o'clock.

5. I try to have lunch at noon.
6. I leave for work at 6 a.m. / o'clock.

Exercise 2.4: Gap Fill & Ordering

before; C　　Then; B　　After the shower; D　　After that; A

Formula 3

Exercise 3.1: Error Correction

1. When I'm not working I really enjoy cycling in the countryside outside my city. It is a very healthy and exciting pastime.
2. I really like to get involved in team sports. They are particularly good for building up co-operative skills and healthy competition.
3. I especially like to spend my free time sleeping and being lazy in my dormitory.
4. My friends and I are really keen on playing computer games. They are a really good way to spend an evening.
5. I enjoy taking part in martial arts like Kungfu; it can keep you fit and make you strong!
6. She enjoys going out to bars on weekends and hanging out with friends.

Exercise 3.2: Word Order

1. I'm quite into watching detective stories on TV.
2. She's a huge fan of romantic comedies.
3. I'm extremely interested in the latest fashions.
4. He's very keen on dancing at clubs with friends.

Exercise 3.3: Sentence Completion

1. satisfying　　2. boring　　3. excited
4. fascinated　　5. interested　　6. satisfying

Formula 4

Exercise 4.1: Rephrasing

1. I hate travelling a lot for work, but my boss makes me.
2. I'm not keen on formal parties where you have to look very smart and behave very well.
3. I can't stand it when my manager criticises me in front of all my colleagues.
4. Susan isn't interested in English at all and thinks it's a complete waste of time.
5. I'm not really a fan of going to expensive restaurants.
6. I don't enjoy watching TV soap operas.

Exercise 4.2: Gap Fill

1. don't really　　2. strongly　　3. really don't like
4. absolutely　　5. thoroughly dislike　　6. can't stand

Exercise 4.3: Error Correction

1. I really enjoy studying English.
2. I like going to the seaside and swimming in the sea very much.
3. I don't enjoy going to parties very much.
4. I really like all parts of my job.
5. Correct

Formula 5

Exercise 5.1: Word Placement

1. A, B or C	2. B	3. B or C	4. A, B or C	5. A, B or C
6. B	7. B or C	8. C	9. B	

Exercise 5.3: Matching

1. D 2. C 3. B 4. E 5. A

Formula 6

Exercise 6.1: Error Correction

1. I really like meeting new people.
2. I particularly love travelling as part of my job.
3. She especially enjoys visiting the famous sights in my hometown.
4. I enjoy taking photographs and sending postcards home.
5. I really like living with my classmates in our dormitory.
6. Correct

Exercise 6.2: Multiple Choice

1. A 2. B 3. A 4. B 5. B 6. A

Exercise 6.3: Matching

1. D 2. G 3. F 4. H 5. B 6. C 7. E 8. A

Formula 7

Exercise 7.1: Matching

1. D 2. F 3. E 4. C 5. B 6. A

Exercise 7.2: Gap Fill

1. elderly people 2. the unemployed; adolescents 3. white-collar workers; wealthy people

Exercise 7.3: Rephrasing

1. A lot of Chinese people regularly play badminton when they are young.

2. Not many women play golf in China.
3. The majority of Chinese people like to listen to music.
4. Very few people / students at my university play table tennis.
5. Most people watched the 2008 Olympics Opening Ceremony.
6. A small percentage of rich people ever ride a bike.

Exercise 7.4: Word Order

1. As a rule, football is more popular with boys.
2. Generally speaking, southern Chinese eat a lot of rice.
3. More often than not university students play sports very regularly.
4. Men tend to like watching sport together.
5. In general, rich people like to drive cars.

Formula 8

Exercise 8.1: Sentence Completion

1. the worst 2. the most beautiful 3. more suitable 4. The most pleasant
5. the best 6. the most fun 7. the most enjoyable 8. the warmest 9. hotter

Exercise 8.2: Gap Fill

1. in the middle of winter 2. at the beginning of 3. during
4. in 5. at 6. on

Exercise 8.3: Matching

1. B 2. E 3. D 4. A 5. C

Formula 9

Exercise 9.1: Table Completion

Age Groups & Generations	Family / Relationship Groups	Work-Related Groups	Social Classes
younger people	parents	retired people	poor people
the elderly	single parents	unemployed people	rich people
the older generation	married couples	white-collar workers	the working classes
school kids	grandparents	housewives	the middle classes
the younger generation	people in a relationship	office workers	the upper classes
adolescents	couples	job seekers	property owners
teenagers	single people		the homeless

Exercise 9.2: Matching

1. G 2. D 3. E 4. F 5. B 6. A 7. C

Exercise 9.3: Gap Fill

1. energetic 2. social 3. Apathetic
4. curious 5. family-oriented 6. studious

Exercise 9.4: Multiple Choice

1. B 2. A 3. C 4. A 5. C 6. B 7. C 8. A

Formula 10

Exercise 10.1: Error Correction

1. The last time I played basketball was when I was at school.
2. On my 25th birthday I went to a Japanese restaurant with my friends and colleagues.
3. I think my boyfriend's parents came to visit around Tomb Sweeping Day.
4. My grandmother gave me the computer as a present last Christmas, so it's still really new.
5. I went to Thailand on vacation about two years ago.
6. Correct
7. I finally passed my driving test in 1997.

Exercise 10.2: Table Completion

Base Form	Past Tense Form	Base Form	Past Tense Form
become	became	lay	laid
begin	began	leave	left
break	broke	let	let
bring	brought	lose	lost
build	built	make	made
buy	bought	mean	meant
catch	caught	meet	met
choose	chose	pay	paid
come	came	put	put
cut	cut	read	read
do	did	ride	rode
draw	drew	run	ran

续表

Base Form	Past Tense Form	Base Form	Past Tense Form
drink	drank	say	said
drive	drove	see	saw
eat	ate	sell	sold
fall	fell	send	sent
feed	fed	sleep	slept
find	found	stand	stood
fly	flew	swim	swam
forget	forgot	take	took
get	got	teach	taught
give	gave	tell	told
go	went	think	thought
have	had	try	tried
hear	heard	understand	understood
hide	hid	wake	woke
hit	hit	wear	wore
keep	kept	welcome	welcomed
know	knew	write	wrote

Exercise 10.3: Gap Fill

1. annoying 2. intriguing 3. stimulating; enjoyable
4. thrilling 5. exhilarating; frustrating

Formula 11

Exercise 11.1: Sentence Completion & Matching

1. started; D 2. drove; C 3. got to grips; B 4. taught; E 5. went; A

Exercise 11.2: Error Correction & Matching

1. I learned English <u>from</u> two really good teachers in middle school. C
2. I learned to use spreadsheets <u>by</u> trial and error. I was not taught by anyone. B
3. I <u>learned</u> how to sing from my mother, A

4. I first was taught to write characters by my father, D
5. I learned how to do Web design by using an online tutorial and going through each section every day on my own. E

Formula 12

Exercise 12.1: Sentence Completion

1. have cut
2. have brought
3. have fought
4. has undergone
5. have spent
6. has become

Exercise 12.2: Sentence Completion

1. are
2. went
3. did not look; looks
4. cost
5. played; enjoyed

Exercise 12.3: Gap Fill

1. better; cheaper
2. faster
3. more fashionable
4. wider
5. more expensive

Formula 13

Exercise 13.1: Matching

1. D 2. E 3. C 4. A 5. B

Exercise 13.2: Error Correction

1. Correct
2. To make my living room more homely, I would put a bookshelf in the corner and some plants.
3. To make the kitchen better I would get rid of the old units and have a totally new, modern kitchen installed.
4. To make my house look more cheerful I would paint the walls of my living room a brighter colour.
5. To let more light in my house and create more space, I would have the balcony extended.

Exercise 13.3: Gap Fill

1. Installing; warmer
2. Hanging; cosier
3. would make; powerful
4. easier
5. Having

Formula 14

Exercise 14.1: Gap Fill

1. especially
2. to some extent
3. completely
4. incredibly
5. fairly

Exercise 14.2: Gap Fill

1. a good way 2. for helping 3. cycling; helps
4. excellent for 5. excellent way 6. can help us

Exercise 14.3: Matching

1. H 2. C 3. G 4. E 5. J 6. F 7. D 8. I 9. A 10. B

Exercise 14.4: Matching

1. D 2. E 3. A 4. B 5. C

Formula 15

Exercise 15.1: Error Correction

1. In the future I would really like <u>to</u> travel in the desert.
2. Correct
3. What I <u>would</u> really like to do when I am older is live in a wooden house in California.
4. I hope <u>to</u> have the opportunity to go fishing in lake Tanzania.
5. What I'd really like to do <u>is</u> learn another foreign language.

Exercise 15.2: Gap Fill

1. manage 2. dream 3. succeed 4. ambition

Exercise 15.3: Sentence Completion

Possible answers:

1. If I pass the test I will go to England on vacation.
2. If I achieve my ambition I will be so proud of myself.
3. If I manage to do everything I want before I am 40 years old I'll have a really happy life.
4. I will be so delighted if I fulfill my dream and travel to the moon.

Formula 16

Exercise 16.1: Gap Fill

1. think that; opinion 2. quite convinced 3. way; believe

Exercise 16.2: Matching

1. H 2. D 3. F 4. G 5. B 6. A 7. C 8. E

Exercise 16.3: Sentence Completion

Possible answers:

1. A tremendous amount of young people don't get enough money and time to travel around the world.

2. In my country, elderly people, in general, like to do exercise regularly every moring.
3. A large percentage of famous people don't get enough freedom and privacy.
4. Nearly all stadents are given far too much homework.
5. The majority of parents today don't give their sons and daughters enough privacy.

Exercise 16.4: Gap Fill

1. ought
2. The best thing
3. would be
4. should
5. good idea
6. It would help if

Formula 17

Exercise 17.1: Gap Fill

1. blogs
2. advertisements
3. newsstands
4. magazines; reviews
5. features

Exercise 17.2: Gap Fill & Matching

1. broadcasts; B
2. browse through; A
3. news reports; E
4. blogs; C
5. find out about; D

Exercise 17.3: Gap Fill

1. biased / one-sided
2. objective / impartial
3. well-respected
4. untrustworthy
5. unreliable

Formula 18

Exercise 18.1: Gap Fill

Mary: not; of the opinion
Mary: do; opinion
Mary: course not; believe

Exercise 18.2: Multiple Choice

1. A 2. C 3. C 4. A 5. B 6. B

Exercise 18.3: Gap Fill & Matching

1. are made; D
2. punish; C
3. have; E
4. are given; A
5. drive; B

Formula 19

Exercise 19.1: Gap Fill

1. incredibly
2. unbelievably challenging
3. fairly frustrating
4. remarkably easy
5. awkward

Exercise 19.2: Multiple Choice

1. C 2. B 3. C 4. A 5. B

Formula 20

Exercise 20.1: Multiple Choice

1. B 2. C 3. A 4. B 5. C 6. A

Exercise 20.2: Matching

1. E 2. C 3. D 4. B 5. A

Exercise 20.3: Matching

1. B 2. D 3. E 4. A 5. C

Part two

Formula 21

Exercise 21.1 Gap Fill

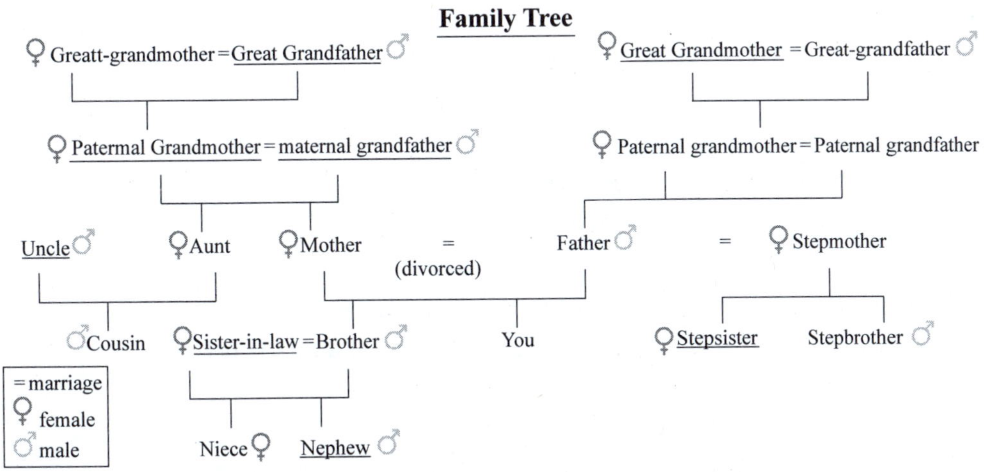

Exercise 21.2 Gap Fill

1. sports personality 2. ex-boyfriend 3. childhood friend
4. friend of the family 5. TV presenter 6. celebrity

Exercise 21.3 Gap Fill

1. who was the President of America
2. who taught us mathematics at school
3. who lived near our family home

4. who now studies at Beijing University
5. who was a civil servant
6. who lived in Los Angeles

Exercise 21.4 Multiple Choice

1. A 2. B 3. C 4. A 5. B

Exercise 21.5: Gap Fill

1. moody	2. supportive	3. immature	4. frank	5. charming
6. ambitious	7. generous	8. reserved	9. humorous	10. bright

Exercise 21.6: Gap Fill

1. seldom	2. frequently	3. every night
4. typically; twice a year	5. every now and again	6. constantly

Exercise 21.7: Matching

1. C 2. E 3. B 4. A 5. D

Exercise 21.8: Matching

1. E 2. B/D 3. F 4. A 5. C 6. B / D

Exercise 21.9: Multiple Choice

1. A 2. B 3. A 4. C 5. A 6. B

Exercise 21.10: Gap Fill

1. have the will to succeed
2. through sheer hard work
3. has a gift for
4. to fight for
5. earn the respect

Exercise 21.11: Gap Fill

1. looked up to
2. felt proud
3. hold; in high regard
4. greatly admire
5. special to me

Exercise 21.12: Multiple Choice

1. C 2. A 3. B 4. A 5. B

Exercise 21.13: Matching

1. F 2. B 3. G 4. D 5. H 6. E 7. C 8. A

Exercise 21.14: Ordering

F, D, B, C, A, G, E

Formula 22

Exercise 22.1: Matching

1. E 2. A 3. F 4. D 5. B 6. G 7. C

Exercise 22.2: Multiple Choice

1. B 2. A 3. B 4. C 5. A 6. C 7. A 8. C 9. C

Exercise 22.3: Matching

1. E 2. C 3. A 4. B 5. D 6. F

Exercise 22.4: Multiple Choice

1. B 2. B 3. C 4. B 5. A 6. C 7. A

Exercise 22.5: Gap Fill

1. in addition to
2. both; and
3. As well as
4. Besides
5. Along with
6. not only; but also

Exercise 22.6: Multiple Choice

1. B 2. C 3. A 4. B 5. C

Exercise 22.7: Gap Fill

1. always; used to
2. had; Whenever; would
3. often; went; was
4. lived; sometimes; took

Exercise 22.8: Multiple Choice

1. B 2. C 3. A 4. B 5. C

Exercise 22.9: Matching

1. B 2. E 3. A 4. F 5. C 6. D

Exercise 22.10: Gap Fill

1. makes me feel
2. important to me
3. provided me with
4. love; because
5. I value; gives me
6. reminds me
7. lets me

Exercise 22.11: Matching

1. D　2. B　3. E　4. C　5. F　6. A

Exercise 22.12: Ordering

E, C, F, A, D, B

Formular 23

Exercise 23.1: Word Order

1. a life-size golden statue
2. a handy antique silver lighter
3. an elegant black silk dress
4. a boring grey mass-produced dictionary
5. a modern spherical glass sculpture

Exercise 23.2: Error Correction

1. I made <u>him</u> a toy car.
2. I bought a painting <u>for</u> my mother.
3. My friend <u>wrote me</u> a story.
4. My father bought <u>me</u> a book.
5. I gave <u>it</u> to a classmate.
6. I asked <u>them</u> to buy <u>it</u> for me.

Exercise 23.3: Sentence Completion

1. bought; was studying　2. saw; was　3. told　4. made; was
5. invented　6. was dating; bought　7. gave; was staying　8. was working; was able

Exercise 23.4: Multiple Choice

1. B　2. A　3. C　4. C　5. A　6. B

Exercise 23.5: Gap Fill

1. are great for　2. are used for　3. provides people with
4. provide　5. is important for　6. it's appreciated because
7. can help　8. useful for　9. are valued for

Exercise 23.6: Word Order

1. I last wore the watch two years ago.
2. The first time I took the subway was in 1989.
3. The last time I watched the film was yesterday.
4. I first used a dictionary a very long time ago.

5. The last time I looked at the painting was last month.
6. I first bought a cell phone in 2003.

Exercise 23.7: Matching

1. B 2. F 3. D 4. A 5. K 6. C 7. G 8. E 9. I
10. L 11. J 12. M 13. H

Exercise 23.8: Multiple Choice

1. B 2. C 3. A 4. C 5. B 6. A 7. C 8. B

Exercise 23.9: Sentence Completion

1. (much) more important
2. not as reliable
3. not as advanced as
4. more
5. not as enlightening as
6. as equally important; as
7. more pleasant
8. warmer; more colourful; than

Exercise 23.10: Gap Fill

1. relaxed
2. sentimental
3. intrigued by
4. nostalgic
5. thrilled
6. inspired

Exercise 23.11: Sentence Completion

1. was made; wouldn't be
2. would play; had
3. would be; were lost
4. hadn't bought; would've been
5. wouldn't have become; hadn't made
6. had been; wouldn't have been

Exercise 23.12: Multiple Choice

1. B 2. A 3. C 4. C 5. A 6. B

Exercise 23.13: Ordering

D, G, E, A, C, F, B

Formula 24

Exercise 24.1: Gap Fill

1. the first time; romantic weekend away
2. legend
3. the time when; road trip

4. speech contest; poems; role play
5. fairy tale

Exercise 24.2: Multiple Choice

1. C 2. B 3. A 4. B 5. A 6. C 7. C 8. B 9. A 10. A 11. C

Exercise 24.3: Multiple Choice

1. B 2. A 3. B 4. C 5. A

Exercise 24.4: Sentence Completion

1. were played
2. was invited; by
3. were read; by
4. was promoted; by
5. were taught
6. had been taken / were taken; by
7. was carried
8. was bought for me; by

Exercise 24.5: Multiple Choice

1. C 2. B 3. A 4. A 5. C 6. A 7. C 8. B

Exercise 24.6: Table Completion

Relatives	Occupations	Relationship	Groups
grandparents	accountant	friend of a friend	a crowd of people
aunt	waiter / waitress	next-door neighbour	loads of people
uncle	musician	colleague	a big group of people
spouse		friend of the family	(sport) supporters
mother-in-law		acquaintance	party-goers
nephew		childhood friend	a tour group
distant relation			audience
			guests
			passengers
			players

Exercise 24.7: Rephrasing

1. Simon, who gets carsick very easily, felt very ill on the school bus one day.
2. Susan, who is very forgetful, forgot her handbag.
3. All of the tennis fans who didn't manage to buy tickets watched the match on TV screens outside.

4. Ralph, who was a friendly old man, used to talk to me every day on my way home from school.
5. All of the passengers who hadn't bought a ticket were thrown off the bus.
6. The members of the tour group who were American didn't understand what I said.

Exercise 24.8: Rephrasing

1. He said that he was Chinese.
2. She said that she wasn't going to study the next year.
3. He asked me if I could go to his house that night.
4. She told him that she didn't love him anymore.
5. I said that I wouldn't be able to leave the party then.
6. My dad said that he had gone to Beijing many years ago.
7. I asked Jack where Jill was.
8. I said to my parents that I couldn't tell them as it was a secret.
9. He said that he had never been to Tian'anmen Square.

Exercise 24.9: Multiple Choice

1. C 2. A 3. B 4. C 5. B 6. A

Exercise 24.10: Matching

1. H 2. C 3. I 4. F 5. A 6. E 7. D 8. G 9. B

Exercise 24.11: Table Completion

Adjectives for Describing Events	Adjectives of Feeling
amazing	amazed
amusing	amused
astonishing	astonished
astounding	astounded
awe-inspiring	awe-inspired
depressing	depressed
disappointing	disappointed
embarrassing	embarrassed
encouraging	encouraged
enlightening	enlightened

续表

Adjectives for Describing Events	Adjectives of Feeling
fascinating	fascinated
frustrating	frustrated
inspiring	inspired
interesting	interested
moving	moved
refreshing	refreshed
stimulating	stimulated

Exercise 24.12: Sentence Completion

1. hadn't been; would've been
2. wouldn't have taken; hadn't travelled
3. had gone; wouldn't have made; enjoyed
4. would've kept; hadn't lost
5. the best; have ever had
6. have always tried
7. the most exciting; have ever been
8. have never arrived

Exercise 24.13: Gap Fill

1. a very stimulating experience
2. I learnt the importance of
3. In the future I will
4. This event taught me
5. I will never forget
6. I wouldn't want to do it again
7. rewarding experience and I learned a lot
8. important for me
9. I would love to do it again

Exercise 24.14: Ordering

1. D　2. F　3. A　4. E　5. C　6. B

Part Three

Formula 25

Exercise 25.1: Matching

1. F 2. A 3. D 4. C 5. B 6. E

Exercise 25.2: Gap Fill

1. believe that
2. strongly believe
3. convinced that
4. certainly do; of the opinion
5. don't think
6. Not really

Exercise 25.3: Multiple Choice

1. A 2. C 3. B 4. C 5. A 6. B

Exercise 25.4: Matching

1. A 2. B 3. D 4. C 5. B 6. A 7. C 8. D

Formula 26

Exercise 26.1: Gap Fill & Matching

1. vast majority; C
2. Most; F
3. A lot of; A
4. large percentage; E
5. political views think; D
6. People with a lot of; B

Exercise 26.2: Multiple Choice

1. C 2. B 3. A 4. A 5. B 6. C

Exercise 26.3: Gap Fill

1. is a better place for relaxing
2. because it's a very therapeutic hobby; energetic
3. keep our natural environment cleaner
4 it is very important that
5. for establishing positive international relations
6. rewarding and fulfilling; better for

7. much wider variety; more convenient
8. necessary for
9. while younger people like
10. I think almost everyone agrees that it's important

Formula 27

Exercise 27.1: Gap Fill

1. agree
2. couldn't agree
3. believe that's true
4. completely agree with

Exercise 27.2: Multiple Choice

1. B 2. C 3. C 4. A 5. B 6. C

Exercise 27.3: Matching

1. E 2. C 3. A 4. B 5. D

Exercise 27.4: Matching

1. D 2. E 3. C 4. A 5. B

Formula 28

Exercise 28.1: Matching

The main advantage of working in an office is you can sit in a comfortable chair all day and drink tea!

The good thing about living in the countryside is that you can take peaceful walks and breathe fresh air.

One of the main benefits of living in cities is that you are able to keep up with the latest fashions, go to clubs, bars and restaurants.

A major advantage of taking the subway is you can travel to work quickly and cheaply.

A key advantage of having regular holidays is that you can give the mind and body a rest from the stress of work.

Exercise 28.2: Gap Fill

1. can get stressful
2. too obsessed with; can give a very bad impression to others
3. might get bored; annoying
4. get bothered by; not good for
5. The disadvantage of; inconvenient for

6. The bad thing; might get stolen
7. can get complicated

Exercise 28.3: Matching

1. C 2. F 3. A 4. D 5. B 6. E 7. G

Formula 29

Exercise 29.1: Multiple Choice & Matching

1. B; C 2. B; E 3. A; D 4. C; B 5. A; A

Exercise 29.2: Gap Fill

1. more important
2. have a higher priority
3. undoubtedly of greater importance than
4. in need of more attention than
5. take precedence over
6. Before thinking; should try to
7. equally as important as
8. much more valuable; than

Exercise 29.3: Matching

1. D 2. C 3. E 4. A 5. B

Formula 30

Exercise 30.1: Multiple Choice

1. B 2. C 3. B 4. A 5. C 6. A

Exercise 30.2: Gap Fill

1. to take steps to
2. ought to provide
3. ought to try harder to
4. should make a real effort to address
5. pay more attention to
6. take measures to
7. could spend more money on

Exercise 30.3: Multiple Choice

1. C 2. B 3. B 4. C 5. A 6. C

Formula 31

Exercise 31.1: Gap Fill & Matching

1. the current rate of international development; B
2. Taking into consideration; C
3. we are constantly improving our education standards; D
4. are spending a lot of money; E
5. are reforming the labour laws; A

Exercise 31.2: Multiple Choice

1. C 2. B 3. A 4. B 5. C

Exercise 31.3: Sentence Completion

1. will be paying 2. will be using 3. will be wearing
4. will have to wear 5. will have 6. will be hosting
7. will all be driving 8. will love